Uncertaii

*an Australian SAS
patrol in Vietnam*

Graham J. Brammer

ALLEN & UNWIN

To 'brothers in arms'

First published in 1997 by
Allen & Unwin
9 Atchison Street, St Leonards NSW 2065 Australia
Phone: (61 2) 9901 4088
Fax: (61 2) 9906 2218
E-mail: frontdesk@allen-unwin.com.au
URL: http://www.allen-unwin.com.au

National Library of Australia
Cataloguing-in-Publication entry:

Brammer, Graham J., 1944– .
  Uncertain fate: an Australian SAS patrol
  in Vietnam.

  ISBN 1 86448 505 1.

  1. Vietnamese Conflict, 1961–1975—Fiction. I. Title.

A823.3

Set in 11/13pt Plantin Light by DOCUPRO, Sydney
Printed and bound by Australian Print Group, Maryborough, Vic.

10 9 8 7 6 5 4 3 2 1

Many good books have been written on the profession of arms, but few in my experience have got to the essence of what the combat soldier really thinks and feels when tired, frightened, pumped up, wounded or exercising the colossal responsibility and loneliness of command.

Uncertain Fate answers this need admirably. Graham Brammer provides a splendidly accurate account of the gut-gripping experiences of a five man Special Air Service Regiment patrol deployed in a behind the lines reconnaissance and ambushing role in the jungles of Vietnam. It includes too, wonderful vignettes of the supporting cast of squadron headquarters officers, staff, gunship pilots, and the higher command.

In writing this engrossing book, Graham Brammer has done himself and a fine Regiment proud.

His Excellency Major General
Michael Jeffery, AC MC
Governor of Western Australia

Foreword

The face of war is not about the manoeuvre of armies, climactic battles and spectacular heroics. It is concerned with the human dimensions of armed conflict—of the reactions, relationships and activities of young men and women placed in extraordinary circumstances.

This is a remarkable book, for unlike many books concerned with warfare it captures the essence of one facet of war in a most realistic manner. That facet is the experiences of young Australian Special Air Service (SAS) soldiers during the Vietnam war. Having read the first three chapters, I put the manuscript aside and reflected on its account of the insertion and infiltration of Sergeant Ashton's patrol and the first evening of the operation. What struck me most forcibly was just how accurately Graham Brammer had captured the atmosphere of SAS operations in South Vietnam. Memories of similar experiences and feelings long lost in the mists of time came back to me very sharply. The description of the insertion, the move to the first night's lying-up place or LUP and the evening activities were exactly as I remembered them. I vividly recalled a similar patrol where we had to cross a well-used track close to the insertion landing zone, although on that occasion an armed group of North Vietnamese regulars moved along it as we approached. Crouching among the foliage as they passed, my thoughts then were similar to Ashton's.

The SAS is a unique organisation. During the Vietnam conflict SAS Squadrons, each comprising a Headquarters, four fighting Troops and an attached communications Troop, undertook an annual tour of duty as part of the 1st Australian Task Force. Each Troop—a lieutenant, four sergeants and twenty other ranks—was organised into five 'patrols'. By 1968 the fourth fighting Troop of each Squadron was provided by the New Zealand SAS. Unlike most other combat units, the Squadron and Troops did not fight as entities. The Squadron Commander deployed the patrols directly, with each patrol operating independently in an assigned area well beyond the protective cover of artillery. Their job was to find and report on the enemy, although increasingly they harassed the enemy deep inside his base areas. Patrols ranged in strength from four to six men, although a combined group of two or three patrols sometimes deployed on an offensive task.

The men who formed these patrols were volunteers in their early to mid twenties, including a number of intrepid conscripts. They joined the Regiment only after undertaking a rigorous selection course that identified those men who were suited to the unique environment they would have to fight in. Training was demanding and highly realistic. For example, fighting drills were practised with live ammunition under conditions that left no margin for error and a final exercise conducted in Papua New Guinea tested all components of the Squadron in a most realistic environment. *Uncertain Fate* vividly portrays the application of that training in South Vietnam. Above all, it captures that unique element that sets the combat soldier, and particularly the SAS soldier, apart from his countrymen—that mixture of loyalty, selflessness, trust, discipline and concern for the well-being of your fellow soldier that binds fighting teams at all levels together.

For those who know Graham, this is not surprising. Firstly, he experienced at first hand many of the types of incidents that Ashton and his patrol confront, having undertaken two tours of duty in South Vietnam with the 2nd SAS Squadron—initially as a patrol scout and later commanding his own patrol. Secondly, he was an exceptionally professional yet unemotive soldier, disdainful of false heroics and utterly reliable in undertaking his responsibilities. Thirdly, Graham is one of those rare people who can penetrate the facades of men, get to the core of a man's character and recognise the worth he has to offer the team.

There are many misperceptions about SAS soldiers. Many of the uninformed see them as 'Rambos'. Nothing could be further from the truth and Graham Brammer does much to correct the myths, portraying those magnificent young soldiers as I remember them.

This is a book about men at war in the genre of Manning's *Her Privates We*, Lawson's *We were the Rats*, Hungerford's *The Ridge and the River* and Forrest's *The Last Blue Sea*. Although it is a novel, *Uncertain Fate* could easily represent the memoirs of many of those who served with the SAS in a conflict fought a generation ago. Indeed, most SAS veterans will identify with this book. Many of them will vividly recollect similar experiences to the events, relationships and anxieties portrayed. I am pleased that Graham has included the activities of the Squadron's Headquarters, whose members supported us so ably and shared our anxiety when those magnificent aircrews of No 9 RAAF Squadron flew out to rescue a patrol in trouble. Graham captures only too clearly the tension of penetrating an enemy camp or bunker system; the dry-mouthed fear that all men experience prior to the firefight; the urgent, sharp, yet matter of fact and controlled actions once the firing starts; and the incredible luck that some of our patrols and helicopter crews experienced—a luck born out of thorough training, audacity and a deepseated concern not to let your mates down. He also captures that remarkable sense of humour of the Australian soldier under stress—as epitomised in Trooper Jim Collier—that disarms the most pretentious of people and lightens a grim situation.

I congratulate Graham for capturing the essence of what it was like to be an SAS soldier on operations almost thirty years ago. *Uncertain Fate* will stand alongside the classics written by men and women who have experienced war at first hand.

Brigadier Chris Roberts
Canberra

Contents

Preface

The events of this book did not occur; but given the right circumstances they might very well have done so. Any member of Special Forces, whether they be SAS, Rangers, SEALS or Green Berets, or any Navy, Army or Air Force unit member who served in South Vietnam in support of Special Forces operations, would attest to this.

There are no Special Forces tactics per se in this book, as I do not believe that such a thing as Special Forces tactics exists. There are, however, a number of options for each element of Special Forces operations from which the patrol commander can choose in order to run his patrol effectively. It is not simply a matter of selecting 'number three from the column of ambush drills' and 'number four from the column of counter follow-up drills' and so on until all the possible options are covered, but it can work a little like that. The selection of options for the commander will often be dictated by the tactical scenario at the time, and the commander who knows of and has practised the most options with his patrol will have the best chance of success.

This is the most widely accepted theory on the success achieved by the Australian Special Air Service squadrons in South Vietnam in spite of the large number of follow-up actions taken against their patrols by the Viet Cong. That no two commanders reacted with the same option in the face of similar tactical adversity was sufficient to sow the seed of caution in all but the most persistent pursuers.

I had more than a little difficulty in writing this book. My

experiences during two tours of South Vietnam in the capacity
of both patrol member and patrol commander did not make the
task any the easier. It was my serious and stated intention not to
write a book about the war in Vietnam—rather, an adventure
novel was what I had in mind. However, as the complex character
of Rowan Ashton developed within my adventure novel, I found
it increasingly more necessary to demonstrate a basis for the
incredible skill and fortitude possessed by him. To that end,
Uncertain Fate was born.

When I asked Brigadier Chris Roberts, AM, CSC, if he would
be so kind as to write the Foreword for *Uncertain Fate*, I did so
in the knowledge that he had seen operational service in South
Vietnam as an SAS patrol commander. He was subsequently a
Squadron Commander in, and Commanding Officer of, the
Australian Special Air Service Regiment and was largely instru-
mental in raising a Special Forces Headquarters in Australia,
becoming its first Commander.

Brigadier Roberts is one of the very few senior officers still
serving in the Australian Army who can provide a perspective on
the full ambit of the tactical, strategic and political development
of Australia's Special Forces that is based on experience and is
unencumbered by pain or prejudice.

Acknowledgements

Bev Seaton and Vanessa Robson
Soul mates and friends . . .
   For keeping me focused.

Captain Julie Simes
Truly a good friend . . .
   For her encouraging readings, her editing assistance and her helping me with my grammatical expression.

Group Captain Mick Haxell, DFC (Rtd)
No 9 RAAF Squadron pilot, who flew extensively on operations in South Vietnam, and former Commanding Officer of No 5 RAAF Squadron in Canberra. One of the many who flew their helicopters 'down the mine' time after time, and often under heavy enemy groundfire, to extract five scruffy individuals who—but for the gallant efforts of these helicopter pilots and crews—could easily have found a place on the Honour Roll of our country . . .
   For his technical advice on what to me are the vagaries of helicopter operations.

Brigadier Chris Roberts, AM, CSC
SAS Troop and Patrol Commander in South Vietnam in 1969–1970. Former Squadron Commander and Commanding Officer of the Special Air Service Regiment and the first Commander of Australia's Special Forces Group . . .
   For so generously agreeing to write the Foreword for this book.

Colonel Don Higgins
Commander Special Forces, Australia . . .
For agreeing to be the security sponsor for *Uncertain Fate*.

and, not least

All the SAS patrol commanders and members I served with on operations . . .
For collectively giving rise to the fictional characters of *Uncertain Fate*.

1

Sergeant Rowan Ashton, commander of the Bravo Nine Sierra patrol, call sign Six-Six, sat on the left-hand seat in the cargo compartment of the No 9 RAAF Squadron helicopter and silently absorbed the activity that was occurring around him. Sitting cross-legged on the floor at his feet was the wiry, dark-haired patrol scout, Billy Wilkins. Along the seats to his right sat the remaining three members of his patrol.

All briefings had been completed and checks done. All was in readiness for his patrols' deployment into the northern area of Phuoc Tuy Province, along the border with its neighbouring province of Long Khanh, and adjacent to the foothills of a large area known to the operations staff as the May Tao mountains.

Rowan Ashton could feel the adrenalin coursing through his body like a small electric current. It terminated at the back of his throat and produced a drying effect on the inside of his mouth. This is the worst time, he thought.

Along the line of helicopters the RAAF crews were undertaking the final pre-flight checks that preceded airborne operations involving their aircraft. The line consisted of five Iroquois (or Huey) helicopters. Three were troop-carrying aircraft, commonly referred to as 'slicks', and the other two were heavily armed helicopter gunships. Ashton looked across the bitumen tarmac area called 'Kangaroo Pad' to the small briefing hut from which they had emerged only minutes before. His eyes scanned the stand of rubber trees beyond the pad and he could make out the shapes of tents and huts that marked the presence of the major Task Force signals units. Also in that area, somewhere, he knew the Australian Task Force Headquarters was located.

Ashton tried always to keep his mind from wandering too close to the doomsday thoughts that occupied the minds of many soldiers immediately before going into combat. This time he idly focused on the helicopter crews as they went about their checks. The designation for the No 9 Squadron troop-carrying helicopter flights was 'Albatross', and each aircraft's call sign was prefaced by that word. Australian helicopter gunships of No 9 Squadron went by call signs prefaced by 'Bushranger'.

Ashton knew almost all the pilots and crewmen of No 9 Squadron either socially or operationally. This was his fifteenth patrol into the jungles of South Vietnam as commander. On eleven previous occasions his patrol had been inserted and extracted from their operations by the No 9 Squadron helicopters and aircrews. Such was the bond between the units that many a pleasant post-operational evening was spent by off-duty SAS members with the RAAF crews at their Vung Tau base.

The sound of the door gunner checking the twin M60 machine guns in one of the crew compartments of the D model Iroquois helicopter brought Ashton back to the present. The two pilots were now strapped into their seats and drawing on their helmets. They were discussing the previous evening's socialising in the RAAF Vung Tau officers' mess. The senior crewman was standing at the right-hand side of the helicopter with his helmet on and with one end of his connector lead in his hand, waiting for the pilots to activate the aircraft intercom system. Ashton watched as the pilots plugged their helmet lead jacks into the electronic system. Their mouths were still moving but the conversation was now lost to him, as it circulated through the intercom and was heard only by the flight crew.

Gloved hands now wandered over the instrument panels, turning a knob here, flicking a switch there. Each pilot appeared to take a turn at testing the tail rotor pedal, the cyclic and collective hydraulic pressures and the controls. Ashton heard the whirring noise as the helicopter's starter motor engaged and spun the engine up to self-sustaining speed. He caught the smell of the initial burn of JP4 aviation fuel from the exhaust efflux as the powerful and reliable Lycoming turbine engine gulped fuel and came to life.

He looked along the line of aircraft and saw that all the rotors were at different stages in their start-up procedure. He noted the rotor blade of the slick in which they were travelling as it made its first pass across the front of the aircraft. Mesmerised, he watched each blade-tip pass in turn across the front—slowly at first, then increasing in speed as the revolution of the rotors increased. The steady increase in speed of the turning blades caused a gradual transfer of energy throughout the airframe.

Rowan Ashton unconsciously pulled his weapon closer to his body as he felt the transfer of energy cause the helicopter to rock gently on its skids—then more violently as the rotor speed increased, before finally settling down as the rotors reached normal operating RPM.

Inside the helicopter the noise became almost deafening as the pilot increased collective pitch to raise the chopper to the hover. Ashton noticed that the two helicopters in front had already become airborne. Both had their tails slightly raised as they accelerated slowly above the bitumen tarmac toward the high fence at its western end. Then, with a more pronounced tail boom elevation, Ashton's aircraft gained translational lift and was airborne too. For an instant, it slid sideways as it was buffeted by the wind.

The pilot continued to manipulate the controls, adjusting tail rotor input, collective lever and cyclic control to counteract any crosswind or turbulence. The chopper responded immediately by straightening, accelerating and climbing. Ashton found himself involuntarily swallowing as the three Iroquois left Kangaroo Pad heading west in tactical formation, with the light fire team of two heavily armed 'Bushranger' helicopter gunships a thousand metres astern, struggling to match airspeed with the much lighter slicks.

As the helicopters continued to climb and gain altitude to cross Provincial Route 2, it became noticeably cooler. Rowan Ashton glanced between the pilots at the instrument panel. Eighty knots and 900 feet. He felt better now that they were well clear of the ground. He could feel the thrusting power of the engine as the helicopter climbed through 1000 feet. They would climb to 1500 feet and level out at 100 to 110 knots. At least that was the brief as he remembered it.

After several minutes they turned north behind Nui Nghe and, with the designated height and speed requirements satisfied, the pilot settled on a course of 360 degrees. Ashton looked around the cabin of the helicopter at the faces of his patrol members and wondered what each was thinking. For a moment he watched the pilots as they carried out their tasks. He couldn't see the crewman on the right-hand side of the chopper but the door gunner behind him looked downright bored. Finally he noticed the co-pilot's flying helmet. DO NOT PUNCTURE—CONTENTS UNDER PRESSURE was stencilled boldly across the back of the helmet. Ashton gave a tight smile—it was just such humour that helped you to keep your sanity in a place like South Vietnam. The stencilled letters slowly blurred in his mind and his thoughts returned to his own people.

Trooper Billy Wilkins sat on the floor in front of his patrol commander and stared intently at the jungle below, his cutdown SLR held across his lap. Ashton knew his scout was a mass of nervous tension, as he always was during the early stages of an insertion. Wilkins' face was grey beneath the heavy camouflage paint. He unconsciously tugged at his headband, rubbed the forefinger and thumb of his left hand together and continuously attempted to swallow saliva that Ashton knew could not be present in a throat so dry. Ashton also knew that as soon as they were on the ground, where it counted, Billy Wilkins would no longer be troubled by such nervousness.

Wilkins was country born and bred and a top soldier. He had been shooting and trapping since the time he could walk. He was 22 years of age, around 5 feet 10 inches tall and weighed in at ten and a half stone. He was lean and wiry and every inch and every pound was as tough as old boots. Wilkins was a genius in the jungle. He could move through the most difficult terrain like a shadow, his feet seeming barely to touch the ground as he moved, and almost nothing escaped his attention. The most notable thing about Wilkins, to Ashton's mind, was the large coal black eyes. Eyes that declared a maturity and compassion beyond his years. For those who knew him well, there was a spark from time to time in those dark eyes that left no doubt that here was a man not to be trifled with.

Ashton's thoughts were disturbed momentarily as the helicopter pilot changed course slightly as the formation manoeuvred. He glanced at the instrument panel—heading 060 degrees at 100 knots. Must be just north of Binh Ba and heading for Thua Tich, Ashton thought, as he glanced out the left-hand cargo door opening and sighted the beautiful village of Binh Gia about five kilometres ahead and just off the left of the Huey's nose.

On the seat next to him, hunched slightly forward to absorb the weight of his pack more easily, was his signaller, Lance Corporal Gusten 'Bluey' Erickson. The Ericksons had migrated to Australia from Sweden one year before Bluey was born. He was now 24 years of age and a veteran of the Borneo confrontation and a previous tour of South Vietnam. He was the most easygoing individual Ashton had ever known. Erickson's weapon was an M16 rifle, which he carried in preference to a heavier calibre weapon on the basis that, with the radio set, he had enough to carry. There was a time when Erickson carried the same weapon that Ashton did, but he'd given it to the patrol's former 2IC at the completion of their third operation.

Naturally, he'd received the nickname Bluey because of the shock of red hair that he never seemed to be able to control. A little taller and heavier than Wilkins, Bluey Erickson was a dependable jungle soldier who had proved his worth in all the contacts with the enemy that the patrol had been involved in. Above all, Erickson was an accomplished communicator who provided the primary link with their Task Force base on which rested the patrol's ultimate survivability.

Jim Collier was asleep, his arms wrapped around the cutdown SLR that stood upright between his knees, his forehead cradled in the crook of his right arm. Much of his face was hidden by the upright rifle stock. The most visible part of Collier's equipment was the fibreglass and metal knife-scabbard taped to the left shoulder strap of his webbing harness. The scabbard, lying upside down along the harness, contained his United States Navy NORD-8115 'Baby Kabar'. Its hollow-ground blade was kept razor sharp specifically to cut through a uniform in order to gain access to a man's wounds, or to slice through the rag tape that squadron members used to fasten the large wound dressings to their rifle butts, water bottle covers or other equipment.

Collier was the coolest, most laidback man Ashton had ever met, and yet he sometimes blew up over what Ashton thought were trivial issues. He had come to the patrol at the same time as Wilkins and Erickson. He had brown, straight limp hair, medium brown eyes and, at 21 years of age and 5 feet 8 inches tall, he was the youngest and shortest member of the group.

Collier was the patrol 'pioneer' or demolitions man as well as the patrol medic and, as far as Ashton was concerned, there was no better demolitions expert anywhere in the world. It was an odd mixture of skills. 'Blow up the baddies and patch up the goodies' was Collier's standard answer to the 'What job do you do?' questions that often come the way of a soldier. Collier carried the most comprehensive medical kit and could inflict devastating damage with a minimum amount of explosives. He spent every waking moment trying to improve his medical skills and to explore new ways to deliver a lethal explosive surprise into the lap of the enemy.

Collier had grown up in the Darlinghurst area of Sydney and the street survival instincts that had served him so well in his youth had easily made the transition to the jungle environment of South Vietnam. Here was a really good soldier—and a scoundrel who needed the very best in leadership and supervision to keep him on the right path.

The newest member of the patrol sat on the seat near the right-hand cargo door opening and in front of the crew compartment. Corporal Gary Dobel at 26 years of age was one year junior to his patrol commander and at 5 foot 10 inches was a full two inches shorter. He was a powerful-looking man with light brown hair and eyes. He carried the same weapon as Ashton, an M16 rifle with an underslung XM148 he inherited from his predecessor when he came to the patrol. The significant difference between their weapons was that Dobel carried a 30 round magazine on his M16 and Ashton used a jury-rigged dual 20 round magazine system.

Dobel had recently been promoted to the rank of corporal to fill the vacancy in Ashton's patrol caused by the hospitalisation of his former 2IC, Allen Cunningham. During the patrol's previous mission, Cunningham had been wounded in action when the patrol tried to bypass part of an enemy bunker system without making adequate security arrangements.

Ashton had argued against Dobel being posted to his patrol as 2IC on the grounds that the promotion of Erickson to corporal was his preferred option. The OC—the Officer Commanding—had not agreed because Erickson had left the army for a brief time after his first tour of South Vietnam and Dobel was the senior lance corporal in the squadron. Naturally, the OC had his way. The OC is always right, Ashton thought with a smile . . . even when he's wrong, the OC is always right.

As a result, there had been some misgivings about Dobel's appointment, even resistance, among the remainder of the patrol. Ashton was forced at one time to take Erickson, Wilkins and Collier aside to remind them of their professional responsibilities. That had worked up to the point where they agreed to give Dobel a fair go. During the patrol's preparations for this mission there were one or two incidents that gave Ashton cause for some disquiet. Even so, he had to admit that, although Dobel was no Allen Cunningham, he had done a fair job as 2IC this far.

The change in pitch of the rotor blades, a decrease in the engine note and a light tap on the leg from Billy Wilkins brought Ashton back to the present. Wilkins made a circling motion with an upright index finger, then pointed over his left shoulder with his fist closed and thumb extended. Ashton caught his meaning and transferred his attention to the right-hand side of the aircraft. One of the other helicopters had broken formation to the right. Just as this registered on Ashton, their Huey began to descend toward the treeline below.

Wilkins looked subtly different now, and the commander could sense that a change had come over everyone in the aircraft. Even the door gunner had lost his nonchalant air. There was activity in both crew compartments as the crewman and the door gunner activated their twin M60 machine guns and reported to the pilot that all door guns were 'hot'.

With the gunships still almost 1000 metres astern, they descended to within ten metres of the jungle canopy. Ashton knew that the aircraft that had led the operation out of Kangaroo Pad would remain at height and guide them to their insertion point. The helicopter that had broken formation would proceed to a predetermined holding point in case it was required in an emergency.

He checked his watch—it was 1425 hours. He looked at the instrument panel. The altimeter did not appear to be registering any height whatsoever but the airspeed indicator was sitting on the red line at 120 knots. The pilot was making numerous course corrections in accordance with instructions from the lead helicopter, and height corrections as dictated by the terrain. This was low flying to the extreme and at its very best; at this speed even the slightest course or height correction exerted some gravitational force on the body.

The increased tension inside the helicopter was caused by apprehension, not fear. The time for fear had passed and all understood the implications of pilot error or mechanical malfunction. Crashing into the trees from this height and at this speed was the equivalent of driving a car into a large tree at over 200 kilometres per hour.

Almost simultaneously, the crewman and the door gunner leaned across into the cargo cabin and displayed one hand to the patrol. The hand was closed with the exception that the forefinger and second finger were extended and crossed. The signal for five hundred metres to run. Time even for personal thoughts was now gone as all available eyes searched the jungle floor below for physical signs of the enemy. Any positive enemy sighting this close to the insertion point would result in the mission being aborted.

The briefing had been precise. The long axis of the landing zone, or LZ, ran in an east–west direction and was just over two hundred metres long and seventy metres wide at its widest point. The slick carrying the patrol would approach from the east, track along the southern side of the LZ approximately thirty metres inside the treeline, wash off all speed in a tight, hard turn at the western end and deposit the patrol in the north-west corner of the pad, with the left cargo doorway facing the treeline.

Now the briefing had become reality. The door gunner tapped the patrol commander on the shoulder and pointed toward the right-hand side of the helicopter. Ashton glanced quickly to his right to identify that it was the correct spot. It was the LZ, all right—the big dead tree in the north-eastern corner confirmed it beyond doubt. He gave a thumbs-up sign to the door gunner and within seconds the slick came round in a hard, banking turn. So tight was the turn that the patrol could sense every mechanical part of the airframe straining against the force of it.

The helicopter came out of the turn slightly nose up and in precisely the correct spot about fifteen metres from the treeline. As the rear of the skids came to within a metre of the ground, the crewman and gunner screamed *'GO!'* in unison. The commander leaned forward to tap the scout on the shoulder but Wilkins was already gone. Ashton and the rest of the patrol followed. The last recollection Ashton had of the insertion was the thought, What a hell of a pilot we've got here.

By the time Rowan Ashton and the remainder of the patrol cleared the aircraft, Billy Wilkins was only five metres from the treeline and in a dead run. Ashton and his group followed at a fast walk, weapons at the ready, watching the northern and western treelines for sign of enemy presence. This was Ashton's drill. As soon as Wilkins was inside the treeline and in a position to provide accurate supporting or covering fire, the others ran like hell for the security of the trees.

The noise was confusing and was designed to be so. As the patrol entered the treeline the first of the gunships passed overhead at red-line speed. None of the patrol members concerned themselves with it as they fought to concentrate on visual signs of the enemy. This was all they could do as it was impossible to detect anything by ear over the sound of the helicopters. Ashton forced the patrol a little further into the treeline. He knew the second gunship would be overhead within seconds and that the slick would pull out of the pad somewhere in front or astern of it, and he wanted to have some trees behind him before that happened.

Suddenly there was silence. The noise of the helicopters could no longer be heard. Even the native fauna had gone quiet for fear that the roaring machines would return to threaten their lifestyle again.

Ashton's patrol was still in single file formation. The last man, Gary Dobel, was only ten metres or so inside the treeline. All were crouched or kneeling, with packs on and facing in alternate directions. Ashton drew himself slowly upright and checked the compass on his left wrist. North was directly through the area where Wilkins was crouched beside a large tree and north was the direction he wanted to go.

Wilkins looked back and caught his commander's eye. Ashton raised his left hand to waist high, forearm parallel to the ground, palm vertical and extended fingers together, pointing north. Then his hand movement changed and he presented his open palm toward the scout with three fingers raised. With an almost imperceptible nod of his head, Wilkins came quietly upright, briefly checked his wrist compass, and moved off slowly in a northerly direction.

Ashton glanced briefly at Erickson and showed him the same three-fingered sign. He waited for acknowledgement, then moved off after Wilkins. He knew the signal would be passed back through the patrol and, by the time it got to Dobel, everyone would know they were only going a distance of thirty metres to the north.

This was a critical time for the patrol. The insertion helicopters would loiter in a holding area some distance out of earshot for twenty minutes. Should the patrol be contacted by the Viet Cong during that time, the patrol's mission would be considered compromised, the helicopters recalled and the patrol extracted under close fire support from the helicopter light fire team. Under normal insertion circumstances, the patrol commander would call the Albatross lead aircraft at the expiration of the holding time and report that operations were normal.

Wilkins stopped suddenly in front of his commander, who looked up. The scout pointed at his feet and nodded his head to suggest that they had come the thirty metres. Billy had not been pacing and was guessing the distance. He always did, it was a game to him. Ashton turned to Erickson closing from behind, caught his eye and made a sign with fist closed and thumb bobbing up and down on top. Erickson moved up to his commander and whispered, 'Thirty metres.' Ashton looked at Wilkins, smiled thinly and mouthed the words, 'smart arse!'

Wilkins grinned in return, stepped two paces forward and knelt down beside a large tree. He loved being right in judging the distance covered without really counting. It was a skill that he had developed in time spent with his grandfather. They played little games like 'How many steps to the milking shed?' and when his grandfather took him hunting, which was often, he made a competition out of judging the distances they travelled through the bush. It gave Billy a superior feeling when he got the distances right on patrol, which he usually did.

Ashton called the patrol members forward one at a time and directed them to the position he wanted them to occupy. When all members were facing outward, Ashton consulted his watch.

Almost twelve minutes had passed since they were inserted. He was sweating profusely, as always, but his throat was no longer dry from apprehension.

He took a water bottle from its carrier and took a long pull, draining nearly half of the contents in one go. This was standard for Ashton. Under his shirt he carried an American five-quart bladder full of water. The adrenalin rush and excitement of an insertion made him lose a lot of body fluid. Many others he knew did the same and by the end of the day most of the contents of the water bladder would be gone.

The short halt gave Ashton an opportunity to study the terrain around the insertion point more closely. There were a number of large bamboo clumps to the east that he had not noticed on a previous aerial reconnaissance of the area. This did not concern him as it fitted in with the small creek system marked on his map.

It was an advantage, in fact, as it was unlikely that the Viet Cong could successfully surprise them from that direction. Also, it would not unduly hinder any withdrawal should he be forced to take the patrol in that direction as a result of a contact with a numerically superior force. He could tuck in between the bamboo and the clearing, using the bamboo as a shield, and force the enemy into a direct follow-up or an assault across the open LZ. This would sufficiently confound any enemy plan to roll them up quickly and would allow the patrol to escape to the east or the south-east.

Ashton studied the area to the north and west. Severely bomb-damaged in both directions, he decided. This meant it was unlikely that the patrol would be molested by the enemy in the general area of the LZ. He relaxed a little and took another pull from the water bottle, nearly emptying it. Possible follow-up was the only surprise that could now be sprung on the patrol. There could be no surprises to the front, for this was the enemy's backyard where anything was possible and they were here to discover whatever, if anything, was there.

His appreciation finished, Ashton took the bladder from his shirt, filled his water bottle from it and returned that to its carrier. He then put his mouth over the bladder's opening and pushed down gently to expel the excess air and to get at the water. He drank greedily in four long swallows while maintaining downward pressure. Having satisfied his thirst, he returned the half-full bladder to his shirt and checked his watch. The holding time was almost up.

Ashton withdrew the PRC 68 ground/air radio from one of the pouches on his belt and turned it on. He placed the unit to the side of his face, pressed the 'Press to Talk' or PTT button and spoke softly into the microphone. 'Albatross Zero-One, this is call sign Six-Six . . . Over.'

There was a brief pause before a voice answered amid a rush of helicopter noise. 'Roger, Six-Six, this is Zero-One, how goes it your end? . . . Over.'

Ashton dropped the call sign and replied, 'We're secure here—you blokes might as well go home . . . many thanks.'

There was another pause before Ashton heard the helicopter noise as the channel opened. 'Zero-One . . . Good luck' was all that was said in acknowledgment before the channel closed.

Ashton turned off the radio, pushed in the aerial and returned the unit to its pouch. He glanced around the patrol locations and made a clicking noise with his tongue. All heads turned toward him and he held up two fingers to signify that they would move in two minutes.

With a nod of the head, members of the patrol acknowledged in turn. Each man then began to refurbish the area in which he had been crouching, in an attempt to restore it to pristine condition, and to make final adjustments to his equipment in preparation for the move.

2

At the end of two minutes, Billy Wilkins stepped off quietly and headed in a northerly direction, the vegetation around him hardly disturbed by his passing. Ashton was keen to put as much distance between the patrol and the LZ as possible before he was forced to camp for the night. The jungle was easy to negotiate at first, but by the time they'd travelled forty metres, they were into the bomb-damaged vegetation he had noted from the LZ. The patrol was fresh but the fierceness had not yet gone from the afternoon sun. Ashton pushed the pace in the hope that this was isolated damage they would break out of quickly.

Billy hated this because it interfered with his ability to scout, made him tire quickly, and the noise concerned him. It was impossible not to make noise with whole trees torn out of the ground, lying like scattered matchsticks in your path. The large trees were not such a problem as the thick secondary growth that thrived as a result of the canopy being torn away, exposing the otherwise sterile growth environment to the sun's elixir of life.

Noise was the number one problem for any patrol. Manmade metallic noises were worst because they travelled further in the stillness of the environment and alerted the enemy. Ordinary human sounds were the next most likely to cause a patrol to be detected. Loud speech, unsuppressed coughing and other such noises were to be avoided as a matter of survival. Naturally, the volume of 'transit noise' created by a patrol was directly related to the terrain being negotiated, the number in the patrol and the personal skill of the individuals. In any case, transit noise created in areas of bomb damage was always of great concern as it transcended the element of individual competence and training.

Wilkins had just eased his body past some particularly thick secondary scrub when he stopped and quietly squatted beside the exposed root system of a large fallen tree. His actions alerted Ashton that something was wrong. A moment of dread gripped Ashton as he realised that he could not cover Wilkins from where he was. He moved forward cautiously toward the thick scrub. Wilkins was in an extended kneeling position beside the root system with his rifle resting on one of the roots. He reminded Ashton of a pointing dog, stock still with eyes fixed on the quarry. Wilkins sensed that Ashton was not in a position to support him and he would not move until he was. It was the lore.

Ashton negotiated the secondary scrub with difficulty and moved up beside Wilkins and squatted. He scanned the area in front for several seconds then looked at his scout. 'All I can see is a big hole,' he whispered, nodding toward the large bomb crater just off to their right front.

'Thirty metres to the front . . . big grey tree,' Billy said quietly. 'Ten metres this way and about two metres left . . . nearly on the rim of the crater. Got it?'

'Got it,' whispered Ashton. 'Looks like the top two layers of a bunker.'

'That's what I thought. Could be old . . . the crater is pretty old.'

Ashton nodded his agreement. 'You'd better go and look at it.'

Wilkins stood up and eased past Ashton, who moved into the position vacated by the scout. A noise off to the left distracted them and they glanced across to see Erickson moving into a fire position several metres along the fallen tree, followed closely by Collier. They made their way around the left side of the scrub to be in a position to support the front pair should it be necessary. Dobel was not in sight.

Erickson grinned and gave a cheeky wink to remind them that they'd nearly left him and Collier out. Wilkins and Ashton exchanged tight, knowing smiles and Wilkins stepped off in the direction of the bunker. Ashton watched him approach within a metre of the spot. He smiled when he detected the release of tension in his scout's body—it was obviously clear.

Wilkins returned to the patrol with a look of acute embarrassment on his face.

'What's up, Billy?' Ashton asked his young scout.

'Its older than you are! Got at least five years of cobwebs growing across the opening.'

'OK,' whispered Ashton, trying to hide his mirth. 'Let's get going or we'll be in this bombed-out shit forever.' He glanced in the direction of Erickson and Collier. Ashton frowned at them and made a sign with two fingers extended against his upper arm followed by a thumbs-up sign. Erickson nodded and indicated with his own thumbs up and a sideways movement of his head that Dobel was still with the patrol and doing his job looking after the rear. Happy with the situation, the commander urged his scout forward.

They passed the bunker opening and Ashton noted that there was barely enough room to walk between the bunker and the lip of the 750 pound bomb crater. And yet the bunker looked to be in good condition. Everything seemed to be in place and the overhead protection was still solid. Makes you wonder just how effective this bombing is, he thought—no doubt anyone inside would have blown eardrums and a hell of a headache. He shook his head in wonder. Soon it was gone from his mind and he checked his compass heading and took off in the wake of his scout.

Shortly after passing the bunker, the patrol encountered its first patch of genuine primary jungle since leaving the LZ. The going became easier and patrolling became almost a pleasure. Ashton was not deluded by this apparent good fortune. The patrol had merely traded an area where they were unlikely to contact the enemy for one where they were most likely to. High primary jungle with its, at best, sparse secondary growth, always made the hair on the back of Ashton's neck stand up in anticipation. He had a name for it: 'camp country'. All his senses became more acute. If the patrol was to encounter an occupied enemy bunker system it would be in country like this.

It was more difficult to distinguish shape and shadow now but it was cooler and the patrol could travel without the psychological pressure of excessive noise. The transformation that had come over the patrol was stunning. Wilkins was patrolling with the precision of an Omega watch movement, individual alertness was at its peak and patrol speed had picked up considerably.

Ashton called a halt fifteen minutes after passing the bunker. They had patrolled for forty-five minutes since leaving the LZ and Ashton felt the need to rest. It was 1550 hours. He waited for his scout to look back and put up his hand in the standard gesture to halt. Wilkins nodded and quickly found the most comfortable position in which to crouch. Erickson and Collier reached Ashton and he pointed to the precise location he wanted them to occupy. When Dobel came into view, he gestured for him to stop and turn around to watch the rear. Then he made his way to Erickson and found out how far they had come since leaving the LZ.

Ashton sat down, withdrew the map case from his trouser pocket and removed the map. He studied it carefully for a brief period and made some calculations. He screwed out the lead on his black chinagraph pencil and made a small dot on the map where he decided their location was. When he finished, he placed the map back in its case and returned it to his pocket.

The commander looked rather absently around the area occupied by his patrol. The terrain had definitely changed, and they were now in the middle of a patch of sparse secondary growth as high as three metres in places. He reached for the top left-hand pocket of his shirt and withdrew a dark green plastic case containing his cigarettes and a Zippo lighter.

Ashton and Collier were the only ones in the patrol who smoked but neither smoked a lot on an operation. A packet of twenty would last Ashton at least two days and Collier never brought cigarettes with him on the grounds that he was giving it up. Jim Collier had been giving up smoking for the fifteen patrols they had completed together. Ashton recalled their first operation and how he had been angry at Collier on the third day of the patrol when his pioneer cum medic had asked him for a cigarette.

'Where's your Durries?' Ashton had asked him.

'I didn't bring any 'cause I'm giving up,' Collier had responded.

'You're giving up smoking on patrol?' The incredulous note in Ashton's voice had not registered with his medic.

'Yep! I figure that if I can give it up out here, I won't have any trouble giving up at Nui Dat.'

It cost Ashton over a packet of cigarettes on that first patrol and he ran out almost a day before they were extracted. It happened again on the second operation and since that time Ashton had always brought an extra packet of cigarettes for Collier. He had considered issuing an order for Collier to bring cigarettes on patrol but he knew, from his understanding of Collier's character, that the order would have been counterproductive.

He looked at the dark green case in his hand. This, he thought, is one of the most useful inventions of our time. The hard plastic case was in two parts and it fitted a packet of twenty cigarettes and a Zippo lighter in a tight, waterproof fit. Ashton had several of the containers in his tent at Nui Dat. He'd found the top was also useful as a cover for the second M16 magazine he had taped to the left side of the one on his weapon. The cover kept water and debris out of the magazine and stopped the top bullet from vibrating forward when the weapon was fired. This allowed him to carry thirty-six rounds in two magazines on his weapon and reduced the time it took him to change his first magazine in a firefight to around three seconds.

Ashton removed the top, withdrew a cigarette and placed it in his mouth. He slowly eased the cap of the lighter from its base so the hinge would not make its customary loud clicking noise and spun the flint wheel. There was a whooshing sound as the vapour ignited and Ashton could taste the lighter fuel as he touched the flame to his cigarette and drew heavily. The cough was almost immediate.

Rowan Ashton suffered from chronic bronchial problems which had dogged him since his early childhood. Because of this he wore a headband made from the sweat cloth that all Australian soldiers kept around their neck. He wore it in such a fashion that a long tail from the headband hung loosely down the left side of his face to about level with the bottom of his breast pocket. On each occasion that he was overcome by a fit of coughing he would place the hanging tail of the sweat rag in his mouth and over his nose to muffle the sound.

On this occasion the cough did not last long. Several muffled, hacking coughs and he was able to settle back and enjoy the remainder of his cigarette. This was not always the case when he was overtaken by a bout of coughing. On several occasions during an average day on patrol he could look forward to spending twenty or thirty seconds on his knees, with his head lower than his chest, trying to drain fluid from his lungs. This occurred whether he was smoking at the time or not. As far as he was concerned it was not a major problem but it was one he was acutely aware of. Succumbing to a coughing spasm at an inopportune time or failing to get the tail of the sweat rag to his mouth in time to muffle the noise could have serious implications for the patrol and its mission, if heard by the enemy.

Ashton drew heavily on his cigarette and thought about the mission. 'Reconnoitre Patrol Zone 624' was the mission given to him by the operations staff, with the limitation to be prepared to engage opportunity targets in the last forty-eight hours. It was a pretty standard mission for a patrol of six days duration, a fairly simple recce/ambush task that normally took the course of four days' finding the enemy and two days' harassing them.

It was now 1600 hours. Ashton attracted the attention of his patrol members with the commonly used 'click-click' of the tongue and held up his hand with all digits spread to indicate that they would move in five minutes. There were many methods used by patrols to attract attention; the double tongue click was one that had a number of variations depending on whether the noise was generated from the front, back or side of the mouth. There was no restriction on methods for attracting attention provided that the noise did not travel outside the immediate perimeter and alert the enemy to the patrol's presence. Patrol Six-Six used the double tongue click because it was simple and everyone could manage it even when the inside of the mouth was dry from nervous tension, apprehension or downright fear.

Ashton watched Wilkins stand up and move his pack to the most comfortable position on his back. His attention was focused on an area beyond his scout when he recalled the changed vegetation. He picked up his weapon and stood up. Shouldering his pack, he made his way to where the scout was preparing to move off.

'What do you make of this light high secondary, Billy?'

'Classic camp country,' the scout confirmed. 'There's two lots of cover from the air here and these small trees are the ideal size for overhead protection poles.'

Ashton agreed. There was better than a ninety per cent chance of finding a big bunker system in this country. That left only one ponderable: would it be occupied by the enemy? He looked around the patrol to ensure that everyone was ready, motioned briefly to Wilkins to wait, and gestured for Erickson to move closer.

'Pass it back, Bluey,' he whispered as the signaller reached him. 'There's a better than average chance that we're getting near a big bunker system. Take it easy and be on the lookout for the signs.'

As the scout and his commander moved off, Erickson nodded and started to drift back toward Collier who had moved on to the anticipated line of march. Erickson and Collier hardly needed to be told—they had been in and around many a bunker system during the past fifteen patrols and Allen Cunningham had been wounded crossing the perimeter fence of a VC bunker system on the previous patrol.

Erickson motioned Collier and Dobel toward him with an urgent gesture. 'Bunker system up here somewhere . . . probably,' he whispered to the two tailend men. 'Better be switched on.' He added, for Dobel's benefit, 'Don't want another Cunningham effort.'

Dobel looked sceptically at the pair in front. He knew the Cunningham story. He had heard it a hundred times in the boozer but figured it had been embellished a fair bit by the volume of Victoria Bitter beer that the Six-Six patrol members had put away on the nights following their return from that operation.

'How do you figure a bunker system up ahead?' Dobel asked, looking intently from one to the other.

'The type of country we're coming into,' Erickson replied, as he moved off to stay in touch with Ashton.

'How can you guarantee that?' Dobel persisted. 'Just because of the type of country?'

'Fuck's sake!' Collier threw at him. 'How long've you been in country, Dobel.' It was a taunt, not a question. Dobel's expression didn't change. He looked quizzically at Collier, his face begging an answer.

He really doesn't know, thought Collier, wondering what experience their new corporal really had. He said, 'This is the *best* country for their bunkers—high primary, with sparse medium height secondary. It gives them additional cover from the air and better security from detection and attack at ground level.' He stared at Dobel for several seconds, then moved off in the direction the others had taken, shaking his head in disbelief as he went.

As Dobel watched him go, he felt a little foolish. But he put the thought out of his mind and quickly checked the area for telltale signs of their presence. There was nothing of note but he made a cursory, and unnecessary, gesture by pushing some more leaves over the spot where Collier had been sitting. This served only to make the area more noticeable to anyone who was tracking the patrol, but Dobel did not appear to care. He took one last quick look around and moved off behind the others.

The day was quickly losing its heat but the patrol's pace did not increase. If anything, it slowed. They had gone two hundred metres since the stop and Wilkins and Ashton were scouting well, but the anticipated indicators of enemy habitation were not forthcoming and the tension was building in the front pair. Suddenly Wilkins stopped, took a half pace back and swivelled his body a little until it was facing a particular direction. Then he squatted like a local Vietnamese villager. He lifted his rifle and placed the barrel across his left knee.

Ashton stopped and did not move. This was Wilkins' standard reaction to coming upon a track that might need serious investigation. Ashton knew the body language well, it was Billy's call. Erickson moved quietly to a position where he had a clear view of what was going on and propped. The rear pair also propped when Collier saw that Erickson had stopped. He put up his left hand in a traffic policeman's gesture to catch Dobel's attention.

Billy Wilkins squatted, motionless, for a full minute. Ashton waited and watched, so did Erickson. Finally, without taking his eyes from the track, Wilkins raised his left hand to just level with his left ear and, with the index and forefinger raised, made a walking gesture.

It was what Wilkins called his upside-down track signal. The signal was meant to be given at waist level with the fingers pointing down but everybody in Patrol Six-Six, with the possible exception of Dobel, understood perfectly that this was merely another variation of trade procedures, adopted out of necessity.

Ashton and Erickson noticed Wilkins' index finger, still held behind his left ear and beckoning for the commander to come forward. Ashton, unaware that Erickson had noticed Wilkins' signal, passed the message to him before he moved forward cautiously toward his scout. Meanwhile, Erickson passed the information to the rear pair and instructed them to close up. Now everyone in the patrol knew of the potential danger from the front and were ready should it manifest itself as a positive enemy threat.

Ashton reached Wilkins and studied the track before them. It was a classic VC foot track, almost half a metre in width, ten centimetres in depth and bare of leaves. Both men studied the ground for almost a minute.

'What do you think, Billy?' Ashton asked his scout in a barely audible voice.

'A lot of traffic has been along here, but I don't think anyone has been down here today.'

'Agreed,' said Ashton, 'we'll cross in a stagger, OK?' It was an order.

Billy nodded but remained where he was. Ashton stood upright and caught Erickson's attention. He held up the index and second finger of his left hand and crossed one over the other. Erickson watched intently as Ashton relaxed his hand and made a series of hopping motions with his forefinger. Erickson nodded and turned to pass the message to Collier before he moved forward.

It was another vulnerable moment for the small group. They would be exposed to enemy presence for the time they were in the vicinity of the track. A small number of enemy moving quietly along the track was all that was necessary to place them in jeopardy. The wounding of even one of the patrol in such a situation could be catastrophic because of the time it would take for friendly assistance to arrive.

The staggered track-crossing was the fastest method known to Ashton that still provided reasonable security for the patrol. It simply involved a concertina action that ensured that one member was facing in each direction until the last man crossed the track. The last two men were then responsible for supporting each other until they were fully clear.

The well-practised drill saw the patrol clear the track in well under a minute. Wilkins and Ashton knew that the rear men would be vulnerable for some time after they crossed so they forced the pace a little to assist them to move away from the obstacle in the shortest possible time.

It was almost 1645 hours and time to start looking for a secure night lying-up place, or LUP. Ashton pushed on for just over fifty metres before he found an area that he felt was suitable for the night. He commenced the ritual of clearing the LUP by stopping the scout on the axis of advance. He physically directed the signaller and medic to where he felt was the most suitable location for them. Finally, he stopped Dobel at a point he considered the correct distance out for a perimeter.

Security during a lengthy stop was paramount. Ashton needed to confirm that the area to the front and to each flank was cleared. He did so by sending members of the patrol in each direction in turn to ensure that there was no physical sign of enemy presence. When he was satisfied, he produced a series of hand signals that ordered the members of the patrol to remove their packs and sit down to listen.

The commander settled back to consult his map. He attracted the attention of his signaller, who provided him with details of the distances they had travelled. He removed the diary from his map case and made a number of entries. He returned the map and diary to the map case and put them away. Then he reached into one of the pouches on his belt and took out a dirty, black-handled shaving brush. He pulled the M16 with its under-slung XM148 across his knees and began to run the soft bristles up and down to remove any dust from the system. It had been a good day so far, Rowan Ashton reflected—on the ground without being sprung, a bit of sign that the VC are about, and we should confirm the extent tomorrow.

He felt good. He felt very, very tired, but he felt good.

3

Corporal Gary Dobel did not share the good feeling that his commander had. It had been a disastrous day as far as he was concerned, even though the insertion had gone well and it was good to be on the ground and reasonably secure. Well, as secure as you can be when you are only five men in the middle of an area reputedly teeming with enemy. And it was sobering to think that no indirect fire support was available to call on, and that any direct fire support from helicopter gunships was, at best, an hour away.

Dobel was no longer sure if he was suited to this job. The others in the patrol seemed to know a lot more than he did. He was embarrassed by the incident at the last stop. If this sort of terrain was indicative of camp country, as everyone here seemed to know it as, why hadn't he learned that in his former patrol? He could not understand how the members of this patrol seemed to know what each other was thinking or was about to do. He had not noticed that on his previous operations.

Willie had been a good patrol commander, the corporal thought . . . liked to do a lot of things himself, but he was good to work with. Dobel pulled a shaving brush from his webbing and began to clean the dust from his weapon. He'd felt that he'd been a good member of Willie's patrol and that he deserved his promotion to corporal. Now he was not so sure, and suddenly he realised that he lacked experience in many of the basic areas of the job.

Maybe I need to be more assertive, take the initiative a little more, he reflected. He knew that Wilkins and Collier in particular resented his being the 2IC of Patrol Six-Six. Both men thought Erickson should have been promoted into the job. He recalled a discussion he'd overheard between Wilkins, Collier and 'Snowy' Jacobs, a member of his former patrol, in the boozer a few nights before they deployed.

'How come that prick Dobel got promoted over Bluey Erickson?' Jim Collier had asked of nobody in particular.

'I don't know,' Wilkins responded. 'Bluey's forgotten more about patrolling than that Dobel will ever know.'

'You *don't know*, do you, you blokes,' Jacobs bought in. 'Dobel's married to the OC's sister! He *had* to promote him or he'd be sleeping alone for the rest of his life!'

They'd broken into wild laughter at that and the conversation had quickly changed to the OC's sex life and ended with some downright derogatory comments on officers in general.

Dobel thought they were pretty low comments but had decided against bracing them up at the time because they were extremely drunk and it would have taken very little to set them all off. Funnily enough, he thought to himself, Bluey Erickson had been really good about it and had been one of the first to congratulate him. If Erickson could accept him, why couldn't the rest of the Diggers? A strong hand, maybe that was all that was needed.

But they were right about his not knowing as much as Erickson. It was Erickson's third operational tour of duty with the SAS and he was vastly experienced in the physical aspects of contact with the enemy. Even between the patrols, the balance was way out for this tour. Patrol Six-Six had completed fifteen patrols and had been involved in six contacts with the enemy. Dobel's former patrol had completed twelve patrols and, although they had sighted and recorded the movements of a lot of VC, they had not been involved in a firefight.

Dobel himself had not gone through the same program of intense training and exercises in Australia that the remainder of the squadron had. He had completed a tour of duty with an infantry battalion three years before. It had been a short tour—he went as a reinforcement, came home with the battalion at the end of the tour and went to the SAS. He was already a lance corporal when he joined this squadron after its major work-up exercise in

New Guinea. Before that he had been in the transport section for almost a year, recovering from an injury he'd sustained during work-up training with another squadron.

It was always going to be a difficult task to fit into a tightknit group such as Ashton had developed, he knew that, but there was a genuine desire within him to do so. His biggest problem was that he was the least experienced in the patrol, and his biggest disappointment came from the way the more experienced junior members of the patrol treated him with what could only be described as absolute contempt.

While Gary Dobel was struggling with his thoughts the remainder of the patrol went about settling into a comfortable but alert defensive posture. Suddenly, without warning, the whole jungle came alive. It happened each evening in South Vietnam. Rowan Ashton referred to it as the 'sunset serenade' because of the way it started almost exactly one hour before last light and lasted in one form or another until darkness started to descend in earnest.

First came the chorus of what seemed to be a million cicadas. It started slowly at first with a dozen or so voices and built up to a crescendo of ear-piercing noise not unlike hundreds of benchsaws operating simultaneously in the immediate vicinity. For twenty minutes or so of each evening at this time of the year it was almost unbearable for anyone out there who had an acute level of hearing.

As the chorus of cicadas began to abate, the unmistakable bark of one of the larger species of deer would reach the patrol members and the sound of the late-evening feeders would occupy the attention of the patrol with their small but distinct noises. The sound of jungle fowl walking slowly across the layers of dead and decaying leaves was unnerving too, as the birds' actions remarkably mimicked the sound of a man doing his best to walk undetected across the jungle floor.

Then, with not more than fifteen minutes of useable daylight left, and as though it had been orchestrated, all sound would cease. After several minutes of silence and almost on cue a low-pitched sound with a tonal waver would start. Very slowly at first—then it would build through the tonal range, culminating at its highest pitch then quickly tapering to a very slow and deep growling sound. The following brief silence would be shattered by a remarkable inflection that, to human ears, appeared to say 'uk–yew'. Because of the elevation from which the noise seemed to come and the similarity of the final inflection to certain words of English origin, the source was christened the 'fuck-you bird'. But a lot of patrol members subscribed to the theory that the source was a grey-coloured lizard with an extremely beautiful blue and red crest.

The sunset serenade always provided disquieting moments for patrol members new to the country, but this was not the case here. Counting the commander's and signaller's previous tours of duty, Ashton's patrol could claim the experience of an average of over twenty operational patrols per member.

Ashton liked to use the period of the cicada serenade to cover the patrol's noisiest activities—the evening meal and the clearing of sleeping spaces. The patrol could then spend the thirty minutes before last light quietly attending to standard security measures. By twenty minutes after last light the patrol was usually secure in its LUP and briefed on what actions to take in the event of contact with the enemy during the night.

One by one, Rowan Ashton threw small pieces of stick in the direction of his patrol members. When the cicadas were active the usual double click with the tongue did not always penetrate that far. Having secured the men's attention, he motioned with his hand near his mouth that they should prepare and eat their evening meal.

It was safe enough for the patrol to use their small cooking stoves and the compressed solid fuel called hexamine. The hexamine came in small white packets each containing eight tablets 45 millimetres square. One packet fitted neatly into the cooking stove.

Mealtime was a ritual in most patrols. Much of the time spent on patrol was mundane and boring and, on most days, the only highlights were the three mealtimes. Each member ensured that only what he wanted for the meal was taken out of his pack. The pack was then secured before preparation of the meal commenced.

Ashton quietly opened the side pocket of his pack. He'd prepared each of his meals in a separate package during preparations for the operation. The patrol was programmed to run for six days and in his pack were eighteen individually wrapped packages. For a six day operation, Ashton would draw three days'

American Long Range Reconnaissance Patrol rations, two days' American 'C' rations and one day's Australian One Man Combat rations.

The last two nights before a patrol were always a relaxing time for Rowan Ashton—sitting in his tent at Nui Dat, loading his fourteen operational M16 rifle magazines with 5.56mm cartridges, rigging the M18A1 Claymore anti-personnel mines and preparing his individual meal packets. Filling magazines and rigging Claymores was a bit of a chore but preparing the meals was a joyful art.

Ashton had his stove alight and an almost full steel cup fighting to get hot on top of it. He looked around the patrol perimeter and beyond. It was important for each member to look up regularly at the part beyond the perimeter that was his responsibility to watch. Most times when a patrol was stationary it was possible to hear approaching movement before it could be detected visually. With the noise of the sunset serenade it was impossible to hear the smaller jungle sounds and so it became more important to look up often from whatever you were doing.

As soon as bubbles started to hang on the inside of his steel cup, Ashton opened the wrapper of the LRRP ration, removed the cup from the stove, and poured hot water into the mixture of dehydrated food. He carefully measured the water into the packet. Too much and it would be the consistency of soup; too little and it would be too dry. He needed to get it right first time as the remaining water in the cup would be used to make tea.

Ashton ate slowly, savouring each mouthful and now and then taking a very small sip of the sweet black tea. When he finished eating he put the tea bag and sugar wrappers into the meal bag, wrapped it very tightly and secured it with an elastic band. He removed a small green plastic bag from his shirt pocket, placed the rubbish in it, wrapped it tightly and put it in the side pocket of the pack where the meal had come from. He leaned back against the large tree that he had selected for himself and lit a cigarette. He braced himself for a bout of coughing but it never came. He smoked and sipped his tea and gazed out into the jungle, contented.

Everyone was relaxed after the meal but each man watched his area of responsibility. The buzzing noise of the cicadas stopped suddenly. There was a silence for a few seconds then it started up again. This was noticed by most of the patrol members, who tuned in a little more closely to the sounds of the jungle. Something had alerted the cicadas. It was a brief alert, but an alert nevertheless. The cicadas did not stop again and, after several minutes, the patrol members felt comfortable enough to relax.

Sergeant Ashton decided it was time to brief his men. He did this three times each day that the patrol was in reconnaissance mode—in the morning, at lunchtime and in the evening. The morning and evening briefing detailed his plan for the next twelve hours and the lunchtime briefing was used to update the patrol on his thoughts. Naturally, any change of plan forced on him by enemy activity would be passed on to the men as soon as possible.

Ashton stood up quietly, bringing his weapon to the crook of his left arm as he did so, and moved off in the direction of his 2IC. The cicadas stopped their infernal buzzing for a brief moment, then started again. He reached Dobel's position and knelt down beside him.

'How's it going?' he asked quietly, as he took the map case from his trouser leg pocket.

'OK.'

Ashton removed the map and returned the case to his pocket. He opened the map for Dobel to see. 'We're about here,' he whispered, pointing to the spot on the map where he believed them to be. 'That foot track we crossed was about here,' he continued, pointing to a dotted line he had made on the map running roughly east–west. He waited for a nod from the corporal.

Dobel gave him a look that he interpreted as agreement, but before Ashton could continue the corporal spoke. 'That was a good track back there. Are we going to do anything about it?'

The question took the commander by surprise. 'What do you mean, "do anything about it"?'

'Well,' Dobel said, 'it's well used—we should observe it for a while.'

'Its not that well used,' Ashton responded. 'It hasn't been used in the last twelve or so hours at least.'

Dobel frowned. 'Looked really worn and you could see footprints on it. How do you know it hasn't been used for that long?'

'Cobwebs!' Ashton replied, a little amused. 'There were big cobwebs just up from where we crossed. They weren't spun today—spiders usually spin at night. And there were a lot of insects in them. They may have been spun last night, but most likely the night before.'

Dobel was half convinced. 'The footprints?' he asked.

'Under the canopy they can stay moist and fresh-looking for a long time.'

The corporal nodded. He seemed happy enough with this, so Ashton went on with briefing him on what action to take if the enemy contacted them during the night. He opened a button of his shirt and slid the map inside after confirming the patrol rendezvous locations. He asked Dobel if he had any questions. Dobel shook his head.

Ashton stood up to move but crouched down again. 'See this tree you're leaning against?' he asked quietly.

'Yes,' replied Dobel, half turning to look at the slender sapling.

'It's too small,' said the commander. 'Every time you move against it, the top shakes.' He grasped a similar-sized sapling nearby and moved it gently near the base. The bushy top, two or three metres from the ground, shook quite noticeably. 'There are no other tops moving,' Ashton pointed out. 'Easy for even a dumb arse VC to pick up.'

Dobel looked acutely embarrassed. 'It's no problem,' Ashton went on. 'You just need to sit against a more solid tree or away from trees altogether if there aren't any solid ones around.'

Rowan Ashton went quietly about the patrol and briefed each member in turn. He found Collier's position last of all. He crouched down beside the pioneer/medic, pulled the map from inside his shirt and said in his familiar tone, 'How's it going, Jimmy?'

'Snowy Jacobs is right, Rowan,' Collier responded trenchantly. 'Dobel is a cockhead.'

'How so?' Ashton inquired, more than a little interested.

'He knows fuck-all about patrolling. Didn't even know that this was camp country . . . and look at that piss-fartin' tree he's sitting against!'

Ashton smiled. His medic had obviously watched him at Dobel's position. 'He must know something about patrolling or he wouldn't be here,' Ashton countered, hoping to draw everything that was bothering Collier out into the open.

'He'll get someone killed,' Collier went on, as though Ashton hadn't spoken. 'Mark my words Rowan, he'll do something stupid and someone will get killed.'

'He needs experience,' Ashton said, slowly and forcefully so that the words would sink in.

'Bullshit!' He's done twelve patrols and half a tour with a battalion—you'd think that would be enough experience.'

'You can't count his battalion tour, Jimmy, you know that,' Ashton said, going to Dobel's defence. 'That's a hundred or more guns on the ground around you in a company group. Some people can't handle this tippy-toe shit—they need the security of all those rifles and machine guns around them. And artillery and mortars too.'

'It's still experience,' countered Collier.

'Some people take more time to learn. A lot depends on how much people are shown or had things explained. Remember yourselves,' Ashton went on as the thought struck him, 'I had to spoonfeed you blokes at the start of the tour. Want to cast your mind back to the first few patrols?'

You prick, Ashton, thought Collier; he remembered all right. Ashton had nearly fired him from the patrol in those early days. He had never been spoken to so vehemently and yet so quietly. Ashton had scared the living hell out of him in just one brief discussion about his behaviour, his future in the patrol in partic- ular, and his future in the SAS Regiment in general.

Ashton decided that Collier's lack of response meant that he was getting through to the Darlinghurst delinquent. 'We need to help him out as much as we can,' he said quietly. 'Explain things to him, instead of getting up him every time he fucks up.' Ashton paused just long enough to cause Collier to look at him expec- tantly. When he did, Ashton finally said, 'Give him a go, Jimmy, we might be able to turn him into a first-rate tailend Charlie.'

You bullshit artist, Collier thought as he looked into the sergeant's eyes and smiled. 'OK, Rowan,' he said, forcing his thoughts to the back of his mind, 'we'll turn him into a first-rate tailend Charlie.'

Ashton knew that Collier was not fooled by his 'Save the 2IC' speech, but he knew that the medic would go out of his way to help Dobel in future. At least, until he decided once and for all that the man was indeed a cockhead, and beyond salvation.

Ashton quickly briefed Collier and brought him up to date with the rest of the patrol. He returned to his central position and sat down quietly. He was pleased to note that Dobel had moved from the sapling to a more substantial tree.

The cicadas had stopped their serenade, or at least the main chorus had given it away for the evening. There was still the odd one or two buzzing from time to time, but the late evening feeders and barking deer had taken over. It was around thirty minutes before last light.

Rowan Ashton called his patrol members in, two at time, to clear their bed spaces. The spaces were cleared in a rough star formation around the commander. Ashton insisted that everyone should be within touching distance—if not from Ashton himself, then from someone that Ashton could touch.

This was important as it enabled everyone to be woken up quickly and quietly should an emergency occur during the night or should someone feel a pressing need to evacuate his bowels. If one member of the patrol was up and walking around during the night, everyone was required to be awake. Sleeping men woken suddenly by someone standing over them in the night can, and usually do, react violently.

As the bed spaces were cleared, the owners took a bearing with their compass along the axis of their sleeping space and moved back to their position on the perimeter. Erickson was the last finished. It was within ten minutes of last light and the 'uk–yew' had started. He was moving back to his position on the perimeter when there was a burst of fire from an automatic weapon away to the north-west. Everyone in the patrol froze. The firing sounded extremely close but each member was experienced enough to know that it was not a direct threat. All eyes turned to Ashton who returned each stare with the silent question: how far?

The consensus was that the firing had occurred between a hundred and four hundred metres distant. Accurate judging of the distance to a sound in the jungle was difficult. In the case of rifle fire it was even more difficult. So much depended on whether the rifle barrel was pointing toward you, away from you or at an oblique angle when it was discharged. Naturally the atmospherics at different times of the day also helped to distort the sound.

Consequently, judging the distance to signal shots that the VC employed was far from an exact science.

The last of the 'uk–yew' sounds split the stillness as darkness closed on the patrol. Ashton could barely make out the shapes of his men on the perimeter. He clicked. There was immediate movement on the perimeter. It was very slow and quiet movement. Movement that could be detected by sight but not by sound. It was good patrol technique, as visual distance was now not more than five metres.

One by one the patrol members moved toward the centre of the LUP with their packs slung by one shoulder strap. Each placed his pack at the end of his bed space nearest the centre of the star and sat down with his back against the pack. There was no sound or movement from the patrol for over fifteen minutes. Everyone was quietly listening to the jungle going through its own nightly shutdown routine and trying to detect foreign sounds on the jungle floor.

It was pitch black. The only noise that could be heard was a small rubbing sound as patrol members spread the tangy American mosquito repellent over exposed areas of their hands and faces. There was a sharp report of a rifle from the general direction of the previous burst. 'How far?' Ashton whispered, to no one in particular.

'Sounds closer than the burst,' Wilkins responded softly. 'About a hundred metres, I'd say.'

Probably from a camp up in that area, Ashton thought. 'About three hundred, I'd say,' he whispered. 'Sounds like they're all coming from the same area.'

No sooner were the words out when they heard a burst of three rounds of automatic rifle fire from several hundred metres to the north-east. Ashton heard Wilkins sniggering softly beside him.

'Bloody big same area.' There was unmistakable humour in the scout's voice. The remainder of the patrol chuckled softly with him.

'Good one, Billy,' Ashton admonished him playfully. 'Now go to sleep, you pricks.'

There were soft rustling noises as they quietly removed their bedding and spread it out. Ashton carried his groundsheet in the right-side trouser pocket of his camouflage uniform. It was a piece of soft, green Vietnamese plastic, a little longer than a man and a metre and a half wide, that folded into a small, flat parcel. He unclipped his webbing belt and removed his webbing. He laid the belt out flat, with the inside facing upward, at the top of his sleeping space and forward of his pack. He removed the long sweat rag from around his neck, folded it, and laid it on the belt so that it covered one of the pouches and the water bottle. He eased his left arm through the left shoulder strap and lay down on his back with his head on the folded sweat rag.

It was customary for Ashton's patrol to sleep like this. One arm through a webbing strap and rifle lying upright and beside the body on whichever side was favoured. The pack was upright with the shoulder straps on the side of the sleeper. Should the VC manage to surprise the patrol during the night all personal equipment was within arm's reach, and it was therefore likely that the patrol could escape without leaving critical items of equipment behind.

Ashton lay for a long time staring at the blackness of the canopy above. He heard another shot from the area to the north-west. Has to be a camp up there, he thought. He looked at his watch. It was 1930 hours and almost thirty minutes after last light. Ashton closed his eyes and drifted off to sleep.

The gunshots woke him again at 2200 hours and at twenty minutes after midnight. Both times there were three-round automatic bursts from the north-west direction they'd noted earlier. On each occasion the burst was answered several minutes later by a single shot from a long way up to the north-east.

At 0200 hours another three-round burst of automatic fire woke Ashton. This time the source was up in the north-east. He noted the time. Several minutes later he heard a single shot from the north-west. He heard other members of the patrol shift in their bed spaces, obviously checking their watches too.

No doubt we'll find out what's up there tomorrow, Ashton thought as he tried to will himself back to sleep. He lay there for a long time, listening. There was no more shooting but he thought he could hear voices way off in the distance—Vietnamese voices, accompanied by grunting and creaking sounds. The sounds were familiar but he could not call them to mind. There was the distinct but very faint sound of metal on metal. Then Wilkins sat up and listened intently.

'What's the matter, Billy?' Ashton whispered.

'Those sounds, I've heard those sounds before but I can't put a name to them.'

'Don't worry, mate, it'll come in time.'

'Umm' was all the response Wilkins could muster as he lowered his head to the webbing belt pillow. Collier and Erickson both stirred briefly and, although they did not appear to wake up, Ashton knew they were also in a state of awareness, listening.

That was the way it was. Ashton never ran a sentry roster at night and there were two good reasons why he felt there was no need to. One was the small, well-concealed, out of the way areas he picked for night positions. The other was the knowledge that in these circumstances everyone remained in a state of semi-alertness all night. The subconscious element of anxiety ensured that. Ashton again looked at his watch. It was nearly a quarter to three in the morning. He pulled the half sock that he wore on his wrist back over the luminous dial of his watch, and drifted off to sleep.

4

Sergeant Ashton opened his eyes slowly. As always, his body felt cramped from sleeping with only a piece of thin plastic between him and the jungle floor. It was still dark, so he lay for a moment looking at the blackness above. He knew without consulting his watch that it was close to first light. Time to get them up, he thought.

Almost on cue, the patrol members began to stir. It took some longer than others to get their bearings and switch on to their surroundings. This was common on the first morning after insertion. Allen Cunningham had usually been first up, shaking and waking the others and making sure the morning routine got off to a flying start. Today there was no Cunningham; he was in the Military Hospital at Vung Tau waiting to recover sufficiently to make the journey back to Australia.

Wilkins was already sitting up, webbing equipment on and rifle comfortably across his lap. Ashton quickly found the right shoulder strap of his equipment and eased into it. He recovered the folded sweat rag he'd used as a pillow before he did so. There was movement behind him and to his right as Erickson and Collier began to stir. The movements were slight but the noise sounded quite loud in the stillness of the pre-dawn. 'Ssssh!' Ashton hissed through his teeth. The noise stopped instantly and the two soldiers continued with their activity with more care and attention.

Dobel had not stirred and this annoyed Ashton. Cunningham would never have allowed himself to be last up. He considered

35

it the 2IC's job to get the show rolling in the morning. Besides, the likes of Wilkins and Collier would have ragged the old 2IC senseless for weeks had he ever been the last to rise.

Ashton leaned sideways toward Wilkins, who sensed this and eased slightly to the right knowing that his commander was going to speak to him.

'Wake that prick up,' Ashton whispered.

'Pleasure!'

Ashton smiled tightly as he heard the stick hit Dobel somewhere on the body. There was a muffled cry of surprise and a long, soft 'Sssssh' as Wilkins carried out the order.

Before the sun provided sufficient light to distinguish shapes with any certainty, all sleeping spaces used the previous night were refurbished, equipment was packed away and all members of the patrol had reapplied a liberal amount of camouflage paint to their face and the parts of fingers that protruded from their patrol gloves.

As the light improved, each member in turn moved quietly back to the position on the perimeter he had occupied the previous evening. All sat silently, waiting for the day to come awake. The early birds were first, looking for the proverbial worm. The small jungle creatures were next, darting about with vigour that increased as the day brightened, as though the sun was the sole provider of their energy.

Ashton always took this opportunity to record the events of the previous evening. He went around the patrol members to discuss what each had heard. While it was too early to determine a pattern of enemy movement in the area, all signs from the night's VC activity indicated that north was the correct direction to be heading. He also briefed each member on what he planned for the coming day and on what emergency procedure to follow in the event that the patrol was split up. As he left each member's position he instructed the man to prepare himself a meal.

Ashton purposely briefed Dobel last. He knelt down beside the 2IC, placing his weapon upright against a small sapling.

'What have you got from last night?' he asked.

'What do you mean?' The corporal had a blank, uneasy expression in his eyes.

Shit, Ashton thought, he doesn't know what I'm talking about. 'All that activity about last night—you got a time, direction and estimated distance for it?' It was not a question, it was a demand.

'No.'

'Didn't you hear any of that stuff last night?'

'Yes, I heard it,' the corporal responded indignantly, 'but I didn't take much notice of it.'

Ashton was flabbergasted. Everybody recorded everything, it was the lore.

'Show me your diary.' Ashton put out his hand for it, still shaking his head in disbelief.

Dobel removed the green notebook from its waterproof wrap and handed it to his superior. Ashton opened it. It was all there, everything that happened the previous day was neatly logged with times, locations and distances. Surprisingly, it looked a lot better than the method he used to set out his own diary.

'This is good,' said Ashton, 'but what about last night's shit?'

'We never had to do that,' Dobel replied. 'Willie always did the night stuff.'

Ashton was amazed. 'Willie' was the nickname that Dobel's former patrol commander, Bevan Willis, went by. 'What happened if Willie slept through the night activity?'

'He never did,' answered the corporal with a wry smile.

Ashton knew Sergeant Bevan Willis as a solid but sometimes nervous type and could understand how he might not get much sleep if there was a prolonged VC presence. He looked at Dobel as he handed back the diary. This is my fault, he thought, I haven't briefed this bloke properly on what I expect of him.

'OK,' he said, 'in future, before you bed down, take a bearing with your compass along the axis of your sleeping space.' He paused to let that sink in. 'As soon as you hear an enemy activity, make a note of the time, distance, direction and what the activity might be.'

The corporal didn't look convinced. 'How am I going to write all that stuff down at night without using a torch?'

'You're not. File it in the back of your mind and write it in your book first thing in the morning.' He looked at Dobel for a positive sign. The corporal merely nodded his understanding.

The system was not foolproof, Ashton would be the first to admit. However, at times when there was enemy night activity only three or four major incidents, at most, would occur, and the patrol members always seemed to provide reports in the morning that confirmed each other's memory.

Satisfied that his 2IC would record future night activities, Ashton briefed him on the coming day's plan. When he was satisfied there could be no misunderstanding on Dobel's part, he picked up his weapon and turned to go. Then, almost as an afterthought, he bent down so that his mouth was level with his 2IC's ear.

'You were last up this morning,' he whispered. The corporal nodded and looked into his sergeant's face.

'Make that the last time it happens,' Ashton ordered. 'The 2IC gets to be first up to make sure the morning routine is conducted properly.' Dobel's frown followed his commander most of the way back to his central position.

Wilkins led off north toward the area where most of the noise had come from during the night. Ashton lagged a little and caught Erickson's eye. The signaller moved up to his commander and propped beside him.

'Tell Jimmy that I want to know what sort of a job Dobel does in refurbishing the position,' Ashton ordered, and moved off quickly to catch up to the scout. Erickson did not have time to acknowledge before his commander was gone. There was no need to tell Collier anything—they were all into making a critical assessment of the 2IC's performance. Everything that Dobel did was compared to how Allen Cunningham would have handled a similar situation.

Ashton quickly caught up to his scout and settled in about three paces behind. He liked to be close up so he could cover the scout while he was going over, around or under obstacles. In essence, they worked more like a pair of scouts than as commander and scout. Erickson, the next in line, usually travelled three times that distance behind his commander. Ashton insisted on this as it gave the back of the patrol more time to react while he and Wilkins were sorting out any enemy problem they might encounter up front. At the same distance again, and bringing up the rear, Collier and Dobel were meant to be operating with the same close cooperation. Ashton always ensured that his 2IC had the idea that he was a 'rear end scout', an idea that was never more important than when a patrol was being followed by the enemy. Of course the distance Erickson travelled behind Ashton and in front of Collier depended entirely on the closeness of the vegetation.

The patrol pushed north without incident or rest for almost two hours. They patrolled five hundred painstaking metres through some severely bomb-damaged country. The going had been noisy and even Wilkins found difficulty negotiating the terrain without making a lot of noise. The last fifty or so metres, though, had been a wonderful change. They had come through another four hundred metre wide patch of bomb-devastated terrain and were again in some classic high primary jungle. Although it was more comfortable there, all were aware that the likelihood of enemy presence had increased.

With a pair of brief signals Ashton ordered Wilkins to stop and sit down. Erickson approached and he caught his eye and held up his watch for the signaller to see. Erickson nodded in understanding that it was time to secure a LUP and report to their headquarters. He brought the signaller in close to him and stopped him there.

The next man in was Collier. Ashton pointed to the spot he wanted him to go to and made a sign that advised him they would be stopping for as long as it took to communicate with their base. Dobel arrived and he went through the same routine. Finally, Ashton and Erickson were together inside a triangular perimeter of which Wilkins, Collier and Dobel formed the points.

While Erickson prepared his radio equipment, Ashton withdrew his map from the side pocket of his camouflage trousers. He leaned over briefly to catch his signaller's attention and, with standard sign language, asked him how far the patrol had come since their night stop. Erickson looked at the oval-shaped pedometer taped to the inside of the pistol grip of his M16 and held up his hand to make two separate signs. One with all digits spread was followed closely by a display of only two fingers. Ashton looked directly at Erickson, reproduced the signals and silently mouthed the words, 'five hundred and twenty'.

Erickson nodded and went back to his task of preparing to transmit. Ashton consulted his map to determine the location of the patrol and wrote it on the waterproof map covering with black chinagraph pencil. The AN/PRC 64 radio was ready; only the aerial had to be run out to operating length for the frequency being used. Ashton was sitting less than two metres from Erickson. He held up the map to display what he'd written. The message would advise headquarters of their 'map grid location and the direction in which they were moving, north.

Erickson copied the message into his book and immediately set about encoding it for transmission. This was Ashton's way. There were other commanders who would not allow their signallers such autonomy but he had absolute trust in Erickson. Ashton believed that, as commander, he was given the mission, it was his mission and he alone was responsible for its success or failure. But he never bought into the professional execution of any task being carried out by one of his subordinates unless there was an obvious breach of competency. Training of the 2IC was an exception. The 2IC was Ashton's understudy and therefore responsible to assume command should anything happen to him. It was Ashton's duty to ensure that Dobel was schooled properly in the running of a patrol and the importance of getting the job done. The maintenance of the aim and the achievement of the mission was all that really mattered as far as Ashton was concerned.

Bluey Erickson stood up slowly. He had a small black fishing reel filled with black aerial wire in his hand. He measured off a little over two metres from the end of the aerial and tied the wire to the tree above his pack, which was sitting with the radio inside its top flap. He checked that the two metres was sufficient for the end to plug into the set, then stooped down and picked up the M16 that was lying across the bottom section of his pack. With the M16 in his right hand and the small reel in his left, he turned to face Jim Collier.

Collier came upright, his SLR held loosely in his hands, and looked at Erickson. No communication had passed between the two men until this time. There had been no need. Collier knew as soon as the signal for a communications stop was given that Erickson would need protection in order to run the aerial to its fullest extent. It was also no accident that Collier was sitting almost directly along the line from Erickson that the aerial had to follow. Ashton had calculated the aerial direction requirement on arrival and had put him in that position on purpose.

Erickson made a clicking noise with his tongue to gain the attention of Wilkins and Dobel. Both men looked at him while he held up the reel for them to see and pointed in Collier's direction. They responded by giving a thumbs-up sign and quickly returned to their task of watching for approaching enemy.

While Collier watched for any sign of danger, Erickson hung the aerial just above head height by draping it over branches that were broken, or by passing the fishing reel through small forks that ran off the trunk. When he reached the end of the wire, he secured it with a slip knot that held tension on the aerial but would release when pulled firmly from the other end.

The task completed, Collier settled back in position to resume his normal vigil. Erickson returned to his pack, attached the aerial, put the earpiece in his ear and turned on the set. He fumbled inside his left trouser leg pocket and came up with the message books. He extracted them from their waterproof wrap, glanced briefly at the operating instructions for that day, plugged in the external morse key and was ready to transmit.

Dit Dit Dah Dah Dah; Dah Dah Dah Dit Dit; Dah Dit Dit Dit . . . Dah Dit Dit; Dit. The sharp sounds were barely audible to Ashton as his signaller interrogated call sign Two Eight Bravo for advice on his incoming signal strength. He liked to sit fairly close to his signaller during comms stops. It ensured that he was on hand to respond to any queries from headquarters and it gave him an opportunity to brush up on his radio skills.

Erickson waited approximately fifteen seconds for a reply from his base station. It never came. He had asked them to advise his signal strength and got no response. He cradled the small brown key again in the palm of his left hand and this time asked them to advise signal strength and readability.

There were several seconds of silence. Ashton was fully attuned to the proceedings now. The unmistakable sound of the base station's PRC 47 set coming on line was extremely loud through Erickson's earpiece. It worried Ashton that the noise might be heard for quite a distance outside the perimeter.

Wilkins had the best hearing of the three on the perimeter and he was slightly further away than the others. Ashton threw a short, thick stick in his direction to attract his attention. Wilkins looked around and caught Ashton's eye. The commander pointed at him, cupped a hand behind his ear, and then pointed to Erickson's pack. Wilkins shook his head to confirm that he couldn't hear any noise from the radio.

Ashton relaxed and lit a cigarette. The small skinks were chasing their prey all over the jungle floor. It was the perennial wonder of the jungle. Would the skink's appetite ever be satisfied? There's a peacefulness about this place, Ashton thought as he watched a jungle fowl pecking at the ground several metres from the perimeter, completely unconcerned about their presence.

The single rifle shot dragged him violently back to reality. It came from the north and sounded very close. Everyone came alert instantly. Erickson was waiting for a reply to his message. It was not a good time for the patrol to have a problem with the enemy.

Ashton was in a crouched position with his weapon in his hand in less than a heartbeat. The adrenalin was pumping and his nerve endings seemed to ache. Each member of the patrol faced north in anticipation until another shot, off to the north-west, brought the conclusion that they were signal shots. They all relaxed a little. Ashton moved quietly to Wilkins' position and knelt down beside his scout. Satisfied there was no immediate danger, the remainder resumed their routine.

'How far?' Ashton whispered, nodding toward the north.

'Between two and three hundred metres.'

'Closer to two hundred, I'd say. Must be a track up there.'

Wilkins nodded. There was no need to remind him that additional vigilance would be required when they moved off in that direction. Ashton returned to his position to find Erickson with the morse key in his hand again. He stood by Erickson and listened quietly. The base station radio boomed in again: QSL . . . QRU.

'That means message received and understood and they've got nothing for us?' Ashton queried. Erickson nodded.

'Pack it up,' Ashton whispered, 'we'll move in five.' He turned to look around the LUP, clicking his tongue in the correct volume and pitch required to get the attention of the remainder of the patrol.

They looked inward and he held up the five splayed digits of his left hand. Each nodded in turn and went about making the final adjustments required for the move.

Ashton was extremely focused now. If there was a track up ahead that was being used by the VC, he might as well get up there and check it out properly.

A fraction longer than five minutes passed before the commander checked that his patrol was ready to move. He moved close to Wilkins. 'Which direction did that first shot come from, Billy?' he asked. Wilkins gestured and Ashton checked his compass against the direction indicated. 'Good,' he said quietly, 'let's go.'

Billy Wilkins had taken three steps before Ashton even realised that he had moved.

5

The sun was almost at 50 degrees in the eastern sky as the patrol moved off in the general direction of the rifle shots. A little west of north was the heading Wilkins followed. The direction was not precisely on a line to the shots but Ashton let him go. By the time they reached where he estimated the track to be, the sun would be almost directly overhead, and it would be time to cease all movement.

It was generally accepted that the VC did not move about in the middle of the day. From around 1100 hours in the morning until 1400 hours in the afternoon the VC observed a rest period, referred to by the Australians as 'park time'. It was standard procedure for patrols to observe park time, as a tactical necessity. Enemy resting quietly during the park time period were in the best position to pinpoint any movement in their vicinity.

In the early years of SAS operations in Vietnam, patrols had unexpectedly come upon enemy groups resting in the middle of the day. The enemy always had the upper hand in such cases and initiated the contact from a secure position. On almost every occasion when this happened the patrol in question had suffered one or more casualties.

It was Ashton's personal experience, though, that the enemy did not *always* stop for park time. On previous patrols while in OP on main enemy access tracks, he had sighted numbers of VC travelling during the park time period. Yet there were other occasions when Ashton's patrol had observed the enemy call a halt at approximately 1100 hours and resume after 1400 hours.

In any case, Rowan Ashton was not prepared to gamble unnecessarily with the lives of his men or the premature compromise of his patrol. There were a number of things about working in a small group that concerned Ashton, but there was very little about it that frightened him. He felt secure in the jungle with his group, secure in the knowledge that, by stealth, they could avoid detection by the enemy until it was time to declare their presence.

He was supremely confident in the patrol's mobility and its ability to evade an enemy's counteroffensive actions. Command and control of a small group in close country operations was a much simpler task than it was in a larger, more unwieldy formation. His small patrol had the ability to strike a severe blow to the enemy and withdraw quickly and quietly before the enemy commander had time to organise his formation to counter the action.

For these reasons, Ashton always observed park time. To his mind, park time was best spent in proximity to a well-defined access track so that any movement along it would be detected by the patrol. It was Ashton's established view that the enemy did not move during park time *unless* they were concentrating in an area in order to undertake a large-scale operation. Two-way traffic by the enemy during park time was an indication of a concentration of force in that general area, while one-way traffic was an indication that a concentration of force was occurring somewhere in the direction the enemy was moving in.

Ashton's feeling of confidence came from the trust that he had in his patrol members. Only Dobel was as yet untested. The remainder had come through a difficult eight months of their designated twelve month tour of duty. They had found many enemy camps that were occupied and had reported the movement of large enemy formations. Their patrol tasks had taken them all over Phuoc Tuy Province and into Long Khanh and Binh Tuy Provinces, and had led to contact with the enemy on six occasions.

The first of these earlier contacts had been deliberately planned by Ashton for the benefit of the two patrol members without combat experience. It was a simple plan: as soon as the reconnaissance task was complete, find a track that was being used infrequently by one or two enemy, engage them with rifle fire, do a body search for anything of intelligence value, and melt into the jungle.

The idea was to initiate the new members of his patrol to the close sound of gunfire in the jungle and the additional adrenalin rush that goes with combat. The success of the plan depended on finding the right location and circumstance to put it into action. It didn't matter to Ashton if the initial 'blooding' of his inexperienced members occurred on the first or the second patrol, but it was important that they were blooded his way and not in an unfortunate action where the enemy held the initiative in the contact.

As chance would have it, the opportunity arose on the very first patrol. They had conducted a detailed and thorough search of their area of operations and, in doing so, had found a situation where a narrow foot track ran along the southern side of a small creek flowing in an easterly direction. The track crossed the creek at a place where the banks of the stream were lowest and then turned back toward the north-west, thereby creating a hairpin bend in the track at the crossing point. This gave the patrol a view down the track for almost thirty metres in both directions.

The only members of the patrol at that time without combat experience were Wilkins and Collier. Ashton, Cunningham and Erickson had been initiated in combat on one of their previous tours of duty. Ashton did not make an issue out of the action he planned for Wilkins and Collier, nor did he explain the purpose behind the action. Not even Cunningham was privy to it.

Ashton secured a small LUP on the north side of the creek forty metres from the crossing point and briefed the patrol on the action he planned at the crossing. The mission statement invented for the purpose of the briefing was: 'To gain information on the enemy forces in the area through the capture of weapons, equipment and documents.'

The execution of the plan was simple. The patrol would move into extended line formation in a covered position adjacent to the hairpin so that they had maximum vision down the track in either direction, Ashton in the middle of the formation with Collier on his right and Wilkins on his left. Cunningham was on the extreme right flank next to Collier, with Erickson on the extreme left flank, next to Wilkins. Ashton stressed that the target size was a minimum of two and a maximum of five enemy.

Ashton was responsible for deciding on the target. He would initiate the action by shouting 'Dung loi! Dua tay len', the Vietnamese words for 'Stop! Hands up'. Collier and Wilkins were to wait for a reaction from the enemy and, if they didn't comply, Collier would engage the first enemy in line—or the one on the right if they were two abreast—and Wilkins would engage the second in line or the one on the left. Ashton, Cunningham and Erickson would engage whoever was behind.

When the action concluded, Ashton would order 'Flanks out' and Cunningham would move forward to cover the area of the north-west track and Erickson the area beyond the creek crossing. Collier and Wilkins would do the body search under Ashton's supervision. Collier would search and Wilkins would cover.

Critical to the success of the action was the patrol's conceal-ment. Waiting at the end of the hairpin, watching the enemy coming down the track toward them would be a nerve-racking experience. In the back of everyone's mind was the knowledge that if someone moved, or in some other way betrayed their presence to the enemy, it could all go very wrong.

As Ashton's briefing concluded and Wilkins and Collier moved back to their positions to prepare for action, the sergeant motioned the other pair to him. 'If they freeze, hose fuck out of the area.' Cunningham and Erickson both managed a smile to accompany their nods.

They moved quietly into the position Ashton selected from a reconnaissance that he and Wilkins had conducted before the briefing. Ashton had an uncanny ability to select the best location for everything they did and this time was no exception. When the members realised how secure the position really was, they lost much of the tension that had been with them as a result of the briefing.

The action was as much to test Wilkins and Collier as it was to blood them to combat operations, and Ashton hoped to find out a lot about his least experienced members. It would also confirm Erickson's ability, as he knew him only by reputation. Cunningham was a different story as he and Ashton had belonged to the same patrol for several months on their previous tour of duty, and the commander trusted him explicitly. Ashton was particularly interested in how long Wilkins and Collier would be prepared to give the VC after he challenged them—not too long, he hoped.

They waited almost twenty minutes that day before the enemy moved toward their position. When they did come, they approached from the north-west. The first indication Ashton had of their approach was the increase in tension that he noted in Wilkins. Wilkins had acute perception and, even though it was his first patrol, his combat senses were already well developed. The knowledge gave Ashton a good feeling.

When the enemy came into view Ashton was ready. There were two of them. Each carried a rifle slung across his back and both wore a light belt with storage pouches. They were travelling very fast and had their heads and eyes lowered, looking down at the track.

They approached within ten metres of the patrol and Ashton opened his mouth to challenge them when a background noise, barely detectable, made him pause. He decided to wait. He knew that Wilkins had heard it too; he could sense additional tension in his scout.

The two enemy soldiers passed through the hairpin bend in the track within three metres of their position. Both were wearing the black 'pyjama' uniform of the Regional Force Viet Cong units. But one carried a World War II United States M2 carbine and the other an ancient P17 rifle, which suggested to Ashton that they were more likely to be Local Force VC.

Ashton watched them disappear across the creek and turn right to follow the track along its southern side. As they disappeared from view, he heard the unmistakable sound of voices in the distance—Vietnamese voices, also approaching from the north-west.

Ashton focused hard on the new enemy threat. They were travelling as fast as the pair in front had been, the soft pad of Ho Chi Minh sandals on the bare earth track preceding their arrival. They came into view and Ashton himself tensed at their approach. There appeared to be a loose group of around ten but it was difficult to tell. The soldier in front carried an AK47 assault rifle and wore a set of chest webbing that stored additional magazines for his weapon. They spoke little and when they did it was soft, with a hint of breathlessness about it.

Rowan Ashton drew a shallow breath through his open mouth and held it. With his mouth still slightly open, he watched the VC approach the hairpin. He could feel the blood pressure pounding at his temples and the side of his neck. The back of his throat was dry. Let nothing happen to betray their presence to the enemy, he prayed. He breathed slowly and quietly through his mouth, his eyes watching the whole group while his mind dwelt on each individual that passed.

There were twelve in the party. Ashton assessed them to be possibly Main Force Viet Cong as they were heavily armed with modern weapons. He was not entirely sure what each man carried but he did notice at least two RPD light machine guns and two rocket-propelled grenade launchers or RPGs in the group.

As the enemy crossed the creek Ashton saw that some wore webbing belts with water bottles, some wore chest webbing and others had bandoliers slung across their body. The men with the RPGs wore specially designed pack frames that carried the B41 rockets for their launchers.

The patrol exhaled easily as the enemy party crossed the creek and turned to follow the two Local Force soldiers who preceded them. Ashton glanced first at Collier and then at Wilkins. Both faces were white beneath their camouflage but otherwise they were expressionless. Neither showed an outward sign of fear or nervousness. Ashton accepted this as a positive sign as he felt the blood returning to his own face. Each member caught Ashton's eye to gauge his reaction. He met each gaze steadily and merely shrugged his shoulders. They would wait.

Ashton thought about the two Local Force soldiers proceeding a hundred or so metres in front of a heavily armed squad of Main Force VC. He thought it odd at the time but, with the pressure of the action still to be carried out, he put it down to coincidence and placed no immediate significance on it.

The patrol waited a further twenty minutes before the soft pad of footsteps alerted them to the approach of another enemy group. Senses became heightened and the tension again mounted within the group. As the enemy appeared, it was noticeable that there was something significantly different about this group. They were travelling a good deal slower than the ones in front had been and they were closer together.

The first two VC travelled almost shoulder to shoulder, with
the one on the left, as the patrol faced them, just one body width
in front of his comrade. Ashton noted that there were four in the
party. The dress of the first VC held Ashton's attention. The
man wore black 'pyjama' trousers and a dark blue shirt with a
headband and chest webbing. His AK47 was slung from his right
shoulder, so that it was upside down and parallel to the ground,
and his hand was on the pistol grip of the weapon so he could
use it in the upside-down position.

The most striking thing about him was the scarf he wore. It
was royal blue with a red border. Ashton had seen such scarves
on his first tour of South Vietnam. D445 Regiment?, Ashton
silently wondered . . . this is the wrong part of the province for
D445. He looked at the second man and noted that he was
carrying an RPD light machine gun. There was a two metre gap
to the third man and another gap to the last man in the party.
Ashton could not see a weapon on the third man but he wore a
distinctive cap and had leather straps crossing the front of a
khaki-grey shirt. The last man in the party had an RPG7 rocket
launcher, with a B41 rocket attached, slung on his shoulder.

The realisation hit Ashton like a hammer. *Headquarters group!*
The man in the cap was obviously a high-ranking officer. There
was absolutely no way he could let this group go by, no matter
what was behind them. The VC were almost on them now. Just
four metres separated the patrol from the approaching enemy.
Ashton took one large nervous swallow, raised his weapon to his
shoulder and shouted in the clearest, most correct Vietnamese he
could muster: 'Dung loi! Dua tay len.'

It was as though a thunderclap had come out of the clear blue
sky. The VC stopped, and for a full second were immobile on
the track. The first to move was the soldier with the blue and
red scarf. He went sideways and to his right in one fluid
movement, the AK47 pointing in the general direction of Ashton's
voice. Collier and Wilkins fired simultaneously.

The 7.62mm bullet from Collier's SLR hit the Viet Cong with
the RPD in the middle of the chest, flinging him backwards for
several feet. Wilkins' bullet struck the VC with the blue and red
scarf low down on the left side of the body, causing him to turn
sharply to the left as he fired his AK47. The burst of fire from
the enemy weapon passed harmlessly across the front of the patrol.

Seconds passed and all firing ceased. Ashton was sure that Wilkins had not inflicted a mortal wound on his target. He took in the scene before him. The officer and the soldier carrying the RPG had been engaged by Cunningham's SLR and Erickson's M16, and both VC were lying, unmoving, on the track. Ashton swore. He was not committing to a body search until all four enemy were accounted for.

He was focusing on the point where he thought the blue and red scarf had disappeared into the sparse vegetation between the track and the creek when Wilkins' SLR fired beside him. Its shortened barrel created additional discharge pressure and caused it to sound much louder than a conventional SLR. The VC with the blue and red scarf cried out as his body was thrown further toward the creek and into plain sight of the patrol by the impact of the heavy calibre bullet.

'He's had it,' was Wilkins' unboasting prediction to Ashton.

'Flanks out,' Ashton ordered immediately, noting the confidence in the young man's voice and accepting his word without question.

Cunningham immediately went forward along the track in the direction the enemy had come and settled into a position where he had best view of the track for an approaching threat. Erickson did not have to move, he had the best view of the track leading west along the creek and he could see the VC with the blue and red scarf from where he was.

Wilkins, Collier and Ashton moved forward together. Wilkins began to head toward the enemy he'd engaged but Ashton put out a hand to guide him in the direction of the VC in the cap. 'Do the officer first,' he directed his two searchers. The enemy officer was lying face up on the side of the track. Wilkins and Collier approached cautiously from his feet end.

Ashton clicked his tongue. 'Approach from the head if they're on their back,' he said quietly, 'and from the feet if they're face down.'

Wilkins nodded, as though he'd just remembered something he had been told before. He moved around the dead officer, approached toward his head and put the barrel of his rifle in the man's mouth. Ashton nodded his approval and started separating the weapons from the dead soldiers as Collier went to work searching the bodies. It was then that Ashton noticed the weapon in a holster at the front of the officer's body. He reached down quickly, unclipped the belt and, by grasping the buckle and holster together, pulled the belt free.

Collier was undoing the satchel straps worn across the officer's body. He watched Ashton pull the pistol and belt free. There was a questioning look in his face and he frowned as his eye caught Ashton's. Ashton merely pointed at his own chest with the index finger of his left hand and firmly forced the belt and holster into his partly open shirtfront.

Bastard, thought Collier as he resumed the search, I nearly had a nice little handgun.

The search was thorough and seemed painfully slow. It took Collier over a minute to search each of the dead enemy. Ashton became agitated at the passing of five minutes. Even Cunningham and Erickson were becoming fidgety in their cover positions, passing frequent anxious looks toward the search party. Five minutes was a long time to be exposed like this in the heart of enemy territory.

Wilkins and Collier were oblivious to the passage of time as they approached the VC down by the creek. The enemy was lying face down. Wilkins approached from the rear and forced the barrel of his rifle between the buttocks. Collier searched the man's trouser pockets and removed the chest webbing to get at the shirt pockets. He withdrew the contents, picked up the enemy's assault rifle and chest webbing and handed them to Wilkins. They moved toward Ashton, who was collecting the remainder of the enemy weapons.

'You get that scarf?' Ashton asked sharply as they approached.

'No,' replied Wilkins, wondering what the big deal was about a scarf.

'Go and get it.'

For a fleeting moment there was an annoyed look on Wilkins' face, but as he turned to comply with Ashton's wishes he saw Erickson kneel beside the body and pull the scarf from the dead VC's neck. He looked back at Ashton, who also noticed what Erickson was doing and nodded his acceptance.

'Look after this,' he ordered, as he handed the RPG to Collier. 'Give the RPD to Bluey and take that AK off Billy and give it to Allen. Then let's get the fuck out of here.'

Wilkins handed the AK47 to Collier and moved off toward the area where the patrol had been briefed over an hour before.

Ashton followed close behind. Erickson was next in line, the RPD slung loosely over his left shoulder. As one of the flank party, he would normally have to remain with Cunningham to see the patrol safely away from the area of the track.

This time the task fell to Collier, who Erickson had been filling in for while he was being initiated in combat operations. Collier had a shirtful of document pouches and bits and pieces taken from the dead soldiers. He carried the rocket launcher slung over one shoulder and the packsling containing three rockets over his left arm and was struggling under their bulk. Soon his effort became evident and Erickson dropped back to assist by helping Cunningham keep watch on their back trail until they were out of sight of the track.

They made their way clumsily to the LUP where Ashton had briefed them for the mission. There was an air of jubilation among them over the success of the action they had just carried out. For the commander, the greatest cause for jubilation was that none of them had been wounded or killed.

Ashton knew there was no time to waste in clearing the area. It had already been far too long since the contact, thanks mainly to the pedestrian search technique employed by Collier. Even so, he took the time to redistribute the load of captured weapons, ammunition, equipment and documents, and by the time they were ready to move off each had a more equitable quota of captured items to carry.

Ashton instructed Wilkins to lead them parallel to the north bank of the small creek, approximately thirty metres from it. They did this for just over a hundred and fifty metres, when the creek turned to the north for a short distance before turning west again. Wilkins stopped for instructions from his commander and Ashton directed him to continue west until they came upon the creek.

The water was around a metre deep at this point so Ashton ordered Collier to dump the three rockets from the packsling, and the one the enemy soldier had been carrying on the launcher, into the creek. It was going to be a difficult task in any case to get the rockets back to their Task Force base as they were altitude-sensitive and were not on the RAAF's most favoured cargo list. For the limited intelligence value the rockets represented, he thought it wise not to tempt fate or the ire of the RAAF by trying to take them on the extraction helicopter.

From there the patrol moved north for almost two hundred metres. Ashton called a halt and under his direction Erickson encoded a lengthy contact report which he sent to the Task Force base.

By encoding the contact report Ashton was effectively telling the OC that his patrol was secure in the area and that there was no need to consider an extraction for them at that time. Unless a patrol commander sent in an encoded report it was customary for a patrol to be extracted immediately their presence in an area was compromised. It was believed that compromise counteracted any advantage that a patrol might have in closing with the enemy to gather intelligence. And of course it severely jeopardised the group's chances of survival.

But this was the second last day of the patrol's programmed duration and the advice Ashton had sent in the contact report was that they had killed an enemy officer and captured two document satchels. So it was no surprise to Ashton when he received an encoded reply advising him to move the patrol to the nearest LZ for immediate extraction.

The group continued north for a brief period and then north-east until they found the southern edge of a clearing large enough to land three or four helicopters comfortably. Ashton quickly secured the area by moving most of the way around the edge of the clearing until they were on the northern side. From this point he had Erickson send a single codeword message to confirm that the patrol was at a secure LZ and ready for extraction.

Within thirty minutes Ashton clearly picked up the sound of Iroquois helicopters in the distance. He moved the patrol to the edge of the treeline, removed the PRC 68 ground/air radio from its pouch on his belt, extended the aerial and activated the on/off switch. Almost immediately there was the unmistakable sound of an airborne helicopter through the rushing noise coming from the small speaker.

'Bravo Nine Sierra Six-Six, this is Albatross Zero-One,' the vibrating voice said. 'Do you read? . . . Over.'

Ashton held the small radio in front of his face so that the microphone was near his mouth and pressed the PTT button. 'This is Six-Six. I have you loud and clear . . . over.' The rushing noise returned almost immediately when Ashton released the button.

'This is Zero-One. I'm inbound for your general area at this time. Advise when you have me visual.'

'Roger, Zero-One.'

The patrol waited just inside the treeline for several minutes before Cunningham sighted the lead aircraft flying at an altitude of approximately 1500 feet, out to the south-west. The patrol became a hive of activity, with members reaching for various items required for their individual part in the extraction drill.

Wilkins and Collier moved out into the clearing for almost ten metres as Ashton took up his radio. 'Albatross Zero-One, this is Six-Six. I have you visual . . . We are two o'clock from your present heading.'

The rushing noise was audible just long enough for Ashton to hear 'Zero-One'. The helicopter in the distance came around on a new heading that would bring it directly over the patrol's location. As the helicopter steadied, the channel opened again.

'Six-Six, this is Zero-One. What is the enemy situation in your area? . . . Over.'

Ashton again spoke into the small radio. 'This is Six-Six . . . We had a contact around three hours ago about four hundred metres to the south-west. We haven't seen or heard any enemy movement since that time—this LZ is secure . . . Over.'

There was another rush of noise. 'Roger, Six-Six. We'll go with one gunship pass as this is your first extraction.'

Ashton smiled. This will be a fitting finale for Wilkins and Collier, he thought.

Several more minutes passed and the helicopter came closer. The communications channel opened again. 'Six-Six, this is Albatross Lead, can we see some light? . . . Over.' It was a demand rather than a question.

Ashton did not reply. He clicked his tongue in the direction of Wilkins, who held up the six by three inch heliograph mirror to the sun and wriggled it a little to find the bright yellow dot that was the sun's reflection. He moved the dot until it played on the cockpit of the aircraft.

The response was almost immediate. 'Roger, Six-Six, we have your mirror. Stand by to throw smoke . . . Over.'

'Six-Six.'

There was a pause in transmissions as the lead aircraft positioned the light fire team and the slick that was to pick them up. After what seemed an eternity, the channel opened again and through the rushing noise Ashton heard 'Throw smoke now . . . Over.'

Ashton clicked his tongue at Collier and nodded. Collier pulled the pin from the smoke grenade he was holding and threw it several metres upwind from the patrol.

Almost immediately the rushing noise came. 'I see yellow smoke? . . . Over.'

Ashton pressed the PTT button and spoke into the small radio. 'Yellow smoke confirmed.'

'Roger, stand by. Albatross Zero-Two will be with you in three-zero seconds.'

Ashton did not reply. His first operational patrol as commander was coming to an end. Vaguely he heard Cunningham yell, 'Here come the gunships!'

The gunships made one pass and each fired two 2.75 inch rockets. The four rockets exploded in the trees thirty metres or so behind them. Ashton smiled when he saw Wilkins and Collier each make an involuntary leap as the explosions took them by surprise. There was no follow-up fire from the onboard miniguns carried by the gunships.

As predicted, Albatross Zero-Two was on the ground near the almost extinguished smoke grenade in thirty seconds. The patrol made a dash for the left-hand door, lurching under the weight of their captured weapons and equipment, with Wilkins leading, followed by Collier, Cunningham and then Erickson. The patrol commander was always last aboard.

Albatross Zero-Two lifted out of the pad and gained height rapidly with Ashton scrambling to get inside. The eager hands of Cunningham and Erickson reached out to pull him, legs kicking, into the cabin.

6

Billy's moving well this morning, Rowan Ashton thought absently. When Wilkins was moving well he appeared to glide through the jungle. It was embarrassing to be behind him and unable to maintain the same degree of stealth. The bond forged on their first patrol had developed to a point where even the smallest change in mood or expression was noticed and understood by the other members. Since the morning's communications stop, Ashton noted, Wilkins' whole manner had changed. Perhaps, he thought with a small smile, it's to do with the enemy somewhere ahead.

A little over two hundred and fifty metres from the communications break Wilkins stopped, took a half pace backward and squatted. Ashton froze: the body language told him 'danger'. He moved a pace forward for a clear view beyond the scout. Wilkins' eyes never wavered from what had attracted him but his left arm came up at chest height behind him with fist clenched and thumb down in the standard signal for 'enemy'.

Ashton's eyes scanned the jungle beyond Wilkins but could detect nothing. He knew they were there because Billy hadn't moved since he squatted. The seconds ticked by slowly while the remainder of the patrol closed up and propped. Erickson waited patiently for some sign from his commander. Collier and Dobel went into a crouch at the rear and watched the patrol's flanks. Ashton became agitated. he hated not knowing what was going on.

After several minutes, Wilkins' body relaxed but he did not change his posture. Ashton moved forward cautiously until he was alongside his scout. Neither man spoke. Wilkins was still concentrating hard on an area ahead. Finally, he turned his head slightly toward Ashton. 'The track is just up ahead, about twenty metres,' he whispered.

Ashton didn't query how he had come to that conclusion. He just accepted that, if Billy said there was a track up ahead, there was a track up ahead. They were in a patch of low to medium height and relatively sparse secondary scrub. Beyond them, in the direction Billy indicated the track to be, the secondary growth was even lighter in density, allowing visibility of up to thirty metres in the world of shadow below the primary canopy.

'Where did . . . ' Ashton never finished the question. Wilkins made a gesture with his left hand that cut his commander short. He followed the gesture with an almost imperceptible nod of his head toward the track. It took Ashton some time before he saw them—only the flash of movement from the light-coloured skin of the palms of their hands betrayed their presence. Finally, the dark, shadowy movements manifested themselves into what were unmistakably human forms. The shadows moved fleetingly at the furthermost reach of Ashton's restricted vision.

Ashton counted a group of three, followed shortly after by a group of four. Both groups moved at a steady pace that could be considered casual by Viet Cong standards. Ashton and Wilkins were too far away to identify weapons and equipment and certainly too far away in the gloom to identify uniforms. The two men waited, motionless, until the shadows disappeared from view.

Ashton pulled back the sock covering his watch and checked the time: almost 1100 hours. He glanced around; it was the thickest scrub in the area and it provided good cover for the patrol. He considered his options quickly and decided that this was as good a place as any for park time.

Ashton put his hand on Wilkins' shoulder with some downward pressure. Wilkins nodded; he understood that he should remain where he was. Ashton came to an upright position and moved the four metres to where Erickson was crouched, waiting.

'Did you see that mob go by?' he whispered to his signaller.

'Only some shadows and palm flashes moving out *that* way.' Erickson motioned with his head.

'There's a few enemy using the track about twenty or thirty metres out. This will be Billy's position. We'll prop the rest back here behind us.'

Erickson stood up cautiously and had turned to retrace his steps when Ashton put a hand on his arm. 'That tree through there, that's my spot.' Erickson nodded in acknowledgment. 'Call the others in,' Ashton continued, 'put Collier out there on the right and you move over there.' He pointed to the locations.

Ashton turned to rejoin Wilkins while the signaller moved to the tree that Ashton had indicated and motioned for Collier and Dobel to come forward. As they arrived, he briefed them on what he knew of the enemy situation and directed them to their positions.

Ashton knelt down beside Wilkins again and briefed him on the decision to spend park time in the thicker secondary growth to the rear. Wilkins nodded; it was sensible to have a good look at the track over a period of time.

There was no movement on the track for over ten minutes so the two men withdrew to the area selected for the park time LUP. After a period of several minutes, Ashton motioned for the patrol members to remove their packs and sit down. As he did so, a single rifle shot shattered the jungle's quiet. It appeared to come from less than a hundred metres to their south-west. There was no need to remind anyone that a degree of silence was required.

Sergeant Ashton quickly made some calculations to pinpoint the patrol's position on his map. He knew he had to get to everyone quickly and ensure that each one knew their precise position on the map and what actions to take should they be surprised by the enemy. It was crucial that everyone had a positive start point because without it it was almost impossible to locate a predetermined rendezvous that might be several kilometres away. It was not Ashton's way to leave such matters as this to chance.

Ashton came slowly to his full height and cradled his weapon in the crook of his left arm. The patrol members were sitting quietly alert for any sound in the vicinity. He made his way to where Wilkins was sitting cross-legged beside a small bush. Another bush a short distance behind him blocked out his silhouette to anyone looking in their direction from the track. He removed the map from his pocket as he approached.

'How's it going, Billy?' It was Ashton's standard opening. Wilkins nodded and smiled at his commander.

'What sort of view do you have of the track?' Ashton whispered.

'Don't know, haven't sighted any movement since we sat down.'

Definitely park time, thought Ashton, as he put his weapon down and moved the map into a position where his scout could see it clearly.

'This is where I figure we are, Billy,' he said, picking up a small twig from behind him and pointing with it to their position on the map. Wilkins nodded his agreement.

'There's no change to the briefing from this morning,' Ashton continued. 'We'll monitor the track out there until about 1600 hours and see how much traffic uses it.'

Wilkins nodded again and thought about it for a moment. Ashton had put the map inside his shirt and picked up his weapon by the time his scout spoke.

'We going to put an ambush on the track?'

'That depends on how much use it gets over the next day or so,' Ashton said as he moved off toward Collier's position.

'How's it going, Jimmy?'

'Good. How's the track look?'

'Don't know yet.' Ashton removed his map to brief his pioneer/medic. 'Might be possibilities for some good intelligence up ahead.'

Ashton briefed Collier as he had Wilkins. He took note of Collier's position in relation to where he believed the track to be and was pleased to note that Collier also sat in a position where the backdrop of bushes concealed any shape and shadow formed by his body.

'The track is out that way,' Ashton said, pointing.

Collier shifted his body a quarter turn to the left to come more square to the direction the sergeant indicated. Ashton gave a thin smile. 'Don't forget this area out to your right,' he reminded Collier, mindful that the medic's attention would now be focused in the direction of the track. Collier shifted a little to the right to keep his patrol commander happy. Ashton smiled again and put a hand on Collier's shoulder to acknowledge his effort. Collier had a cool head and a serious side to his personality that Ashton liked to put to a subtle test from time to time.

When Ashton instructed Erickson to put the patrol members on the ground, he had already configured the defensive perimeter so that Wilkins and Collier were in the best position to view the track. That left Erickson and Dobel in position to take responsibility for watching the rear and flanks, thereby releasing Wilkins and Collier to concentrate on their task. Collier had not realised this and Ashton's byplay with him did not even register.

Ashton had picked up his weapon and straightened up to move to where Erickson was sitting when there was a loud *bang* from west of the patrol's location. Ashton froze in midstride and the others immediately became tense as they strained to identify the sound. It sounded again, *bang*. And again, *bang*. It was an oddly familiar sound, one that Ashton knew but could not pick at that moment.

The sound appeared to be coming from several hundred metres to the west, but it was difficult to tell under such a close canopy. It occurred rhythmically as Ashton made his way to Erickson's position and knelt down beside him to face the direction from which the noise was coming. He did not put his weapon down as was his custom. Instead he laid it across his raised knee and bent his head slightly to speak to his signaller. 'What do you make of that, Bluey?'

As he spoke, there was a rattle of metal on metal that identified the noise beyond doubt. 'Sounds like someone trying to open a 44 gallon drum with a hammer and cold chisel—and missing the chisel with the hammer!' Erickson relaxed noticeably and a hint of devilment crept into his voice.

'OK, Bluey.' Ashton also relaxed now that identification of the sound was positive. 'So how far, smart arse?'

'Has to be three or four hundred metres.' The lightness had gone from Bluey's voice.

'I'd say that,' Ashton agreed. 'With this canopy helping the noise along, it could be even further.' Erickson nodded. Wherever it was, it was no threat to them at that moment, but it did point to the strong possibility that there was an enemy bunker system nearby.

The sound started again as Ashton briefed Erickson. There were several more banging sounds and another rattle as the worker mishit the chisel again. Erickson smiled as he listened to the briefing, nodding as he did.

'We'll leave here at 1600 hours and head south-west for a while. I'll give you something to encode and send while we're here.'

Erickson nodded again. 'Lunch?'

'We'll eat cold for lunch,' Ashton replied. He made a mental note to remember to tell Dobel about eating cold. There was no need to tell Wilkins or Collier not to light their stoves; they understood that any light from either position would easily be seen from the track and that there was just a chance the unmistakable smell of the hexamine might also be detected.

Ashton stood up to make his way to Dobel's position when there was another rattling sound of hammer missing chisel. 'Clumsy prick,' he heard Erickson mutter softly, and smiled at the irony of it. There could be hundreds of VC in that camp, he thought, and we're out here looking for them . . . They're meant to be hiding from our superior forces and they're banging fuck out of 44 gallon drums . . . We're meant to find them and we're frightened even to fart for fear of getting our arses shot off . . .

'How's it going, Gary?' Ashton was back into his routine by the time he reached Dobel.

'What's going on?' the 2IC responded in an anxious whisper.

Ashton went down on one knee, placing his weapon upright against his leg. He was concerned at Dobel's anxiety but said nothing. He withdrew the map from inside his shirt and opened it. 'We're here,' he said, pointing to the place with a small twig. 'There's a track about thirty metres to our front where we sighted at least seven enemy.'

Dobel nodded without comment so Ashton continued with the briefing, bringing his 2IC up to date by confirming emergency actions should the patrol be contacted and become separated. He added, 'We'll leave here at 1600 hours. Eat anytime you like, but no cooking while we're here.'

Dobel nodded again as his commander stood up to leave. Ashton put the map into his trouser leg pocket, cradled the weapon in his left arm and returned to his place in the centre of the defensive position.

When he was settled, he examined the defensive area that he'd hastily selected some twenty minutes before. The area was as large as a two car garage. A little small, perhaps, but it did provide good cover from detection while allowing a reasonable view of the track. Most important, it was tactically suitable, with flat ground between them and the track and ground that sloped away slightly on the other three sides. At this stage Ashton was only interested in the volume of movement on the track, not what was being moved, and the LUP was adequate for that.

Ashton again extracted the map from his pocket and, with protractor in hand, confirmed their military grid location. He removed his field notebook from the map case and jotted down the grid reference. Then he thought for a moment about the message that he was going to send to base. The message would say that the patrol was located at grid reference 495 884 and that they had sighted seven enemy at 1055 hours that day on the north-east/south-west track in front of them. It would also advise that the patrol had not been able to identify any of the enemy's weapons, dress or equipment and that they thought an enemy camp existed some 300 metres to their west. Finally, the message would tell headquarters that Ashton intended to monitor the track the following day unless HQ advised otherwise.

Ashton noted that it was almost 1200 hours. He needed to get the message off to base and have a reply by 1400 hours because he suspected that enemy movement might resume around that time. He knelt down beside Erickson and opened his notebook, pleased to see that Erickson already had the codebook out in anticipation. It was a fairly short message for its content and, as was his way, Erickson copied the message directly from Ashton's notebook into the codebook.

'Get Dobel to help with the aerial,' Ashton commanded when Erickson finished copying the message. He determined that the aerial would need to be run between Collier's and Dobel's positions and, although Erickson would have a natural preference for the medic's assistance, it was critical that Collier remain at his position on the perimeter in case the enemy decided to use the track while the aerial was being run out.

Ashton left Erickson with the encoding and returned to his central location. It was more than possible that headquarters would want the patrol to pinpoint the location of the enemy camp and determine its dimensions and defensive layout. This was not one of Ashton's favourite tasks as it meant splitting the patrol in order to create a support base while he and Wilkins poked about the perimeter of the camp.

The worst part about looking closely at a camp was the time it took to do the job properly. It could mean two or three days right in the enemy's living room under constant fear of being discovered. He closed his eyes and could almost visualise the VC's reaction to a scruffy pair of Diggers in or near their camp.

The idea made him think of something. Taking his signal mirror from his pocket, Ashton checked the quality of his camouflage paint. He retouched areas of his face and neck with paint from a small tin and checked them again in the mirror. Satisfied, he returned the mirror to his pocket and worked the camouflage cream on to the fingertips protruding from his patrol gloves. Finally, he closed the tin and put it away.

Bluey Erickson stood up with the small black fishing reel in his hand. Collier sensed the movement and looked toward the signaller to find Erickson was not looking his way but in the direction of Dobel, trying to attract his attention and not having much success.

Useless dozy prick, thought Collier, as he began to rise to assist Erickson with the aerial. Ashton caught his eye and motioned him to remain where he was. Collier glared in the direction of Dobel but sat down.

'Click-click', went Erickson's tongue. Ashton watched Dobel closely. There was no response. 'Click-click'—still no response. Ashton picked up a twig and threw it. It hit Dobel on the leg and his head turned sharply, a look of irritation on his face.

Erickson held up the fishing reel for the 2IC to see but Dobel only frowned. Erickson held up the reel again, this time motioning with it toward the direction it had to go. For a fleeting moment Dobel's face indicated he understood, then he frowned, shook his head and gestured in Collier's direction.

'*Click-click.*' This time it was Ashton's tongue. Dobel glanced in his direction and was startled by the anger in the commander's face. Ashton pointed in his direction and made a sign like the running of his thumb and forefinger along an imaginary horizontal wire. There could be no mistaking Ashton's intention that Dobel should assist Erickson with the aerial. Dobel rose and moved to assist with the task.

Ashton did not know what to make of his 2IC's actions. Surely he must have seen that Collier was not in a position to assist, he thought, and wondered if Dobel was thoughtless, lazy—or just a worthless prick as Collier liked to describe him. Whatever the answer, he was not shaping up as someone who could be an effective patrol 2IC.

Erickson tapped out the message to headquarters. Ashton did not even take the trouble to eavesdrop and test his skills. He spent some time pondering the worth of Dobel, going over in his mind all the things Dobel had done so far that had drawn attention to his shortcomings. It was a fairly damning list, Ashton had to concede.

Ashton heard the standard 'wait out' signal come from Erickson's radio. He looked at his watch—just after 1240 hours. Things always take longer when you don't want them to, he thought. There was bound to be a significant wait while the message was decoded and considered at headquarters.

The minutes ticked by. Five minutes ran into ten and ten minutes into fifteen. There was no answer. There was another loud noise from the direction of the suspected enemy camp. It was the 44 gallon drum again. This time there was no sound of hammer on cold chisel, only the sound of an empty drum being hit with a piece of wood. Once! Twice! Then silence.

'Click-click.' It was Wilkins. Everyone looked in his direction. His arm was extended behind him, fist clenched and thumb down. Ashton crawled part of the five metres to Wilkins' position, then slowly stood up. He could see shadows moving in the distance. He crouched down again from habit, turned and made his way back to the centre of the LUP.

Time seemed to creep by and Ashton consulted his watch several times before he heard the hum of the base station radio as it came on line. Erickson quickly adjusted the volume as the noise coming through his earpiece sounded unusually loud. He began the task of receiving and decoding the reply to Ashton's message. There was another double click from Wilkins' direction— more enemy were passing along the track. We could be in for a busy afternoon, thought Ashton.

At 1322 hours Erickson caught Ashton's attention and motioned him over. Ashton picked up his weapon and forced himself upright. The look on Erickson's face indicated that the reply contained nothing to be thrilled about. He made his way carefully to Erickson and knelt down beside him. Erickson opened his notebook to display the decoded message to his commander.

'Fuck!' Ashton exclaimed, almost to himself. The message said: CLOSE RECON PD CAMPREP ASAP PD GOOD LUCK.

To Ashton the abbreviated signal meant: 'Conduct a close reconnaissance of the enemy camp STOP Require a detailed camp report as soon as possible STOP Good luck.'

Erickson looked at Ashton in bewilderment. He had never seen his commander react this way to a message. After all, it wasn't the first time that they'd been ordered to complete this type of task.

Ashton sensed his signaller's confusion but could not tell him that he had some doubt concerning Dobel and his ability to carry his end in such a task. He thought momentarily of confiding in Erickson, of making a decision to excuse Dobel from his duties and to elevate Erickson in his place. Instead, he picked up Erickson's notebook and studied the abbreviated text again. He looked into Erickson's eyes and gave a tired smile.

'Why not?' he whispered with a shrug. 'After all, that's what we're here for.'

7

The message from base forced a change of plan and Ashton moved the patrol away from the track at 1530 hours that afternoon. He decided to start the close reconnaissance after breakfast the following morning. This would give everyone an opportunity to prepare physically and mentally for the task. Close reconnaissance of an occupied enemy camp was not something you just went off and did without adequate planning and prep-aration.

Ashton had been involved in similar tasks on his previous tour of duty as a patrol member, and they'd been sighted by the enemy and engaged in a firefight on three occasions out of five.

On this tour he had successfully undertaken close reconnaisance twice. A third occasion had resulted in the wounding of Allen Cunningham while he was withdrawing the patrol to plan the reconnaissance. He felt uneasy about the coming task but did not let it concern him unduly. He felt it was better to be a little uneasy and cautious than to relive some of the drama he had experienced previously.

They moved south, then west, looking for a secure area in which to establish a LUP to prepare for the task and to spend the night. Ashton found one not more than seventy metres from where they had monitored the track during their last stop. That put them almost one hundred metres south of the track. In Ashton's estimation, this was more than sufficient distance from the enemy camp and would allow them to carry out their preparations in relative safety.

He had not advised the patrol of the nature of the upcoming task, so Erickson and he were the only ones who knew what the immediate future held. It was not Erickson's way to discuss the patrol's message traffic with anyone and Ashton did not plan to brief the remaining members until they had secured the LUP.

The decision on a night location made, Ashton stopped the patrol, secured the area and gestured to them to remove their packs and sit down to listen. He made his way to where Wilkins was sitting, not bothering to kneel down or open the conversation with his usual greeting. Instead, he bent from the waist until his head was level with Wilkins'. 'How many did you count go past on the track while we were there?' he whispered.

Wilkins took out his notebook and did a number of quick calculations. 'Six groups,' he said, 'two threes, one four, two sixes and one over twenty.' He paused while he did some fast arithmetic. 'Forty-four . . . about. Maybe a couple more.'

'Thanks mate.' Ashton left Wilkins' position and headed for Collier.

He knew that Collier would want to have a say about Dobel. No doubt he'd noticed what transpired between Erickson, Dobel and himself over the running of the aerial. Collier never misses a trick, he thought, pity he doesn't have Erickson's and Wilkins' inclination to keep his own counsel.

He moved close to Collier, placing the barrel of his weapon on the toe of his right boot, and leaned from the waist toward him. Collier looked around, mouth open as if to speak, but the look in his commander's eyes was sufficient warning for him to say nothing.

'How many did you count up on the track?' Ashton asked, an odd inflection in his voice.

Shit! thought Collier, as he reached for his notebook, he's uptight this afternoon. He took the notebook from its waterproof container and opened it for his commander to see.

'Tell me,' Ashton said, dismissing Collier's attempt to involve him in the arithmetic. Collier looked defeated. His lack of skill in mathematics was legendary within the squadron. 'OK,' Ashton said with a thin smile, 'give it here.' He reached for the notebook. 'I've got a message to get out before dark.'

Collier gave up the notebook willingly. One thing about Ashton, he thought, you can always tell when he's pissed off and you can always bet his mood won't last long. Ashton had been the greatest influence in Collier's life and there was virtually nothing he would not do for his commander.

Ashton quickly totalled up the enemy numbers from Collier's diary entries. A total of forty-eight enemy in six groups. The group numbers tallied with Wilkins' count but Collier had four more enemy.

'Billy got forty-four enemy, Jimmy,' Ashton said, 'and you've got forty-eight.' There was the hint of a question in his quiet voice.

'That Billy Wilkins never could count properly,' Collier responded with a grin.

Ashton nearly broke into a fit of laughter but managed to hold himself in check. Forty-four or forty-eight—it didn't matter that much but he decided to play Collier along a little.

'What am I going to do about this discrepancy, Jimmy?' he asked in the most serious voice he could muster.

Jim Collier's mathematics may not have been good but it didn't take a genius to work out the discrepancy. For Collier, it was like getting change at the corner shop, and he had never been shortchanged in his life.

'That'll be the two I got that Billy missed,' he said with a straight face. He looked Ashton in the eye and added, 'Take the two off that I got and add them on to Billy's for the two he missed.' A small smile began to form in the corner of his mouth as he watched his commander digest what he'd said. 'That would make forty-six,' he said finally, 'how's that sound?'

Ashton was not astonished by Collier's turn of logic. The medic's quick wit and keen sense of self-preservation prevailed in most instances. It was one thing that Ashton understood about Collier—he was a survivor.

'Forty-six sounds about right,' Ashton said, as he lifted the rifle barrel from his boot. 'We've had a change in task, Jimmy,' he went on before Collier could initiate a conversation about Dobel. 'I'll brief everyone before last light.'

Ashton smiled to himself as he turned to make his way back to the centre of the LUP. That'll keep his mind off Dobel for a while, he thought.

The commander alerted Erickson that he was about to send a message to headquarters. He needed to advise the extent of enemy movement on the track, so he quickly drafted the message, checked it, and then moved to where Erickson was waiting with the codebook in his hand.

Ashton left him to organise the transmission and made his way over to Dobel, who was sitting on the perimeter. The corporal turned his head at the sound of the approach and relaxed a little when he identified his patrol commander.

'We've had a new tasking order,' Ashton said, watching closely for a reaction. Dobel merely nodded.

'We are to conduct a close reconnaissance of the camp over there.' The sergeant spoke slowly, quietly, dramatically. It worked—there was an instant reaction from Dobel; his eyes flickered and his brow creased in a frown.

'Close recce?'

'That's right. We'll start after breakfast tomorrow.'

'How are you going to tackle it?' The corporal appeared to be showing interest.

Ashton was surprised. He had Dobel figured as one who had been promoted long before he was ready and who would extend himself just enough to avoid incurring the wrath of his superiors. This show of interest was a bonus.

Ashton withdrew his map case and extracted the map. On one side of the cutdown map was a 1:25,000 pictorial coverage of the area and on the other side was a 1:50,000 standard topographical coverage. He turned the map to the 1:50,000 side and took out his retractable chinagraph pencil.

'We're here,' he started, making a small cross on the clear plastic covering. 'The enemy camp is over here a hundred metres or so.' He drew a circle to indicate its presence. He looked at Dobel to ensure that he was following what was being drawn. The 2IC appeared totally engrossed. 'There's a track coming into the camp from the north-east, I suspect . . . like so,' Ashton went on, 'so there must be at least one track coming out.' He looked at his handiwork. 'Any problem with that?'

'No,' Dobel responded with a shake of his head.

'We'll patrol around the camp like so,' Ashton continued, drawing a dotted line in a box shape around the outside of the perimeter, 'and keep a distance outside the perimeter as we go.'

He knew that it was not possible to circumnavigate the camp without bumping into the perimeter at least two or three times and that the plan was subject to the camp's having a visible perimeter structure or track. The fate of Allen Cunningham would still be fresh in Dobel's mind and Ashton didn't want him putting unnecessary pressure on himself by worrying about what might happen around a perimeter fence.

'Why go all the way around there?' Dobel asked innocently.

'I want to put a box around the camp,' the sergeant said patiently, 'an accurately paced out box so that when I divide the area into quarters for the recce, I'll have a better idea of its true dimensions.'

Dobel nodded, but he didn't look convinced that this was necessary.

'It'll also give us the advantage of having a feel for the area we have to cover on the way back,' Ashton added when he noted that his 2IC was having difficulty with the concept.

'OK,' Dobel said, after considering Ashton's words, indicating that he was happy with the final explanation.

Ashton shook his head, his mind working overtime. Why should I have to explain this to a corporal? he thought. A corporal should know the fundamental principles of this shit, even if he's only just been promoted.

'How many close recce jobs have you done, Gary?'

'None.'

'Did Willie have a basic close reconnaissance plan?'

'Not that I know of.'

Ashton knew that Dobel had to be briefed on the basic plan before things went too far. He admonished himself for not having done it back at Nui Dat. After all, Dobel was the patrol 2IC and should anything happen to Ashton he would have to assume command. Ashton could not, for the life of him, visualise Collier willingly giving his undivided attention and respect to Dobel. How Erickson and Wilkins would deal with it was another matter. Ashton believed that loyalty would prevail in both cases and they would provide the 2IC with sufficient, properly constructed advice to get him through.

'The basic close recce plan works like this . . .' Ashton launched himself into the explanation, drawing a line under the existing chinagraph markings on the map and making a small circle below it. 'This is an enemy camp, OK?' He looked at Dobel for acknowledgment and found he had his full attention.

'We patrol around the camp to determine its rough size.' He drew a box around the circle and looked again at his 2IC, who nodded. 'Then we make the box into quarters and recce one quarter at a time.' He drew the quartered divisions inside the box.

'How is the recce done?' Dobel asked.

'Each quarter is done in three phases,' Ashton said, drawing lines in and out of the camp perimeter. 'On each phase, you, Erickson and Collier provide fire support near the perimeter to cover Billy and me while we poke about inside.'

'OK. So when one phase is finished we move the fire support group to cover the next phase?'

'Basically that's right. Billy and I will come back to your group at the end of each phase and I'll reposition your group before the next.'

'Sounds like a good plan.'

'It's OK as plans go, but remember, it's only a guide and plans can change.' He put a hand on Dobel's shoulder as he got up to leave. 'And sometimes they even work!'

As Ashton moved away from Dobel's position he noted the tension in the radio aerial go slack. This signified that communications had been completed. He looked in Erickson's direction and his signaller confirmed it by giving the thumbs-up sign. Rather than distract Erickson from the task of packing his equipment, Ashton decided it was time to put Collier's curiosity to rest.

'How's it going, Jimmy?' he whispered, as he knelt down beside Collier.

'What's going on, Rowan? What's the new task?'

'Close recce, Jimmy,' Ashton replied softly. It concerned him that Collier, who was usually so cool about physical situations, had become so anxious about information. Collier was acting out of character and had been since the patrol's first night in. He had never seen Jimmy take a dislike to anyone as he had to Dobel, and it seemed to be having a detrimental effect on his normally casual personality.

'Close recce,' Collier repeated, nodding his head emphatically. 'That'd be right—me and Bluey stuck with that useless cockhead while you and Billy stuff around in the camp.'

'That's *right*.' Ashton fixed him with a stare, becoming annoyed with this bullshit. It wasn't like Collier at all and he couldn't find a rational explanation for it. 'Dobel is going to be boss of the support group and Billy and me are going to stuff around in the enemy camp.'

Collier knew he was pushing it, he could feel the anger begin to radiate from his commander. He knew it was time to quit on the subject of Dobel but he couldn't. He had a bad premonition about this patrol and Dobel was the only cause of it he could accept.

Before Collier could pursue the matter further, there was a commotion from the area where Ashton suspected the enemy camp to be. Shouting and high-pitched laughter broke the otherwise sleepy quiet of the jungle. It took them by surprise and everyone froze momentarily until instinct told them there was no immediate threat. There was a burst of automatic rifle fire from the camp and then silence.

'What do you make of that, Jimmy?'

'Sounded like a very short party!' Collier knew Ashton wanted his view on distance to the noise but was too annoyed to provide it.

'*How far?*' Ashton was not amused by what he considered to be a juvenile attitude and his agitation was plain for Collier to see.

'Around a hundred.'

'That's what I'd have thought.' If Wilkins was the guru of accurate judgment in point-to-point distance covered on foot by the patrol, Collier was the equal of anyone in judging the distance to a sound source in the jungle. Ashton took a quick bearing on the source with his compass for future reference.

'When do we start?' Collier's question jolted Ashton out of his thoughts.

'Directly after breakfast in the morning. With any luck we should box it by park time and then start making our way back in the afternoon.'

Collier nodded but still had a troubled look on his face. Ashton could not share his foreboding; he was optimistic that Dobel would hold his end up when and if the time came.

'I'll make Dobel and Erickson responsible for our packs in case of an emergency,' he went on quietly. 'That will leave you to control any direct fire support that Billy and I might need.'

There was a slight flicker of pleasure in Collier's eyes as he smiled at his commander. He was overjoyed by the responsibility given him. It was the responsibility that had normally been vested in Cunningham—and in this case should have been given to the new 2IC.

'I'll finalise the briefing in the morning before we move off,' Ashton said. He was happy to give the job to Collier. Collier had had sufficient experience and was very capable in a gunfight.

Ashton left him and sat down next to his pack in the centre of the LUP. It was 1655 hours and almost time for the sunset serenade. He looked across at Bluey Erickson and made a brief sign asking how the communications with their base had gone, and was answered by a thumbs-up from the signaller.

He took the green plastic holder from his shirt pocket and extracted a cigarette and the lighter. He lit his second cigarette for the day and waited for the coughing reaction that never came. In its place was a dizzy sensation as the nicotine flooded his body after some hours absence. Ashton leaned sideways against his pack and closed his eyes, the dizzy feeling departing almost as quickly as it had come.

'Click-click.' As Rowan Ashton got everyone's attention he held up his hand and motioned as if to spoon something into his mouth. They all acknowledged by sign. Satisfied, Ashton reached into his pack for one of the evening meal packets. As he did, the cicadas began their nightly serenade.

By twenty minutes before last light all was in readiness for what Ashton hoped would be a restful night. While the final preparations were under way, Ashton had caught the smell of Asian cooking blown on a soft north-westerly breeze.

As nightfall began to descend in earnest, Ashton called his patrol members to their close night positions. Collier was the last man in and as he reached the group there was a burst of gunfire from the area of the suspected enemy camp. The firing was followed by several raised high-pitched voices, then there was silence.

'Psssst,' Ashton hissed softly into the half darkness. When he felt that he had everyone's attention he said, 'Stay put in the morning and I'll brief on the close recce.' He sensed more than saw the nods of assent. He sat down at the top of his sleeping position while the remainder of the patrol did the same. They sat and waited, listening to the sounds of the jungle, listening for the sounds of enemy movement toward their position. They could hear the enemy moving about, not toward their position, but on the track some hundred metres to their north. It was difficult at first to determine which direction the enemy were travelling in. They sat and listened quietly for over fifteen minutes and still could not tell. Then came the sound that Ashton and Wilkins had heard the previous night. A creaking, groaning and straining noise, accompanied by the faint ringing of a small bell and encouraging Vietnamese voices.

'Ox carts, Billy!' Ashton identified the sound that had eluded him the night before and he rolled to one side as he whispered to his scout. Nobody answered and Ashton felt a bit embarrassed at his excitement. He should not have been. Ox carts meant the movement of weapons, ammunition and equipment and that was a most positive discovery.

Soon Ashton could determine their direction of movement with some certainty. They were moving away from the camp in a north-easterly direction. Into Long Khanh Province most likely, Ashton thought, as he tried to estimate the size of the group. It was much too difficult to judge with any certainty—but it was big. He thought about the sounds they'd heard the previous night. Had the ox carts been coming into the camp from the province to the north? Had they been bringing in equipment and sup-plies—or were they shifting them out tonight? He pondered the possibilities for several minutes before giving up.

Ashton cursed softly to himself in the darkness. If it wasn't for the new tasking order, he would be sitting in OP on the track right now and could have the information back to Nui Dat immediately after first light. He shook his head. Sometimes you were there and sometimes you weren't. That was the way it was. He signalled for the patrol to bed down. He knew there wouldn't be much sleep through the night if the VC continued to pass in such numbers. There were the customary slight scuffling sounds as his men eased into their places.

Ashton settled down but could not sleep. He went over the plan he had devised earlier in the day. It was a reasonable plan although much depended on how many were inside the camp and where. It would take a lot more time than he had allocated but, with an ounce of luck, they would get all the way around the camp and he and Billy would get in and out without getting sprung. He was happy with his overall plan and felt a little better for having gone over it again in his mind. His eyelids were getting heavy and in the background he could hear the enemy still moving in groups along the track.

It's one thing sneaking around Charlie's backyard looking at his vegetable garden, he thought, but it's quite another to sneak into his house to find out where he keeps his valuables.

8

Major Colin Deane sat poised over his war diary. The curtain was going down on another day at the Australian SAS Squadron Headquarters at Nui Dat. Colin Deane was a well-built man with dark, close-cropped hair and hazel eyes that sparkled with intelligence and could burn with passion, depending on his mood. He had commanded the squadron since its formation and knew almost every man in it by his first name.

Deane had the respect of all who knew him because he set high standards of personal conduct, was consistent when dealing with everyday problems and would back any officer or soldier to the fullest extent of his power on the strength of their word. As long as their word was honest, nobody had anything to fear.

He had been studying the results of his squadron's time in Phuoc Tuy Province while bringing his diary entries up to date. For their efforts so far, they had registered sixty-four enemy confirmed killed in action. Deane considered this to be quite high for a small unit whose charter was not to intentionally become involved in the blood and death side of warfare. Their primary job was to gather information for use by large infantry formations, who were best equipped to deal with the enemy by closing with and destroying him in his own backyard.

The gathering of information was not the easiest of tasks when you were faced with mobile guerrilla warfare. The Viet Cong did not remain in one location for extended periods and any information gathered by Deane's squadron was, at best, useful only for a few days. And specific information on the enemy's movements was particularly difficult to obtain by observation alone. The most valuable information was obtained either from VC informants or from documents and letters taken from the bodies of dead enemy soldiers.

Colin Deane had inherited the modus operandi of his squadron. The difficulties of collecting information had long since been recognised and the technique of recce/ambush as an information-gathering tool was established by the time his men arrived in South Vietnam. It was not the only type of operation conducted by his squadron but it was the one most often employed.

Most recce/ambush patrols were of five to seven days' duration. Each patrol would be provided with a free-fire zone in which to operate. This was an area of operations, or AO, where no Vietnamese civilians were permitted to be. Around the AO was a one kilometre deep border and the area within was referred to as a no-fire zone. This was a buffer designed to protect the patrol from wayward friendly artillery as well as harassment and interdiction fire and ground/air fighter-bomber strikes.

The patrol would reconnoitre their AO in the hope of finding a large concentration of enemy to report. In the absence of a major VC concentration, the patrol commander would search for a suitable well-used access track and set an ambush during the last twenty-four hours of his patrol's allocated duration.

The information gained in this way was often useful to the Task Force Commander in the planning of future battalion operations, but in most cases the information was not acted on for several weeks. Such tardy reaction annoyed Deane because the enemy would have long since left the area and the credibility of his patrol's information would be brought into question.

Deane glanced at his watch. He had just under twenty minutes to be at Task Force Headquarters for the Task Force Commander's conference. He stood up and reached behind him for the belt and holster containing the Browning 9mm pistol. He had buckled the pistol belt around his waist and was reaching for his sandy-coloured beret when Lieutenant Peter Hanson walked into his office.

Hanson was a man of average height with a shock of blond hair and pale blue eyes. He had come to South Vietnam as a reinforcement Troop Commander for the previous squadron and had tried to stay on with Deane's squadron to command one of his Troops.

Deane would have none of it because he was happy with the Troop Commanders he had been allocated. But an injury sustained by the designated operations officer had forced him to withdraw from the tour at late notice and Deane offered Hanson the job in operations when the withdrawal was confirmed.

Hanson had completed seven operational patrols as a patrol commander with the previous squadron. He was a mature twenty-four years of age and a competent staff officer, an ideal choice for the operations position in a new squadron. Unfortunately, Hanson's twelve month tour was up in a week; his replacement was due to arrive in country in two days time.

'Message just in from Ashton's patrol, sir,' Hanson said casually.

'OK, OPSO,' Deane said, looking directly at the lieutenant, 'what does Sergeant Ashton have to say?'

'Forty-six VC passed him this afternoon, sir. He intends to start the close recce first up in the morning.'

'Thank you, Peter.' The major quickly noted the information in his conference book. Then he said, 'Look, I'm almost late for the conference—we'll speak about Ashton when I get back.' He scooped up the book and his area map and left.

Deane thought about Rowan Ashton as he drove toward the Task Force CP. Ashton was one of his most reliable patrol commanders, but he was becoming worried about the degree of responsibility he had asked the sergeant to shoulder over the past months. It seemed that each time a difficult task came up it was given to Patrol Six-Six. Ashton had been tasked with three operations more than the other patrol commanders of the squadron.

Hanson watched his Squadron Commander driving away and hurried to the operations room, where the sergeant was preparing the daily handover brief for the oncoming duty officer. Sergeant 'Sticks' Rawle was the thinnest man Hanson had ever known. His medium height and fragile-looking frame belied a truly robust strength of character, an agile mind and an insatiable capacity for work.

'Where's the operations file on Ashton's patrol, Sticks?'

'On my desk, sir. I've been bringing it up to date.' He paused to ensure that the officer was looking in the right spot. 'Just had to put in Corporal Dobel's details.'

'Is it completed?'

'Yes sir.'

'Thank you,' Hanson said, as he made his way to his desk with the file in his hand. He would have liked to head over to the mess for a predinner beer, but he knew that Deane would be back in an hour or so and, from the way he'd spoken, would want to know everything there was to know about Ashton and his patrol.

At 1700 hours the oncoming duty officer walked into the room to receive his briefing for the evening. Lieutenant John Andersen had a number of old patrol reports under his arm and a recently issued operations order for a new mission in his hand. The reports were from patrols conducted previously in his new AO and he would study them later for information to assist his planning.

'Hello, Peter,' Andersen said as he entered.

'Oh! Hello, John,' Hanson replied, pleased. Andersen was Ashton's Troop Commander and would be able to update him on the man and his patrol.

Sergeant Rawle quickly briefed Andersen and after bidding both officers a good evening headed for the mess. Andersen was confirming patrol locations on the battle map when Hanson spoke.

'Ashton's your Troop Sergeant isn't he, Peter?' The operations officer was studying the file as he spoke.

'Yes he is.' Andersen looked away from the board and toward Hanson. 'Why?'

'The boss wants to talk about him when he returns from the conference. I'm not sure what it's about, so I'm reading up on his blokes.'

Andersen looked puzzled. 'The boss hasn't spoken to me about Ashton.'

'Maybe he'll want to speak to both of us,' Hanson replied. It seemed the sensible thing to do.

'You there, OPSO?' It was the voice of Major Deane calling down the corridor.

'Yes, sir,' Hanson responded, 'in the Ops Room.' He got up to make his way to the door but the voice stopped him.

'Stay there, I'll be up shortly.'

Hanson looked at his watch, 1745 hours. Good chance of missing dinner again, he thought, as he walked to the door and looked at the empty corridor leading to Deane's office.

'Have you eaten, sir?' he called down the corridor.

'No I haven't, Ops. Do you think you could organise the kitchen to keep us something?'

'Yes, sir.' Hanson picked up the phone and ordered two meals to be set aside. He was cradling the handset as Deane walked in and spied Andersen at the duty officer's desk.

'Ah, John!' he said, 'glad you're here.' He pulled the swivel chair in front of Hanson's desk toward him. 'You might as well be in on this.' Both officers stared at their commander as he gathered his thoughts. Finally he looked directly at Andersen and said, 'How is Ashton going since the Cunningham affair?'

'He's fine, sir,' Andersen said hesitantly, not sure where the conversation was heading. 'There doesn't appear to be any change in *him*, at least.'

'What does that mean, John?' The major was instinctively on to the inflection in Andersen's voice.

'Well,' Andersen replied thoughtfully, 'there seems to be a big change in the morale of the patrol since Cunningham was wounded.'

'They don't strike me as the type of chaps who would fall apart because one of their mates was wounded.'

'I don't think it has anything to do with Cunningham, sir.' Andersen knew he was getting into an area where he didn't want to be. 'It's Corporal Dobel, the new 2IC.' Andersen took a deep breath. 'None of Ashton's blokes want to work with him.'

'You don't think he should have been promoted?' the Squadron Commander said quietly. It wasn't exactly a question, more a challenge.

Andersen and Hanson knew the circumstances surrounding the promotion of Gary Dobel. Ashton was angered that Bluey Erickson had not received his second stripe and the sergeant and Deane had argued about it. Mostly Ashton had argued, while Deane had simply made up his mind. There was no argument about it as far as the Squadron Commander was concerned.

'It's not a matter of Dobel's promotion so much as putting him in Ashton's patrol,' Andersen answered cautiously. 'Ashton would have been better off with Erickson as a lance corporal 2IC and given one of the new reinforcements to train.' He was glad it was out—he just hoped it had come out right.

'Why didn't you come to me with this before, John?' Deane queried.

'I let Ashton do that, sir,' Andersen responded. 'It's his patrol.'

'Well, Ashton botched the job,' Deane said with a smile. 'Had he approached me differently he may have got his way.' He fixed his stare on Hanson. 'I run this squadron, eh, OPSO! Not Sergeant Rowan Ashton.'

The lieutenants' eyes met and both men smiled. It was called the profession of arms. One body was responsible for the squadron, one body that could demand the loyalty of the hundred or so soldiers on the hill, and that body was Major Colin Deane. The Dobel incident had been a refresher in loyalty for Ashton, there was no doubt about that.

Deane knew that he could demand the loyalty of his subordinates but their respect had to be earned. He and Ashton were the same people, with the same principles, and they had a mutual respect for each other that would survive the most stringent of tests. That is why Dobel is out there with Ashton now, thought Deane, and that's why Ashton will give Dobel every opportunity to make it as a 2IC.

'Anyway, that's not what I wanted to speak to you about.' The major brought his subordinates' attention back to the present. 'I want to discuss wear and tear on Ashton's patrol.'

'Yes, sir,' Hanson said, not knowing what else to say.

'How many contacts has Ashton's patrol had?' Deane asked.

'Don't know, sir.'

'Around six, sir . . . I think.' Andersen tried to help out his brother officer.

'If you count the time Cunningham was hit,' Deane continued, without acknowledging Andersen's contribution, 'this will be his fourth close recce?' He paused long enough to see both men nod in agreement. 'There's only been one other really close recce done this tour. Is that right, Ops?'

'That's right, sir,' Hanson responded quickly. He hoped that Deane wasn't going to ask him who had done it because he was having a memory collapse at that moment.

'I know that Ashton hasn't been on R&R yet. When is his patrol due to go?'

'Next month, sir,' Andersen answered. 'About five weeks time.' He knew because he and Ashton had discussed it; they were allocated weeks following each other on the R&R roster.

'I think by the time he gets back from this patrol he will need to go on R&R,' the major said authoritatively. 'Is it a problem to organise that?' He looked pointedly at Hanson, challenging him to find a problem.

'No, sir, he's due out in four days so I'll organise it for next week.'

'Good, let's go and eat.'

'Dobel's not due for R&R,' Hanson said before Deane could rise. 'He had his with Sergeant Willis' patrol in July.'

'That's fine,' said the major as he rose and slid the chair back against the desk. 'We'll find a patrol for him to operate in while the rest of his team are away.'

Deane and Hanson walked from the building and across the volleyball court that separated the headquarters area from the officers' and sergeants' mess. 'What do you think of the Ashton thing, Peter?' Deane asked his operations officer. The two men had become quite close as the tour progressed and Deane had come to rely on the younger man as a sounding board on operational matters.

'Which part of the Ashton thing, sir?' Hanson queried, guardedly.

'The Dobel part. Was it too severe a lesson in loyalty for Ashton?' The major searched Hanson's profile. 'Did he really need it?'

'No!—to both points, sir,' the operations officer answered without hesitation. 'But we all need to be reminded from time to time,' he continued with a wry smile, 'even the Squadron Commander!'

'You're absolutely right,' Deane said, mindful of the confidences that the operations officer kept on his relations with some of the senior officers at Task Force Headquarters. They took the accepted shortcut through the mess. The bar had closed for the evening meal and the barman was in the process of reopening it—otherwise the room was empty.

'Who are the stand-by patrol commanders tomorrow, Peter?' the major asked.

'Sergeant Connell is stand-by one, sir, and Sergeant Norris is stand-by two.'

'Please brief them in the morning to be prepared in case Ashton really gets himself into trouble.'

'Yes, sir.' The lieutenant thought he'd do so that night, in case the sergeants decided to go on a drinking spree.

The two officers walked slowly across the dirt road toward the dining hut. Peter Hanson glanced at the major. There was a good deal of tension in his superior's face. Hanson realised it was because Deane had committed Ashton to his fourth close reconnaisance task for the tour and the potential consequence of that decision was eating him up inside.

9

The first hint of light struggling through the jungle canopy aroused Gary Dobel from a fitful sleep. He lay with his eyes open and stared at nothing in particular. Today would be an experience for him, an experience he would rather do without. He felt the uncertainty in every fibre of his body. What if Ashton and Wilkins get sprung in the camp and I don't know how to get them out, he thought. What if I freeze, or make the wrong decision. That was his worst fear—making the wrong decision.

'Make that the last time it happens.' Ashton's words echoed through his mind. He sat bolt upright and looked around at the bodies on the ground. He was sure Ashton had spoken but it could not have been, everybody was still asleep. He remembered then that Ashton had admonished him for being last up on the first morning. God, he thought, was that only yesterday?

He thought briefly about who was sleeping where. Wilkins was on one side of him and Erickson on the other. He reached over to where the frame of Billy Wilkins was just visible in the early light and shook him slightly. Wilkins stirred a little but did not respond in the manner Dobel thought he should.

'Psssst,' Dobel hissed and shook Wilkins again.

'OK,' Wilkins said, 'I'm awake.'

'Time, fellows,' Dobel whispered to nobody in general and everyone in particular as he shook Erickson.

Ashton smiled to himself in the half light of the new day. It was not normal for the patrol to oversleep but they had had a very difficult night. A large number of VC had come from the direction of the camp during the night and headed north-east. More VC than Ashton thought could possibly be in the province—a continuous stream from just after last light until a few hours ago. The last group had left the camp around 0330 hours.

Ashton had thought seriously about running out the radio aerial and trying to get through with the information while the movement was occurring, but commonsense and experience had prevailed. Communications at night with the low output, high frequency AN/PRC 64 radio was never an option and even daytime reception had been particularly bad for the past six weeks or more. He knew he would have to get the information on the enemy's night move to headquarters as soon as possible after daylight. It was a nuisance that interfered with the recce plan he had made for the day.

They came awake slowly but there was no hesitancy in the way they packed their equipment to be ready for the first move toward their perimeter positions. Ashton's regular members knew there was no need for haste this morning because the commander was going to brief them on the recce while they were still at their sleeping positions.

Ashton picked up his weapon and, using it as a crutch, forced himself on to his knees, turning inwards to face the centre of the group. He was confronted by a tight group of heads in an area not more than two metres square.

'Before I start—we're going to be here longer than I planned while we report that stuff from last night.' Nobody spoke but Ashton noted the nodding of heads. 'All right, we'll then move north-west from here until we hit a perimeter track or that access track up there'—he waited for that to be assimilated—'then we'll find approximately where the track runs into the camp and patrol a tight box all the way around the camp, looking for access tracks as we go'—he paused again briefly—'until we're at the north side where the access track up here joins the camp.'

There were nods of understanding all round so Ashton continued. 'I'll decide where the first support base will be and Billy and I will go in for a look.' He paused to allow them to picture what was being said. 'I'll move the support base after each probe or whenever I think it necessary until we've finished the task.'

'How long will that take?' Dobel asked. Collier snorted and it was light enough for Ashton to see Erickson give him a dig in the ribs with his elbow.

'Could take two or three days,' the sergeant replied truthfully. 'No point in rushing death!'

'How come we're starting the recce near the track?' Dobel asked with a troubled note in his voice. This time nobody scoffed. It was a better than fair question.

'We're not. We'll move back from the track a bit before we start.' Ashton shifted a little as he spoke. 'I just need to make sure that Billy and I know exactly where it is so we can keep an eye on it while we're poking about in there.

'Any problems so far?' he asked after a moment. There was no response so he continued. 'Actions on!' he whispered hoarsely, and felt the tension rise in them immediately. They were all listening intently—this was the part they all needed to know. To get it wrong could result in one or more of them becoming a casualty.

'At any time if we are contacted by the enemy I will consider the task compromised and we'll extract ourselves from the firefight using our normal procedures.' Ashton paused for effect.

'If Billy and I get sprung in the camp'—looking directly at Wilkins—'the support group is to move, if necessary, to provide effective fire support.' He shifted his position again to ease the pain in his knees. 'Gary, you will position the group and Jimmy will direct the fire to wherever it will do most good.' He watched the back of Dobel's head for a reaction; there was none. 'Any problems?'

This must be tedious for the older hands, he thought, but it won't hurt them.

'If the support group is sprung while Billy and I are in the camp, we will move to the best spot to provide you with cover to get out.' He looked at them. There was no reply.

'Whatever happens, both groups need to get into visual contact as soon after the initial firefight as possible and stay that way until the best opportunity to marry up presents itself.' There was another long pause and the patrol members waited. They knew there was more to come.

'Rendezvous!' Ashton spat the word out. 'There is no change to the RVs given in the initial patrol brief.' He liked to keep the same rendezvous points for the duration of a patrol. It was less for people to remember. Continually changing the RVs led to confusion and could have the effect of preventing a split patrol getting back together quickly. Ashton accepted that there might be circumstances where changing the RVs had some commonsense basis, but a normal run of the mill recce/ambush operation in South Vietnam was not one of them.

'Equipment! When Billy and I go into the camp, we'll leave our packs with the support group.' He looked again at Dobel's back for a reaction. There was a slight shift in the 2IC's posture. Stand by for another question, Ashton thought. 'If there's no pressure on in the contact but we can't link up quickly,' he continued, 'Gary will grab my pack and Bluey,' he paused, looking at Erickson, 'you grab Billy's pack and we'll marry up as soon as practical after we clear the camp.'

'Aren't we leaving our packs here?' Dobel asked. It seemed as good a place as any to him. That way there would be less noise moving around the perimeter and therefore less chance of being detected.

'No,' said Ashton patiently, 'we'll take them with us.' He looked directly at his 2IC. 'We may need to sleep on the other side of the camp for a couple of nights.'

'It will be too noisy with our packs on,' Dobel said seriously. 'The VC will hear the racket and come out looking for us.'

It was a teaching that you should never take your pack on a close recce—that was true enough. But it was a matter of interpretation of the word 'close'. Ashton had no intention of taking his pack on his part of the recce. That's why he was leaving it with the support group.

'If the VC come looking for you, Gary,' Ashton said with a straight face and a hint of devilment in his eye, 'you have my permission to shoot them.'

The patrol moved from their LUP at 0930 hours. It had taken a long time to encode and send the necessary information on the enemy activity of the previous evening. There had been a number of queries from headquarters over the content of the message. Finally, they were satisfied and Erickson recovered his aerial, packed up the radio and was ready to go.

They moved a little west of north. Very slowly they proceeded toward the area where Ashton thought they might pick up the track before it ran into the camp. It had been quiet all morning and nothing was heard from the camp. Still, they moved quietly; Dobel's fear over the noise created by their packs was without foundation in the open primary jungle.

Suddenly, without warning, they found the low narrow entanglement of sticks and leaves that represented a perimeter fence. Ashton stopped the patrol and quickly moved them back to where Collier was crouching. He motioned for Dobel to come forward to join them. They were in sight of the perimeter and any enemy that was within twenty metres of it.

Ashton quickly removed his pack and motioned to Wilkins to do the same. He moved to where Dobel was crouched, watching the rear. 'The perimeter fence is just up ahead,' he briefed his 2IC, 'familiarise yourself with the surroundings quickly. Billy and I are going to plot the track into the camp.'

'How long do you think you'll be gone?' Dobel asked. Ashton thought it a very poor question in the circumstances.

'As long as it takes, Gary,' the sergeant responded flatly. 'We're leaving in the next few minutes.'

Ashton caught the attention of Collier and Erickson, made a gesture to himself and Wilkins and then circled his fingers around one eye followed by the silent signal for a track. Both soldiers understood perfectly that he and Wilkins were going on a short reconnaissance to find the track. He motioned Wilkins toward the direction he wanted him to go and nodded.

They'd travelled forty metres when Wilkins' body language told Ashton they had found the access track. Ashton moved to his scout for a better view and suffered an involuntary rush of breath at his first glimpse of the track. It was wide and deep, with two sets of wheel ruts to allow ox carts to pass. There was room for people to walk in between and it was deep enough to indicate that an extremely high volume of traffic had passed along it over a long period of time.

'Shit,' Ashton whispered to Wilkins, 'this is nearly as wide as the Firestone Trail.' It wasn't true but Wilkins knew what his commander meant. 'Mark it, Billy,' Ashton went on. 'How about that large tree with the big growth about five metres up the trunk?'

'OK,' Wilkins replied; it was perfect. They would be able to see the big, natural bulge on the tree from a long way off.

Ashton squatted several metres from the track and let his eyes wander over the area. 'I've seen enough for now,' he finally said. 'I'll cover you out.'

Wilkins moved without Ashton even noticing. He waited, searching with his eyes for the telltale sign of enemy movement.

'Click-click.' It was Wilkins signalling that he was in position to cover his commander.

They covered each other away from the track and some of the way back to the support group. When they arrived, Ashton quickly briefed the others on what they had seen. The tree with the growth was not visible from this point, but Ashton was confident it would be a useful marker when they made it around the other side of the camp.

The patrol moved off slowly and quietly in a due westerly direction, keeping the perimeter fence in sight until it began to bend toward the north. They had gone almost three hundred and twenty metres from a line where the tree with the large growth had been. Ashton allowed another ten metres of travel in a westerly direction before turning north to again parallel the fence. Within fifty metres, Wilkins stopped and went into his step back and squat routine. Ashton immediately sent the signal back that they had found a track before moving forward to Wilkins. This track was only half the size of the one at the other end of the camp, a single ox cart track running away from the camp in a south-west direction.

They used the maximum security drill to deal with the track and within forty seconds they were across, leaving no sign of their passage. It was a most vulnerable time, in sight of the perimeter fence and exposed to a chance encounter with the enemy moving in either direction along the track.

They continued north barely in sight of the fence. After eighty metres, Wilkins again went into his step back and squat routine, it was a rerun of the previous track crossing. The patrol moved swiftly and surely again to clear the second track quickly. It was another single ox cart track, this time running north-west away from the camp.

Soon after crossing the second track, Ashton noticed the fence bending away to the east. He looked at his watch. It was almost

1230 hours. He continued for a further twenty metres and stopped the patrol. He figured they were forty metres from the track and over sixty metres from the fence and he was confident enough, given the surroundings, to allow his men to have a hot meal.

The patrol relaxed a little from the tension that patrolling the perimeter had so far brought. Ashton busied himself with estimating the dimensions of the first two sides of the camp and sketching what he'd seen. All things being equal, he thought, the camp should be about three hundred metres long and around one hundred and fifty metres wide. He wondered how they had fitted all those VC in there last evening—presuming they had camped there for some part of the day.

The patrol had a leisurely lunch. Ashton was in no hurry to rush the reconnaissance. If he got some of it done today it would be fine; if he didn't, it didn't matter. His primary concern was Dobel and how he would handle it. This was new to Dobel and it was important that he be eased into it at a pace he could adjust to. Ashton decided to give him a further briefing before they moved out.

The sergeant was puzzled by the lack of activity at the enemy camp. He had given a deal of thought to the reasons why there had not been any movement from the camp at all that day. The most likely reason was that the camp had been emptied the previous evening when the large force moved out. While it puzzled him, it did not concern him too much. And if there were no occupants the most hazardous phase of the task—getting to the start point on the north side of the camp—could be completed easily without the patrol being detected.

10

They moved off at 1400 hours. The perimeter fence was barely visible and on occasion they lost sight of it completely for minutes at a time. There was some comfort in being away from the fence but Rowan Ashton was aware that out of sight of the fence did not necessarily mean out of sight of the enemy. To believe otherwise provided a false sense of security that represented enormous danger for the patrol. The Cunningham incident was sufficient testimony to that.

The three hundred metres to the north-east corner of the camp was the easiest movement the patrol had experienced so far. After half the distance there was an obvious change in vegetation. The area of the north-east corner was almost devoid of secondary growth and the perimeter fence could be seen from twenty metres. It was good for stealthy movement but not for security.

The area was studded with large trees fifteen to twenty metres high, with trunks a metre or more in diameter. The branches and leaves were entwined at the top, creating a dense mat of foliage that blocked out the sunlight. The filtered light that did manage to penetrate the canopy was insufficient to provide the photosynthesis needed to maintain strong plant growth on the jungle floor. Although the area was almost devoid of undergrowth, there were enough large trees to provide protection from enemy fire.

The patrol reached a point where Ashton decided the first support base would be. He motioned for Wilkins to stop, moved to where his scout was standing and quickly removed his pack.

He gestured to the remainder of the patrol to close up into a loose, all-round defensive position. Wilkins waited for the position to be secured before removing his own pack.

The commander caught the attention of his patrol and gave the thumbs-up signal to each in turn. They responded simply with a nod of the head. Wilkins was the last man he looked at. Their eyes met briefly and, in a joining of the minds, Wilkins' eyes registered his understanding. This was it. Without further gesture, Wilkins moved off toward the perimeter fence. Ashton followed five metres or so behind. He would have been closer in normal circumstances but the country was so open beneath the dense jungle canopy that five metres was the minimum he dared to be from Wilkins.

When the two men departed, Dobel organised the position into something he thought would best provide the support Ashton and Wilkins might require. There was no argument from Collier, but the medic was taking note of all the 2IC did and subconsciously giving him a mark out of ten for each action or decision.

Ashton and Wilkins moved south at a good pace and crossed the perimeter fence at the bend where it turned and ran parallel to their heading. As though by direction, Wilkins propped beside a large tree just inside the perimeter fence. It was not a defensive or cautious action, so Ashton moved to the side of his scout and positioned himself so that they both had maximum protection from the tree.

'According to my calculations,' Ashton whispered, 'it should be about a hundred metres to the big ox cart track.'

'OK, you taking the sharp end from here?'

'Yes, I'll take the sharp end,' Ashton confirmed and, realising that Dobel's group could not support them as effectively as he'd first thought, said, 'You'd better hang back a little in this open shit.'

Ashton was right; it would be a difficult task in this terrain to do an effective support job. He'd made an error of judgment in leaving the other three so far behind—the size and placement of the trees was a problem. Although the trees were perhaps twenty metres apart, there were so many that they reduced clear lines of sight. Where clear lines did exist, they were what the military called natural fire lanes and natural fire lanes could be used to great advantage by a competent machine-gunner.

Wilkins noticed it at almost the same time as Ashton did. 'I wouldn't like to be in the mob that attacked this place,' he said quietly, 'just look at some of these fire lanes.'

Ashton had a decision to make: keep on with the recce or return to the support group and bring them forward to make a two-group recce party out of the patrol. It was not an easy choice as there were advantages and disadvantages in either course of action. The biggest disadvantage in *not* bringing the remainder of the patrol up was that Ashton and Wilkins would have no direct fire support in a contact. The biggest disadvantage of bringing the other members forward was that, in the event of a contact, the group could find themselves in a fire lane covered by a machine gun, without realising it until too late.

Wilkins watched as his commander wrestled with the problem. He knew that any decision made by Ashton could be wrong in a given set of circumstances. Don't waste the time going back for them, Rowan, he thought, we'll be better off on our own, more mobile, and less likely to get caught in a fire lane.

'You ready?' Ashton asked his scout suddenly. He had made his decision. The two of them could do the job faster and more accurately without the cumbersome distraction that a closer support group would provide.

'Yep!'

'Mark a tree then, and let's get going.'

Wilkins pointed to a tree nearby. It was one of relatively large diameter, with an unusual dead branch angling downward near the top of the trunk.

'OK,' said Ashton, 'that'll do.' He was up and moving as he spoke.

They continued south, with Ashton leading. After twenty-five metres they encountered the first of the bunkers. He turned and caught Wilkins' eye and placed the clenched fist of his left hand under his chin. Wilkins acknowledged the bunker signal and moved closer while Ashton checked it. It was empty. Ashton plotted its position as accurately as possible on the sketch he had prepared previously.

He studied the area carefully and noted the crawl trenches terminating at the bunker near where he was standing. One trench ran off generally in the direction they were heading in, and the other ran off toward the south-west.

They continued south and found two more bunkers before they encountered the large ox cart track at a point near the tree with the large growth they had noted from the other side of the camp. All the bunkers were connected by crawl trenches. When he was satisfied about the camp dimensions, Ashton plotted both bunkers and the crawl trenches. The pair turned north-west and paralleled twenty-five metres from the track for a hundred and fifty metres, finding another bunker just before they came to a large, cleared central area.

From the edge of the clearing the area appeared a little smaller than a football field and had an odd-looking mound of dirt in its north-east corner. Ashton was puzzled by the mound as he had not encountered anything like it before. He looked over his shoulder to see Wilkins crouching just beside him.

'There's no one here, Rowan. I'd be willing to bet on that.'

'We already have, Billy,' Ashton responded drily. 'I'm going to investigate that mound of dirt over there.' Ashton made the fifteen metres to the mound in quick time and was surprised to find that it was a bunker, an odd bunker, but a bunker nonetheless. There was an entrance at one end and Ashton removed a small torch from his shirt pocket and eased himself into the entry way.

It was a tight squeeze with his webbing on but he got his head and arm into the opening and turned on the torch. The bunker was five or six metres long and two metres wide. The inside was clear of anything that might indicate habitation. At the far end of the floor, in the corner diagonally across from the entrance, there was a hole. The top portion of a light bamboo ladder protruded from the hole, indicating that it led to another level.

Ashton was not prepared to investigate the bunker further. He withdrew his head from the entrance and spied an unusual cone-shaped bamboo structure a dozen metres away. He studied it for several seconds until a spark of recognition leapt in his mind. A fireplace cover! He had seen such a cover on his previous tour, but it had not been so large.

He rejoined Wilkins and they continued to probe the extent of the quadrant by turning north, away from the centre. This was a most vulnerable time and Wilkins had difficulty watching for an enemy that could surprise them from any one of several directions.

They found another bunker twenty metres before the perimeter fence by following a crawl trench north-west. Ashton picked up an AK47 assault rifle magazine filled with ammunition. The bunker was otherwise empty. They turned east, following another crawl trench toward their start point, and discovered a further bunker fifty metres along. Ashton eased himself into this bunker and emerged with a portion of the linked belt from an RPD light machine gun. The belt contained twelve Soviet 7.62mm cartridges. There was also a scarf which Ashton thought must have belonged to a member of the 274th Main Force VC Regiment.

Forty metres further along they reached the reference tree they had marked for this section of the quadrant. Ashton plotted the central area with its strange bunker and fireplace. He also plotted the final two perimeter bunkers and crawl trenches they'd found. He looked at the partial sketch in his notebook and realised they had just completed the entire quadrant in one triangular-shaped sweep. His watch told him it was 1620 hours.

'Let's go back to the others.'

Wilkins nodded, checked his compass and moved off in a due northerly direction. It was important that they return to the support group's location from the same direction that they'd left it. Many times, in many wars, soldiers had returned to a start point from a different direction, only to be mistaken for enemy and shot in error.

In the jungles of Vietnam, where the enemy was likely to pop up at any time and from any direction, there was always a degree of nervousness whenever anybody, friend or foe, approached a static location. Here, on the outskirts of a camp that had given refuge to a large enemy unit not 24 hours before, nerves could be stretched to breaking point, and in some cases triggerfingers could become a little twitchy. Ashton was not normally one who needed to test the reactions of his patrol. But with the wounding of Cunningham in mind, and now the presence of an unknown quantity in Dobel, going back to basics was the only sensible thing to do—and coming back from the same direction that you went out was as basic as it came.

Ashton did not speak to anyone when he and Wilkins returned. He wanted to get away from the area quickly and secure a LUP for the night. He gestured to them to shoulder their packs. In less than half a minute Wilkins was leading them away from the camp. After twenty metres Ashton directed him to head west and they breathed a sigh of relief when they were finally engulfed by the secondary growth adjacent to the north-western quadrant of the camp.

Because of the lateness Ashton wanted to stop the patrol just inside the line of secondary growth. But he pushed on for another fifty metres to ensure that anyone seeing them enter the scrub would not have the advantage of a cleared area in which to sneak up on them during the night. It was a little after 1730 hours and within five minutes he had the patrol in a night LUP.

Immediately the position was secure, Ashton had Erickson and Collier run an aerial to let headquarters know that they were OK and to ask for any message traffic to be passed. The cicadas had started almost as soon as the patrol pulled up and the noise that was normally an asset was now of concern—it could just as easily cover the approach of an enemy who had sighted them moving from the open area into the scrub.

The message traffic took over fifteen minutes. There was no encoding to be done but the atmospherics made the signaller's job particularly difficult. Finally, Erickson tapped out Dit Dah Dit Dah Dit, which signified that he was finished. Ashton immediately gave the signal for everyone to eat; they were well behind schedule on their evening routine and he was trying to speed it up before darkness beat them.

One thing about these more open secondary areas, Ashton thought, there's not a lot of clearing to be done for sleeping spaces. He realised he still had to do his round of the patrol and was hurrying his meal. He washed down the last mouthful of food with the dregs from his modest cup of tea and silently put his cup and empty ration container away. He got up unsteadily, picked up his weapon and made for Dobel's position.

'How was *your* day, Gary?'

'I was a bit worried when you blokes got out of sight and we couldn't support you,' Dobel hesitantly confided in his commander. 'I was going to move the group but I wasn't sure exactly where you went.' It was evident that Dobel was concerned that he had not done the right thing by remaining at the support base.

'That's OK, Gary.' Ashton put his mind at rest. 'It was a bit tricky further into the camp and having the whole patrol down there might not have been a good thing.' He was careful not to imply that Dobel would have been in the way.

'We saw you coming back from the west along the fence,' Dobel said with some relief. 'How much did you get done?'

Ashton withdrew the field notebook from his pocket and showed the partially completed sketch to his 2IC. He pointed out specific areas and explained the symbols he'd used on the sketch. 'When it's all done we'll have a full camp sketch,' he said.

Dobel was impressed. Not so much by the sketch as by the way Ashton and Wilkins had gone into the camp and moved around a quarter of it in an hour and a half. 'What's the go for tomorrow?' he asked.

'I'd like to finish it tomorrow. And there's no reason why we can't. My biggest concern is the area between the two tracks at the western end.'

Dobel nodded. He was becoming more comfortable in Ashton's presence. It was the way Ashton had of putting people at ease by lessening the impact of their mistakes and quietly providing alternative solutions to their problems.

Ashton briefed his 2IC on the emergency actions to take should they be contacted by the enemy during the night. He put his notebook away, picked up his weapon and headed in Collier's direction. He could see that Collier was itching to discuss something and made a mental note not to bet against Dobel being involved. From his shirt he withdrew the scarf in which he'd wrapped the AK47 magazine and linked belt. He placed these on the ground where they could easily be inspected.

'What's that tell you, Jimmy?'

'They must have plenty of ammo,' Collier said, 'or they're slack pricks for losing gear.'

'They did leave in the dark last night,' Ashton reminded him. 'You think this is a 274 Regiment scarf?'

'Looks like. One of Andersen's blokes had a 274 scarf that looked like this one.' Collier picked up one corner and turned it over in his hand. 'He calls it his Dong Nai rag.' Dong Nai Regiment was another name for the 274 VC Regiment.

Ashton allowed a pause in the conversation so that Collier could clear his mind if he desired. The medic said nothing so Ashton brought him up to date with what the recce had achieved and briefed him on the emergency procedures for the night. Ashton wondered why Collier had not brought up Dobel's name during the conversation. He slowly wrapped the VC equipment in the scarf and returned it to his shirt before he stood up.

'Nothing to report on Dobel today, Jimmy?' Ashton could not contain himself.

'I thought we were going to give him a chance to develop into a halfway decent 2IC,' the medic threw at him with a touch of impertinence in his voice.

Ashton nodded several times as he stood up to disguise his embarrassment at being outfoxed by the younger man. He looked across at Wilkins, lying against his pack near a large tree. Something was odd about the scout. He felt a momentary anger as he realised that Wilkins was asleep.

Ashton stopped beside his scout and gazed down at his sleeping form. Both hands were by Wilkins' side and his map was lying in his lap. In Ashton's memory, Wilkins had never slept during the day on a patrol without specific direction to do so. It was not the done thing in the patrol to sleep when you had a portion of the perimeter to watch. The anger left him as he realised that Wilkins had put a great deal of effort into the day's reconnaissance. The continual tension of covering someone's every move for a solid hour and a half was extremely tiring.

He reached down slowly and picked up the cutdown SLR beside Wilkins. He checked that the safety catch was in the safe position and nudged the scout in the middle of the chest with the barrel. Wilkins came awake with a start, reaching for his rifle as he did so. He quickly focused on reality and froze when he saw the displeased look on his commander's face. He looked sheepishly away as Ashton crouched beside him.

'I could have been a VC, Billy.'

Wilkins regained his composure quickly. 'Sorry, Rowan,' he said, struggling to sit upright, 'today must have taken more out of me than I thought.'

Ashton caught Wilkins' map as it slid from his lap and handed it to him. There was no point making an issue of the incident at that time. Ashton would wait until an appropriate moment to let the story out to a group of Billy's peers. That would ensure his attention for the remainder of the tour.

'Are you ill Billy?' he asked with concern.

'No, mate, just knackered.'

'OK,' said Ashton, the disappointment fast fading from his expression. 'That long-looking bunker in the centre of the camp—any ideas?'

'No, never seen or heard of anything like it.'

Ashton dismissed the bunker issue and briefed his scout on the recce plan for the following day and the emergency procedures for that evening.

'Any questions, Billy?' he asked finally, as he got up to leave.

Billy shook his head but motioned for the sergeant to come closer. 'You won't tell the other blokes I was asleep, will you?'

'Of course I will, Billy'—Ashton put his hand on Wilkins' shoulder—'first opportunity I get.' He gave him a brief, reassuring pat as he left.

Ashton's mind was back on the bunker as he approached Erickson. Something about it intrigued him and he knew he would not be able to erase it from his mind until his curiosity was satisfied.

'How did the recce go?' Erickson asked.

'Bloody open in there,' Ashton replied, pleased that his signaller had led him into his brief, 'but we got the whole quadrant out of the way today.' It was good news to Erickson but he sensed that something was troubling the boss. He decided not to question him on the matter as he knew Ashton would eventually get around to addressing it.

Ashton briefed Erickson and then queried him on the unusual bunker in the middle of the camp, drawing another negative response. He had not asked Dobel or Collier about the bunker and made a mental note to do so when they concentrated in their sleeping area.

He got up slowly and left Erickson's location. The impending darkness would disrupt their normal routine. It was a few minutes before last light and Ashton remembered he had not had a cigarette since park time. The clearing of the sleeping spaces would have to be done after last light.

Ashton felt as tired as he had ever been in his life. The tension of being in the enemy camp with only one gun for support began to leave him and its place was taken by a wave of exhaustion. For some odd reason he found himself thinking about life back at Nui Dat and how the soldiers of the squadron were mad keen to play simple tricks on each other. Like purposely misleading each other about the name of the nightly movie.

The movie was one of the highlights of the day for those preparing for—or recovering from—patrol duties. The name of the movie was intended to be secret in order to surprise everyone, but there is no way that such secrets can be kept from soldiers. The few scallywags who took the trouble to hunt down the name had a decided edge over anyone who made a casual inquiry in the mess queue. Many had been caught by the squadron pranksters as they laid their clever trails of false information. On some evenings there would be several titles to choose from and the number of people who attended the nightly screening in antici-pation of viewing such classics as 'Zulu' or 'Bonny and Clyde' would be bitterly disappointed when the classic turned out to be a B grade black and white flop.

It was so bad at one time that the Squadron Commander issued a directive forbidding anyone from spreading rumours. This improved the situation for a while but also gave rise to jocular exchanges.

'What's the movie tonight, mate?'

'The House Across the River.'

'Oh yeah? Who's in it?'

'No one! It's been deserted for years.'

Ashton smiled to himself as he thought that it didn't really matter in the least what movie was screening. It was the only show in the area and everyone who was in camp usually got out their folding deckchair, filled a small ammunition liner with as many beer cans as they were allowed or were available, and went along to Ocker's Opry House no matter what.

The black abyss of sleep began to gather him in as his thoughts turned to the following day. I hope Billy and I are right, he thought, and the enemy camp is just like the house across the river . . . deserted.

11

The gentle pressure on his shoulder roused Ashton from the deepest sleep he had experienced in two tours of South Vietnam. Dobel's soft but persistent effort had taken several seconds to get a response from his commander. There were still minutes until the first rays of dawn struggled through the jungle canopy and the remainder of the patrol were already awake, packed up and listening. Ashton quietly folded and packed his groundsheet and cursed himself for being the last to rise.

As daylight forced the curtain of darkness from the jungle floor the patrol members seemed anxious to be on the move. Although he had some desire for urgency Ashton resisted it strongly, preferring caution. He had slept the sleep of the dead and had heard nothing from the area of the enemy camp. There was good reason to examine the happenings of the night before proceeding with the recce.

Rowan Ashton picked up his weapon and drew himself up on to his knees to face inward. The remainder took his lead and did likewise. Thanks to his lack of familiarity with the finite procedures of the patrol, Dobel was the last to realise that a briefing was to occur. When everyone was in position and leaning slightly inward there was less than a metre's distance between heads.

Ashton seldom briefed his patrol in this manner. He preferred the more leisurely method of rounds to brief the patrol as it gave everyone an opportunity to have his say in private. The 'facing in' method, as it was called, was expedient and relatively secure as each member was required to maintain vigilance by watching the perimeter beyond the man facing him.

'Any movement or noise from the camp last night?' Ashton whispered, looking at each of the faces in turn.

'I heard some shots a long way to the south,' Erickson offered, 'but nothing from the camp.'

There were nods of agreement all round as Ashton produced his field notebook with the partially completed sketch of the camp. This was the most uncomfortable time for all at this type of briefing as the need to look at the book distracted their attention from the primary task of vigilance. He orientated the sketch so that they could view it from the appropriate perspective.

'Seems as though the VC have all gone from the camp.' The others indicated agreement. 'We might be able to finish the job quickly by taking the whole patrol into the camp for a look-see.' Nobody acknowledged Ashton's statement. They were waiting for him to provide details of the plan.

'We'll move down to the perimeter fence in single file,' Ashton continued, pointing to the notebook with his pencil as he spoke, 'then go into a diamond formation for the search.' He looked around the circle of faces and noticed that Dobel was frowning.

'Problem, Gary?'

'*Diamond* formation?'

Ashton knew instantly that he was at fault. The patrol had not practised the diamond formation during their preparations for the mission. It was not a formation he used often in the close confines of the jungle; they had used it on only two occasions during the tour so far.

'You've never used the diamond, Gary.' It was a statement rather than a question.

'That's right,' responded Dobel, a little embarrassed.

Collier had a lopsided grin on his face that clearly said: 'Stuffed up, Ashton!' Ashton deftly turned the page on the notebook and presented a fresh page to the group. 'OK,' he said, smiling to hide his discomfiture, 'a refresher in the diamond formation for all.' He looked around at his men. Then, drawing five dots on the page to represent the patrol members, he explained the position of each.

'The diamond formation is more of a square turned 45 degrees, and it's only useful in some circumstances,' he ended, looking directly at Dobel. 'It will work fine in the more open country that we're liable to find inside the camp.'

Dobel nodded his understanding but the look on his face suggested that he was still confused. Ashton looked him in the eye for a brief moment, then moved the notebook closer toward him in a gesture of concern. With his pencil he drew a circle around the dot in the middle of the diamond.

'This is me in the middle here. I can recce in any direction by taking the member at that point of the diamond with me.' He made a line from the centre to the outside in three directions through the dots representing Wilkins, Collier and Erickson, and waited for a nod from Dobel before continuing. 'When the recce party leaves, the remainder close up a little for control and to provide a support base.'

Dobel seemed happy with the concept as Ashton explained it. His brow drew tight as the obvious thought crossed his mind. 'What about contact drills while travelling in the diamond formation?'

'I move to the side and go slightly forward into the gap between points in the direction of the threat,' Ashton explained patiently as he drew further short lines to emphasise each part of the drill. 'The guns at the points, here and here, support us out of the contact.'

Dobel nodded. It was really quite a simple drill and very similar to the one they had practised in the event of a contact while lying up. He looked into Ashton's eyes. 'Just like the LUP contact drill?'

'That's right—and getting as soon as possible into two fire teams commanded by each of us is critical.'

Ashton turned the page back to the sketch as he looked around the group. Using his pencil as a pointer, he roughly outlined his plan for the remainder of the recce. At the conclusion of the briefing all were aware of the plan and the actions to be taken if there was a contact that caused them to be split up.

'Better get out to your positions on the perimeter,' Ashton instructed them. 'Have breakfast, and be prepared to move in thirty minutes.'

Rowan Ashton stopped the patrol a little over ten metres inside the perimeter fence to identify a prominent tree as a reference point and to shake out into the diamond formation. He'd planned for the patrol to move through the area making a number of halts from which to conduct a two man reconnaissance.

They moved south into the camp with Wilkins at the forward point of the diamond. Collier and Erickson made up the right and left flank points respectively. Dobel was at the rear with Ashton in the centre a little toward the front. They found the first bunker of the quadrant after forty metres. The commander noted that a crawl trench ran off to the north-west and another toward the west. He could plainly see the central clearing with its strangely shaped bunker and the fireplace cover.

Ashton took Collier from the right flank and checked the trench leading off to the north-west. They found a bunker. It was empty. To save time, Ashton decided to continue along a trench that led away generally to the south-west. They found another bunker near one of the westerly access tracks into the camp—it also was empty.

He had Collier watch along the track to the north-west while he scouted a little forward toward the perimeter fence. His mouth went dry momentarily when he discovered himself in front of a huge tree with a large scarf—a V-shaped incision—cut into it just above head height. Inside the scarf was a neatly positioned Chinese D10 directional anti-personnel mine. It faced the approaches to the access track.

Ashton swallowed nervously and moved to the base of the tree. He moved around the tree until he found the electrical initiating cable that ran down the trunk on the side nearest the track. He followed it toward the bunker where Collier was propped near a neat round hole, watching him closely. The electrical cable ran under the ground several metres from the bunker and there was no doubt that the initiation point was somewhere inside or near the bunker. Collier was too far from Ashton in the poor light to see the cable or to know what he was doing. Ashton beckoned him forward and Collier moved quickly and quietly to his commander's side.

'This is the initiation cable from a D10 in that tree over there,' Ashton whispered as Collier joined him. The demolition man's interest heightened. He moved slightly forward to investigate the mine and followed the electrical wire back to where Ashton crouched, covering him.

'Probably runs to that foxhole near the bunker,' Collier offered quietly as he reached down and exposed thirty or forty centimetres of the previously buried wire.

'What foxhole?' Ashton asked, not having seen a hole near the bunker.

'Show you on the way back.' Collier gently separated the two strands of electrical cable a little over halfway along the exposed portion. He produced a small pair of wirecutters from somewhere among his webbing equipment and neatly cut one of the strands. Ashton smiled as Collier reburied the cable and refurbished the area to look as near as possible to how he found it.

'That'll surprise fuck out of them when they try to detonate the mine,' Collier whispered with a mischievous grin.

Ashton smiled his agreement and motioned with his head that they should return to the remainder of the patrol. Collier pointed out the foxhole as they went past. It was well camouflaged and would be almost impossible to detect by anyone approaching the camp from along the track.

Good spot for a sentry post, Ashton thought as the pair made their way back to the support group, maintaining a wary eye as they went.

Ashton plotted the location of the bunker, the anti-personnel mine and the foxhole in his notebook before taking the patrol across the most northerly of the two access tracks and into the area between them. Although the patrol was always focused while inside an enemy camp, as soon as they crossed the top track their alertness became much sharper. The enemy could return in force at any time and discover them inside the camp. Between the tracks was not a place to be if that occurred, as the enemy would be able to encircle them quickly and quietly by the intelligent use of their internal track or crawl trench system.

Here was a problem that required a different approach. In this case Ashton decided that it made more tactical sense to take the support group south of the bottom track while he and Wilkins conducted the recce of the area between the tracks. The vegetation was a little thicker here and moving the support group to a position below the tracks provided more advantage than disadvantage as far as the ultimate security of the patrol was concerned.

He briefed his men on the revised plan and detailed the precise route that he and Wilkins would take on this next recce. He knew there would be times during their recce that the groups would not be able to provide effective cover for each other and any immediate counter action would be up to the individual group. It was a calculated risk that Ashton was prepared to accept in the circumstances.

The patrol made the two track crossings without incident. Ashton and Wilkins remained on the northern side of the second track and covered the support group across it. They passed beside two bunkers on the way that were connected by a crawl trench; a close inspection proved both to be empty. Ashton was becoming completely confident that the camp was unoccupied, but he waited until the support group was in position before moving west beside the track and toward the perimeter fence. The pair moved quietly and quickly in the knowledge that their back was covered by the support group.

Several metres before they reached the fence, the two man recce team came across a perimeter bunker positioned to guard the approach along the bottom access track. It was empty, but the foxhole beside the bunker showed sign of recent occupation. A small, empty tin had been discarded near the hole.

Ashton picked it up gently and examined it. There were Chinese characters on the label and it was covered with ants. He placed it back precisely where it was and flicked the ants from his hand by wiping it on his trouser leg. He examined the foxhole more closely and found the bare wires that he suspected ran to another D10 mine.

Ashton had Wilkins wait by the bunker as he made his way forward to check the approach properly. This time he suffered no reaction when confronted by the mine neatly positioned in a tree. Unlike the previous mine he and Collier had found, this one had foliage placed in the scarf to conceal it. He searched around the tree until he found the wires cleverly placed into a small groove cut in the tree. Obviously some greater effort had been made to camouflage this mine.

Ashton followed the wire for less than a metre before it went underground. He did not have the neat little wirecutters that his demolitions man always carried; instead, he reached into a small pouch on his belt and produced a pair of secateurs that he carried for cutting through bamboo and thick vine country. They were not sharp as Collier's side cutters, but were nearly new. He exposed a half metre of the buried wire and, with care and adequate pressure, snipped one of the thin wire strands. Wilkins watched his commander with more than a little interest. Ashton reburied the cable and moved back to Wilkins' location.

'What was that all about?' Wilkins asked when Ashton joined him.

'Initiation lead for a D10. Can't leave those things just lying around armed—someone might get hurt!'

Wilkins smiled and Ashton indicated that they should make their way back to the support group.

Ashton knelt beside his 2IC, laid his rifle against a small sapling and took out his notebook. 'There's a bunker or something up near the clearing.' He started drawing as he spoke. 'Five or six metres long, two metres wide, mound of dirt on top, and a hole with a ladder in one corner leading to another level maybe. Any ideas, Gary?'

Dobel thought about the description for several seconds. 'Could be,' he replied finally, 'I'll need to have a look at it though, it was a while ago.'

'Let's go,' Ashton urged without hesitation. He came upright, bringing his weapon to the crook of his left arm. He signalled Collier and Erickson that he and Dobel were moving forward to look at the bunker and they were to watch the space vacated by the 2IC.

The commander and his deputy moved past the position occupied by Wilkins and Ashton led Dobel to the open end of the strange construction and pointed to the entry hole. Dobel did not hesitate. He removed his webbing, squeezed himself into the opening with great difficulty and disappeared into the bunker.

Ashton waited several minutes by the opening but Dobel did not reappear. He knelt down and put his head inside the opening. Dobel was not in the upper chamber. Ashton began to feel apprehension gripping him. He sensed movement behind him and sat upright to find Wilkins settling into a position near him.

'What are you doing?' he growled at the scout.

'You blokes are hopeless,' Wilkins responded with a cheerful grin, 'both heads down with no real cover.' The grin was replaced by an admonishing look. 'That's a good way to get your arse reamed.'

Ashton opened his mouth but thought better of it. Wilkins was right, they were vulnerable here on the edge of the clearing without close cover. He was about to say so when Dobel's head appeared from the bunker.

'What do you think?' Ashton fired the question at his 2IC.

'It's an escape bunker. Seen them in Bien Hoa last tour.'

'Explain!'

'Oh,' Dobel said, taken by surprise at the sharpness in Ashton's voice, 'there's at least three levels in the bunker with openings at alternate corners at each level.' He gestured at each end of the bunker as he spoke. 'And an escape tunnel runs off from either the third or fourth level to somewhere out there.' He made a sweeping gesture indicating the area outside the perimeter fence.

'Which level does this one run off from?'

'Don't know, I only went to the second level.' The look on Dobel's face challenged his commander to go below the second level personally.

'OK,' Ashton nodded as he spoke, 'let's get out of here for a break. It's park time.'

The patrol moved south until they found the perimeter fence. Ashton headed Wilkins south-east for sixty metres and stopped the patrol in an area of relatively thick scrub. He looked at his watch. It was 1120 hours. Ashton had a feel for the area by now and decided it was safe enough to forgo the formality of securing the position, so he immediately signalled the patrol to remove their packs and sit down for park time.

They moved north again after the midday break. Although Ashton had felt reasonably safe at their park time location he had not allowed them to light their small stoves for a hot meal. Something was worrying him, a voice reminding him to stay within the basic rules. The feeling was so strong that he decided to revert to the original plan for the recce of the last quadrant and to leave the support group south of the perimeter fence. He stopped the patrol short of the fence and he and Wilkins went forward to conduct the final phase.

They nominated a reference tree at the point where they crossed the fence and Ashton turned east almost ten metres inside and followed a crawl trench. They passed an empty perimeter bunker and shortly came to the point where the large track entered the camp. Ashton went forward of the fence and looked back. It was no surprise to find another D10 in a tree overlooking the track. He located the wire and cut and reburied it as they had the others.

They found a foxhole not far from the tree and Ashton noted with some puzzlement that the hole was over ten metres from the bunker. He plotted the bunker and foxhole and the location of the mine before moving parallel to the track along another crawl trench for a little over seventy metres. Here they discovered another bunker close to the track.

Ashton went down on his knees and looked inside. It was empty. He was facing the bunker opening, his rifle on the ground beside him, and was reaching for his notebook to record the bunker and the crawl trenches leading away from it when he sensed the pad of feet behind him.

'Pssst.' It was Billy. The warning was very low and had an urgent note to it.

Ashton knew it was the enemy even before he looked up to see Wilkins with his fist clenched and thumb down. He felt a momentary sensation of blood draining from his body as he slowly flattened himself toward the ground, eyes and mouth open, hardly daring to breathe.

He heard one of the Viet Cong speak and wished he knew the words. A second voice answered the first. They were very close. Shit, thought Ashton, they're right next to me. He lifted his eyes and strained for a glimpse of Wilkins, who was sitting by the bunker, his rifle facing the direction of the approaching enemy. His right hand was wrapped loosely around the pistol grip, finger on the trigger. There was a tense look on his face.

Ashton tried to remain calm. He knew that Billy would not engage the enemy unless the VC saw either of them. He needed to know how many there were. He could hear the padding of footsteps coming closer; the VC were still talking. The blood returned to his body, he could feel it pounding in his temples, and the dryness in his mouth was almost unbearable. He was three metres from the track and totally exposed. Ashton felt himself on the verge of panic. With much difficulty he suppressed a strong urge to act.

Suddenly, the footsteps and voices had passed. He strained for the sound of more footsteps or voices coming from behind but there were none. He turned his head slowly to the right and looked up to see the two figures disappearing toward the cleared centre area of the camp. He looked at Wilkins, amazed by his expressionless face. Their eyes met and a silent prayer passed between them. They had probably been saved from detection by the way the track ran at an oblique angle to the bunker.

Wilkins smiled and gave his commander the thumbs-up signal that all was clear. They were both shaken by the close and sudden nature of the encounter. The voices were still penetrating the silence of the jungle camp. The VC appeared to have gone to the other side of the cleared area. Ashton could make out one or two words—ngu and cai vong—and thought he knew them. They were still talking as Ashton drew himself upright and picked up his weapon.

Ashton's and Wilkins' eyes met briefly and Ashton nodded. Wilkins moved south toward the support group. He propped after several metres and covered Ashton away from the danger that the track presented. They continued to cover each other in tactical bounds until they came to the crawl trench that ran parallel to the perimeter fence ten metres on its inside.

Erickson was the first person Ashton saw as they approached the support group. He watched the signaller give the thumbs-up to the remainder of the patrol. Ashton could feel the tension escape from the group as he and Wilkins entered their tight perimeter. He was pleased to see that Dobel had them standing-to with packs on. The 2IC and Erickson had the packs belonging to himself and Wilkins beside them, in case they were required to withdraw.

They quickly donned their packs and Ashton gestured to Wilkins to head south. After forty metres he had Wilkins change course to south-east for a further forty metres and then due east for another eighty. Ashton considered this to be far enough from both the camp and the large access track. It was close to a previous LUP they had occupied, but he went through the procedure of clearing the location anyway.

The patrol settled down quickly from the adrenalin rush produced by their near discovery in the camp. Ashton glanced at his watch—it was 1540 hours. The whole business had taken just one hour and forty minutes since park time. He picked up his weapon and moved to where his scout sat quietly, legs crossed and leaning slightly forward.

'That was a near thing, Billy.' Ashton still could not understand how he had not been detected by the VC in such an exposed position. Even the oblique angle of the track could not fully explain his good fortune.

'Nah,' Wilkins responded with a degree of bravado, 'I'd have got both of them.'

Ashton said nothing, but there was no doubt in his mind that Wilkins would have done just that.

'You nearly shit yourself, Rowan,' Billy smiled, encouraged by his commander's silence.

'And you went to sleep the other day!' Ashton countered without malice. 'What were those two carrying?'

'Both had small packs. One had an SKS and the other had one of those Russian burp gun things.'

'PPSH,' Ashton corrected him.

'They had black gear,' Wilkins added. 'Could be anything . . . Engineers, Main Force VC, or just caretakers.'

'Probably caretakers on their way back from guiding that mob that left here the other night.'

Ashton placed his hand on Wilkins' shoulder in a gesture of thanks as he got up to make his way to the centre of the LUP. Wilkins nodded as he watched him go.

The commander sat down at his customary place in the centre of the position and put the finishing touches to the camp recce sketch. He knew they had missed at least one bunker in the last quadrant so he made a best guess at its position. Still, it had been a successful recce thanks to the near absence of VC in the camp. Now he needed to tell headquarters what they had found out about the place, and to ask for directions. He took the layout book from his pocket. This book told him in abbreviated terms precisely what HQ needed to know.

Ashton drafted a message, got to his feet with the aid of his rifle and made his way to where Erickson was relaxing against a large tree. He handed his notebook to the signaller who studied the content of the message briefly before reaching for his codebook.

'We'll get this off tonight,' Ashton told him. 'Get it encoded and Collier and I'll run the aerial.' Erickson nodded and reached into his pack for the small black fishing reel.

12

'Camp report coming in from Patrol Six-Six, sir,' the Signals Troop Sergeant, Harry Filer, shouted through the pigeonhole in the wall between the operations room and the communications centre.

Bugger you, Ashton, Lieutenant Hanson thought. He had just concluded a briefing for the oncoming duty officer and was looking forward to making his way to the mess for a nice cold beer before dinner. But his denunciation of Ashton was far from being serious. There was no better news for Hanson than an incoming camp report from Patrol Six-Six. It meant that Ashton's patrol had finished in the enemy camp and the headquarters staff, principally himself and the OC, could rest a little easier.

It had been a trying two days for Deane and Hanson. Having a patrol inside the enemy's living room, so to speak, provided a degree of anxiety. Now that the patrol was out of the camp, a great weight was lifted from their shoulders.

At that particular moment Peter Hanson was the senior officer at Squadron Headquarters. Major Deane was away at the Task Force Commander's daily conference and Captain Joe Larkin, the squadron's 2IC, was out of the war zone on R&R. It was obvious to Hanson that Ashton would not have initiated communications at this time of day unless he had important information to pass or needed some direction on future operations.

Sergeant Filer went to the 'K' Telephone switchboard in the furthermost corner of the communications centre, plugged in one of the telephone jacks and turned the handle three times in rapid

113

succession. There was a long pause but no one answered. He turned the handle again.

'Hello! Sigs.' The voice on the other end was familiar.

'Better get down here, Squeaker,' Filer said, idly watching the duty signaller writing down the coded message as he received it. 'Ashton's mob are just sending in a camp report.'

'Stuff it!' was Corporal Ian Doyle's immediate response. 'OK,' he said, almost without a pause, 'I'll be right down.'

Corporal Doyle hung up the phone and went to the opposite end of the tent to collect his eating tray, knife, fork and spoon, and plastic cup. Why doesn't Ashton pack up at five o'clock like everyone else?, he asked himself, as he left the tent and headed down the steep pathway through the bamboo that connected the headquarters area with the Signals Troop lines higher up on the Nui Dat feature.

Squeaker Doyle was the squadron cipher clerk. He was half an inch over six feet tall, with dark hair greying at the temples. He'd earned the nickname 'Squeaker' because of the high-pitched inflection that often found its way into his normal baritone voice when he was excited.

'No point in your hanging around, Harry,' Hanson said to the signals sergeant as Doyle entered the communications centre. 'Squeaker and I will sort this out.'

'Thank you, sir.' Filer picked up a clipboard and headed for the door. 'See you in the morning.'

'How long, Squeaker?' Hanson asked as the duty operator copied down the final corrections to the message and gave the patrol the signal to wait for an answer.

'About fifteen or twenty minutes, sir,' the cipher clerk responded, beckoning to the duty operator to move his chair to the front of Doyle's desk.

'Back in ten minutes, then.' Hanson left the room and headed for the officers' and sergeants' mess.

'Like a beer, mate?' John Andersen asked with a smile as Hanson entered the bar.

'No,' Hanson replied, shaking his head, 'but I could go a "goffa"—lemonade will be fine.'

'Another "long green" for me and a lemonade for our drunken OPSO here,' Andersen called to the barman, a huge grin on his face.

'How was your day, John?' Hanson asked his friend with interest.

'Really good. Did the VR over near Binh Tuy this afternoon—the area looks pretty interesting. I'm doing my orders and rehearsals tomorrow and we're on the ground the day after.'

Hanson watched idly as the barman gave Andersen his change. He already knew the details of Andersen's program but realised that his friend was caught up in his battle preparations and was at the stage where his mind was cluttered with the many possibilities of success and failure.

'Morning or afternoon insertion?' he asked.

'Morning,' Andersen responded vaguely. 'By the way, any word from Ashton?'

'He's out of the camp. There's a report just coming in now.' There was a noticeable sign of relief on Andersen's face and Hanson realised that Andersen had been carrying the additional burden of concern for Ashton along with the pressures of his own patrol preparations.

'Rowan is a big boy, John,' Hanson said quietly, 'with a very capable bunch of blokes to help him.'

'I know, but he's been in the thick of it more than anyone else and a couple of his contacts have been pretty horrendous.'

'That's true, but he's got skill and his luck has been pretty good.'

'General Custer had skill and luck, Peter, and look how he finished up!'

'Well, he's off on R&R as soon as he gets back from this one.' From his pocket Hanson pulled a number of crumpled MPC script—a substitute currency—and selected three red-coloured five cent notes and threw them on the bar in front of Andersen. He didn't much like the direction in which the conversation was heading.

'Have a "long green" on me, mate,' he said to his friend. 'I have to get back to the Ops Room and take a look at Ashton's report.' He left the mess with the half full can of lemonade in his hand.

'Almost done, sir,' Squeaker Doyle said as Hanson entered the communications centre. 'Not much in it.' He handed over the completed message on a standard message form.

Hanson read it carefully. It was a comprehensive report. The detail given on dimensions and defences was most useful. Hanson pondered the miscellaneous information section which told him that the camp was a staging area for VC deployments and was being looked after by a pair of caretakers.

Peter Hanson picked up the folder containing all the messages received from Ashton over the duration of this current operation and, returning to his desk in the operations room, sat down with the folder. He read quickly back through the messages to refresh himself on what the patrol had reported so far.

Ashton had asked for direction from HQ and, from the messages Hanson had in front of him, there appeared to be four tasks that could be given. One option was to send the patrol back into the camp to dispose of the two caretakers. That made little sense as it would alert the enemy to the fact that the camp had been discovered, without achieving much else. Another was for Ashton to link up with an infantry company and move in to demolish the camp. This would not be possible in the present operational climate as the bulk of the infantry units were already deployed on search and destroy operations in other parts of the province.

The remaining options were to move the patrol out of the area and extract it to Nui Dat or, alternatively, to have Ashton ambush the main access track leading away from the camp into Long Khanh Province. Hanson pondered Ashton's situation and considered the two options open to him. His discussion with John Andersen was still fresh in his mind and the concern Andersen had shown for Ashton was clouding the issue. Hanson was leaning heavily toward sending Ashton on the relatively safe task of reconnaissance in the east of his area of operations, with an extraction planned from the LZ at which his insertion had taken place. The lieutenant shook his head: it was the safest option, but it was not one you selected for someone like Rowan Ashton.

Hanson considered the ambush option carefully before deciding that Ashton should ambush the track far enough away from the camp so as not to arouse suspicion about its being discovered. He felt good about the decision when he concluded that, in the circumstances, Ashton was only likely to ambush a small caretaker group, if anything. That should satisfy everybody, he thought, as he quickly drafted a reply to Ashton's query on tasking.

'You still there, Squeaker?' he called out.

'Yes, sir.'

Hanson picked up the message folder and went into the communications centre. He put the folder back into the Patrol Six-Six box and handed the short draft message to Doyle. The corporal quickly entered it into the codebook and began encoding. Hanson saw that it was 1750 hours and began to feel a little hungry. He left Doyle to his encoding, stepped outside the headquarters building and headed for the mess. He noted that Colin Deane's Land Rover was parked at the side of the building.

'Peter!' It was Deane's voice. Hanson stopped at the threshold of the mess and turned to see his commander coming toward him but didn't answer.

'Anything new, Peter?' the major asked as Hanson allowed him to go inside.

'Ashton's out of the camp.'

'That's a relief! What's the word on the camp?'

'Looks like a fair-sized transit camp, but there's only a couple of caretakers left.'

The two men walked slowly through the deserted mess without noticing the absence of the usual early gatherers. It was almost five minutes before opening time and even the barman had not yet made an appearance. They emerged from the mess, still walking slowly toward the dining hut.

'What's Ashton doing now?' Deane asked.

'I tasked him with ambushing the access track that runs into Long Khanh.'

'We could have tried for an extraction for him tomorrow,' the major said. 'He's done a pretty fair job.'

It took a moment for Hanson to realise that his commander had stopped walking. Hanson knew that Deane was fishing for an explanation as to why he'd given Ashton the ambush task, but Deane's body language hinted that he also wanted to talk about more important operational matters.

Matters of importance that were not for the general knowledge of the squadron were often discussed in this manner. Headquarters was located in a Kingston hut, which did not provide the privacy that some matters required. Deane and Hanson had many of their more private discussions in the open or in Deane's tent.

'Pulling Ashton out tomorrow didn't enter my mind,' Hanson said. 'I did consider having him recce the remainder of his AO, but I felt that with such a big camp in the north-west it's unlikely there would be anything to recce in the east or south-east.'

'Good.' Deane nodded his approval. 'It's unlikely that we'll get early extractions in future without a lot more justification than we've provided previously.'

Hanson looked sharply at him. This must be something from the Commander's conference, he thought. Aloud he inquired, 'Why is that, sir?'

'We're burning up too many of the Task Force assets, especially air hours. Nothing formal yet, of course, but I anticipate something from the Commander shortly.'

'But there's a war on here, sir! And we need a *lot* of assets to conduct our type of operations.'

'Yes Peter, I know,' the major said, and began to walk toward the dining hut. 'But the war is costing the government a million dollars a day and they're trying to hold the lid on cost escalation.' He glanced at his operations officer. 'These big battalion operations currently going on are burning up the dollars and we're been directed to have a close look at our insertion and extraction methods.'

'They can't be serious about no early extractions,' Hanson replied, falling into step beside Deane. 'We'd have to stop patrolling altogether in that case. You can't put patrols in, even by foot, without some guarantee you can get them out.'

'I've made the Task Force Commander aware of that. The present patrol program will most likely stand but we'll need to have a close look at next month's program.'

The two men walked slowly through the dining room, oblivious to the activity, and stopped at the kitchen servery. They collected their meal and made their way back to the dining area where Hanson's replacement, the newly arrived Bill Griffiths, and the SSM were sitting.

'How is the patrol program going?' Griffiths asked after the introductions were complete.

'Things have been moving along fine,' the major responded. 'We've had a dozen or so wounded and a number of cases of VD and malaria, but we haven't lost anyone KIA as yet . . . touch wood!'

'Got many patrols out?'

Deane glanced toward Hanson, looking for assistance.

'We've got four patrols out at the moment,' Hanson offered on behalf of his OC. 'Three are due for extraction tomorrow. And two are due for insertion the day after.'

'That's not many,' Griffiths observed.

'That's right,' Deane agreed. 'The Task Force have "two battalion minus" search and destroy operations on the go at the moment, and the brigadier doesn't want us involved in them at all.'

'Why not?' Griffiths inquired, a puzzled expression on his face.

'No idea,' the major replied, a little untruthfully. 'Perhaps he thinks we'll get in the way.' Deane drew a deep breath before continuing. 'I believe one of the enemy units the battalion operations hope to come to grips with went into Long Khanh Province the night before last.' Deane shook his head in wonder. 'I raised it at the conference as a possibility yesterday but got laughed at for my trouble.'

'It's definitely 274 VC Regiment that went out the other night, according to Ashton,' Peter Hanson interjected suddenly, realising the significance of one of the points in Ashton's report.

'It was,' Deane said, more a question than a statement, but seeking confirmation.

'That's right,' Hanson confirmed. 'It's in Ashton's camp report—they picked up a regimental scarf belonging to someone from 274 Regiment, he thinks.'

'That proves nothing,' Colin Deane said. 'What about the D445 scarf that Ashton picked up on his first patrol—the VC they got turned out to be 274 Regiment.'

'But it isn't likely to be D445 Regiment that far up north wearing 274 VC scarves just to confuse us,' Hanson suggested logically.

He's right, of course, thought Deane. Then he said, to no one in particular, 'That means that one of those battalions is out there looking for something that isn't there.' He pondered the implications of his statement for a moment before getting up and heading for the door.

'Come on OPSO,' he ordered, 'let's have a look at Ashton's report. The Task Force CP might be interested this time.'

Bluey Erickson attracted Sergeant Ashton's attention and motioned to him that there'd been a response to their message. Ashton moved across and took the signal from him. It read: AMB TRK LAST 24 HR PD GL. Translated, it said: 'Ambush the access track for the last 24 hours of the patrol STOP Good luck.'

The next morning was the start of the final 48 hours of the patrol and it meant that Ashton had most of that day to recce the track for a good ambush position, brief the patrol and complete the preparations to occupy the ambush. A quick appreciation indicated that, at best, he could not hope to occupy an ambush position until first light on the following morning.

Ashton returned to his position. Last light was fast approaching. He called the patrol members in when the time was right and they sat in silence in the descending darkness with only the odd lingering 'uk–yew' to shatter the peace of the evening.

13

'We've been tasked to ambush the access track up here,' Ashton whispered to his group as they sat waiting for daylight to filter through the canopy. 'We'll head north-east for three hundred metres, then turn north to the track.' He listened intently for any indication of uncertainty and heard none. 'There's no change to the emergency procedures,' he added, 'and we'll have breakfast here before we leave.'

The patrol members moved out to the LUP perimeter as the light strengthened, and each man sat quietly brushing the dust and sand from the outside of his weapon. Ashton could not remember cleaning his the previous day and admonished himself. He worked his shaving brush back and forth, paying particular attention to the thin, improvised leaf sight for the launcher.

When Ashton was happy with the external cleanliness he forced the butt of the M16 under his right arm and squeezed it tight. With his right hand under the ejection opening, he opened the XM148 sufficiently to expose the base of the 40mm high explosive projectile and gently pulled it free of the chamber. He ran the brush quickly around the rim of the chamber and thoroughly cleaned the locking latch and extractor. He replaced the projectile and slowly returned the chamber to the locked position. There was a slight click as the locking latch engaged but the noise was not loud enough to be heard on the perimeter, less than ten metres away.

121

Ashton then turned his attention to the M16. He removed the top half of a plastic cigarette case from the left magazine, quietly and carefully depressed the magazine release catch and allowed the twin magazines to ease into the palm of his left hand. He placed the magazines on the ground beside him and put his left hand through the opening created by the carrying handle so that his fingers were over the ejection port's dust cover. With his right hand, he pulled the cocking handle rearward for several centimetres to withdraw the 5.56mm cartridge slightly from the chamber. The dust cover flicked open noiselessly against the fingers of his left hand, exposing almost half the cartridge case.

He then eased the cocking handle forward until the bolt face rested loosely against the chamber. He turned the weapon on its side so the ejection port was uppermost and allowed the dust cover to click softly against the receiver. Using his left hand on the rifle bolt for stability and his right thumb on the weapon's bolt assist, he carefully and quietly locked the bolt into position.

Ashton wiped the ejection port with the brush and placed a thin film of light grease, from a small tube he carried for that purpose, around the area where the dust cover clipped into position. He carefully eased the dust cover closed, picked up the magazines and brushed the top of each before carefully placing them on the weapon. The final act in the ritual was to replace the plastic cover on the exposed magazine.

His weapon taken care of, he set about preparing breakfast. The sun was beginning to send oblique rays of light through the less dense canopy to the east of their location.

When he finished eating he packed the residue of the meal away, sat back and took the cigarette case from his pocket. He lit a cigarette and braced for a reaction; it did not come. A wisp of smoke drifted upward from the end of the cigarette and reminded him of the danger such carelessness presented. He drew heavily on the cigarette and exhaled the smoke down into a small bush beside him. The branches dissipated the smoke and it did not rise to be held in the light of the early morning sun's rays and act as a beacon for anyone within a hundred metres to see.

Ashton drank the last of the tea from his steel cup and placed it in his webbing. He forced the stub of the still burning cigarette a full finger distance underground and sealed the hole. He looked around the patrol and noted that everyone had finished eating.

He caught their attention with the familiar 'click-click' of his tongue and held up five fingers. All nodded their understanding that they were to move in five minutes.

Wilkins stopped suddenly, took half a pace to the rear and squatted quietly, his rifle held comfortably in his right hand, ready for instant use. He raised his left hand to shoulder height and made his unique upside-down track sign. Ashton's awareness heightened and he propped momentarily, caught Erickson's attention, and passed back the signal. He moved forward cautiously, knowing the patrol was closing up behind, ready to provide fire support if necessary.

They had moved the three hundred metres to the north-west in quick time—the sparse secondary growth and the sandy terrain had invited them to do so. They turned north just before they were forced to cross a dry creek with steep sides. The terrain after this point remained flat but the secondary growth became thicker as the soil changed to a richer texture. The creek line began to drift away to the north-east and they lost sight of it before they went thirty metres. They travelled north for almost a hundred metres to reach the spot where Wilkins was now crouched.

'What have we got here?' Ashton said quietly as he knelt on the right hand side of his scout. He could barely see the track several metres in front of them.

'It's that double ox cart track that runs down to the camp.'

Ashton strained for a clear view but the scrub was too thick. He nudged Wilkins forward so he could get a better look and they'd moved almost on to the double track before Ashton could see enough to make an effective inspection. Apart from the engineer-cleared trails throughout Phuoc Tuy Province, it was the widest track he had encountered in two tours of duty. The two lane ox cart track was a little over five metres wide at this point.

As an ambush position, the area left a lot to be desired. Any portion of track selected in the immediate area would lack sufficient length for a good killing zone. Even with the devastating M18A1 Claymore mines, the killing zone needed to be covered by rifle fire should the mines fail to detonate, or should any enemy not immobilised by the mines decide to make a fight of it.

An ambush position should also have a relatively clear view of the approaches to the killing zone. This gave the patrol ample warning of the enemy's presence and provided the opportunity to determine numbers, disposition and weaponry. This area provided none of those things. Ashton put his hand on Wilkins' shoulder and they returned to the others.

Ashton gathered the support group around him as Wilkins continued to watch in the direction of the track. There was no point in looking further down toward the camp. Here they had three hundred metres distance from the camp and that was the minimum requirement as far as Ashton was concerned.

'It's hopeless just out here,' he told them, 'we're going east from here for about fifty metres, where you blokes will prop and Billy and I will recce for a better spot.'

They made their way cautiously toward the east. All were mindful that they were only twenty metres from the track. It took the best part of thirty minutes to cover the fifty metres even though the scrub became more open after they'd travelled a third of the distance. Ashton propped the patrol in an area of thick scrub and sat down with the relevant information on distances travelled that he received from Erickson. He plotted their precise location and moved about the patrol to confirm that everyone understood exactly where they were. He purposely left Wilkins until last so they could depart on their recce as soon as he finished briefing. No sooner had he crouched beside Wilkins than they heard a three round burst of automatic rifle fire a long way off in the distance.

'That's the first we've heard since the big mob was in the camp,' Ashton whispered. 'How far do you reckon that was?'

'A couple of clicks, at least,' Wilkins responded cautiously.

'That's what I'd have thought.' Ashton took the map from his shirt front. 'We're about . . .'

The single shot caused Ashton to break in mid-sentence. He looked at Wilkins and they traded knowing smiles. The shot had come from the camp. Another lot of signals like that, Ashton thought, and I'd say there's another mob about to transit through the camp. And with any luck, we'll be in position to hurt them.

'We're about here, Billy,' he said, his attention returning to the task at hand. 'We may not be able to go much further east because of this dry creek.' He pointed to the creek line that ran almost due north nearly a hundred metres from their position.

'You ready to go?'

'Yep!' Wilkins came to his feet.

'Click-click,' Ashton signalled. The others looked as one in his direction and Ashton held up one finger of his left hand, then pointed to himself and finally made a circle with his thumb and forefinger around his left eye. All three gave the thumbs-up sign to indicate they understood the recce was about to commence.

'This looks OK, Billy,' Ashton said as he took in the scene before him. The track here ran a little east of north-east and bent gently toward the north a few metres along from the place he'd selected for the killing zone. This gave the right flank a clear view of the track for a good thirty metres and the view for the left flank man would be much better. The sixty metres of vision along the track in that direction was excellent to have because that was the direction of the enemy camp.

The area the patrol would occupy was around seven metres long and four metres from the track, with a large fallen tree that paralleled the track in the centre of the area. The Claymore mines would be placed between the log and the track and the patrol would be behind the log.

The six killing group mines and the two flank mines would be in best position to inflict maximum casualties on anyone in the killing zone or anyone who tried to counterattack the patrol from either flank. The area where the mines would be laid had marvellous camouflage potential, so the possibility of the ambush position being detected before Ashton detonated them was minimised.

'It's good, Billy,' Ashton repeated. 'I just want to have a look over in the creek behind us—mainly to see how far it is.' As he spoke, Ashton pointed roughly in the direction he wanted to go. The terrain between the track and the creek was open secondary scrub with patches of close country and large bamboo clumps near the creek. They reached the creek in ninety of Ashton's paces—about seventy metres.

Ashton studied the area of the creek with interest. The bank was not steep here as it had been at the point where they turned north earlier. The creekbed was fairly wide and clear of major obstacles. A little further down the creek to the south-west a large clump of bamboo threw its long tentacles across the creek in umbrella fashion. Ashton went beyond the bamboo clump and found the creek to be clear for as far as he could see, in spite of several more overhanging clumps.

'OK,' he whispered, 'let's head back to the ambush site and then to the patrol.'

They approached the site with caution, confirmed its location in relation to the creek, and headed to where the remainder of the patrol were located. They checked their bearings regularly and rejoined the LUP from roughly the same direction they'd left it.

'We've found a fairly good place for the ambush,' Ashton told his 2IC as he knelt beside him. He pulled back the half sock covering his watch and was surprised to find it was 1140 hours—time had got away from him considerably. He rolled the sock back across the watchface, put his rifle against a small sapling, removed the map from his trouser pocket and opened it for Dobel to see.

'This is where we are at the moment,' he said, pointing to their position with a small twig. He looked to Dobel for a response and found him nodding in agreement.

'We found the ambush position here,' Ashton went on, pointing to the area. 'We had a look over here along this creek as well'—moving the twig to the area around the creek as he spoke 'There appear to be good escape routes out that way as well as to the south.' Dobel nodded his understanding and seemed to be looking forward to the task. Ashton was pleased with the outward response from his 2IC but wished that he would do more than nod his head.

'When do you figure putting the ambush in?' The question took Ashton a little by surprise.

'First light tomorrow. We're going to have to move a little further south to complete our final preparations. I'll brief immediately park time is finished.'

Ashton made for Erickson's location with his map still in his hand. It was unlike him to expose his map as he went between positions during rounds, but there was a degree of expectation, even excitement, running through him.

Ashton gave Erickson the same brief he had given Dobel and he included the briefing time so that he would not have to field any questions. If he was going to be ready to brief at 1400 hours, he needed to get on with it. He briefed Wilkins and Collier in quick succession and by the time he made his way to his central location the other members of the patrol had their packs on and were ready to move.

They set off in a southerly direction and Ashton stopped them after thirty metres. He waived the requirement for further security procedures and quickly put the patrol members into position. Then he sat down to prepare lunch and to write a quick set of confirmatory ambush orders.

Confirmatory ambush orders were not a difficult item to produce. Ashton's patrol had practised the mechanics of laying an ambush on many occasions. They had conducted several practice runs for Dobel's benefit during the rehearsals for this patrol. Ashton and Wilkins were extremely accomplished at laying a bank of Claymores. During battle preparations, the killing group mines were especially set up so they could lay, arm and camouflage the six mines in less than twelve minutes from a standing start.

At 1400 hours Ashton motioned for the patrol members to leave their packs on the perimeter and move into the centre. It was not his preferred method of briefing but there was no other way to conduct an ambush briefing than to have all the participants present.

'Situation!' Ashton said the word quietly but forcefully. 'As I've told you, we have been tasked by headquarters to ambush the main ox cart track to the north-east of the enemy camp.'

'Mission! Ambush the track in the vicinity of grid reference 498 889.' Ashton waited several seconds and repeated the mission statement.

'Execution! General Outline!' He emphasised all three words. 'We'll leave here just on first light tomorrow, establish an ambush on the track at 498 889, initiate the ambush as or if required, conduct a body search and withdraw to the south, south-east.' He again waited for the information to sink into their minds, before moving on to the more detailed aspects of the execution— timings, routes to the ambush site, occupation of the site, springing of the ambush, the body search, and withdrawal from the area. He took questions after each phase so that any uncertainty could be dealt with.

The points Ashton emphasised most related to the initiation of the ambush. The first point was that only the Claymores were to be used. There was to be no rifle fire unless the ambush went wrong and the commander opened fire or gave the order to do so. It was Ashton's view that one explosion in the jungle sounded much like any other explosion. There were always large explosions in the jungles of South Vietnam. Harassing artillery fire and heat-detonated blind bombs were some of the causes. Rifle fire directly after an explosion certainly signified an ambush in the area and it was not in Ashton's plan to provide that much certainty to the enemy.

The second point was that Ashton was prepared to initiate the ambush against a group of up to twenty enemy. The decision would be his exclusively. He was of the opinion that an ambush party should hit whatever size group came along. One or one hundred, two or two hundred—he had said it many times. It was only a figure of speech though, as it would be folly to ambush a group of one or two hundred in a killing zone capable of containing a tight group of at most twenty or thirty enemy.

Ashton then detailed all the actions he expected the patrol to carry out in the event that all went well and in the event that things went wrong. He dealt with malfunctioning Claymores, flanks out, body searches, taking of prisoners, dealing with wounded enemy, dealing with friendly casualties, and action to be taken should the enemy follow the patrol after the withdrawal from the area. He looked from face to face when he finished and asked if anyone had any questions. There were none.

'Administration and logistics!' Ashton detailed who was to carry what equipment and who was responsible to check the allocation. The patrol had just sufficient water to last until the morning after next.

Much of the logistics for the task revolved around the preparation of the Claymore mines. Collier carried five lengths of detonating cord, ten percussion detonators and two white phosphorus hand grenades. One of the phosphorus grenades had to be given to Dobel to put in front of his flank Claymore when it was laid and Collier would place the other in front of his flank mine. The idea was to set fire to the flanks as well as to spray the area with 700 small steel balls from each Claymore should the enemy attempt a flanking manoeuvre.

Each of the lengths of detonating cord carried by Collier was ten metres. He also carried a detonator for each end of all lengths and was responsible to fit and crimp the detonators and to distribute the leads to Wilkins before the commencement of the patrol's evening routine.

'Command and signals!' There was little to brief the patrol about on this aspect of the orders as Erickson carried responsibility for patrol communications. Ashton and Dobel had PRC 68 sets for speaking to aircraft and to the armoured personnel carriers of the Cavalry Regiment.

The matter of Erickson's radio and the way Ashton refused to consider setting it up in an ambush caused great concern to Gary Dobel. The point had been argued at rehearsals when Dobel had brought it up. The corporal felt strongly that the sooner headquarters learned that an ambush had been sprung the sooner they would dispatch helicopters to pick up the patrol. Ashton had countered that that was fine if the patrol *wanted* to be extracted. But what if the patrol wanted to stay in and ambush the track at another location?

Collier, Wilkins and Erickson had had great joy watching Dobel's attempt to come to grips with the idea. It was obvious that Dobel considered that extraction of the patrol should inevitably and immediately follow a contact with the enemy or any other serious compromise of the patrol.

It was difficult for Ashton to shake the absolute faith that Dobel had in his training, where he'd learned that the signaller should always have his radio ready to operate during an ambush. Ashton was happy to have the radio functional in a composite-patrol ambush, where there were five extra guns to protect the signaller if things went wrong, but in his view a five man group needed to be fully mobile.

During the rehearsals Dobel had persisted in his view to the extent that finally, in absolute despair, Ashton agreed that when Dobel was in command of the patrol he could employ the signaller in any way he wished.

With the briefing completed and no questions of a serious nature forthcoming, Ashton ordered the patrol back to their places to finalise preparations for the task. This allowed him to go over the mechanics of the occupation sequence in his mind.

Collier was in his element, trimming the last centimetre from the end of the detonating cord where the explosive powder train had fallen out and gently forcing a detonator on to each trimmed end in turn. Finally, he grasped the detonator several millimetres from the end and gently secured it to the detonating cord by means of a crimping tool.

As Collier painstakingly prepared the detonating systems, Dobel went around the patrol redistributing the Claymores so that the eight ambush mines carried by the patrol ended up with the correct members. Dobel and Collier were required to have one Claymore each—already prepared in the manufacturer's carrybag during patrol preparations. Each mine could be laid and armed quickly and the initiation cable was rigged for rapid deployment from the mine's position on a flank to the firing point in the ambush party.

The remaining mines would be carried into the ambush by the patrol commander. Ashton would have two mines that were rigged in the manufacturer's carrybag as Collier's and Dobel's were. The remaining four mines had no bag, no initiating cable and no M57 initiator, or 'clacker' as it was known. These were called 'nude' mines as they were a standard M18A1 painted with dark green and black paint for camouflage.

Ashton would carry the four nude mines down the front of his shirt and the two manufacturer's bags containing prepared mines would be slung around his neck by the bags' carry straps. Wilkins would carry the five lengths of detonating cord with the detonators attached and feed them out to Ashton as required. Their system was fast, quiet and efficient.

The ambush preparations were completed by the time evening routine commenced. Their attention had been distracted several times throughout the afternoon by bursts of automatic weapon fire. The automatic fire and the answering single shots were noted by the patrol with a degree of excitement. There certainly appeared to be another buildup in the enemy's transit camp.

Darkness came quickly as the patrol made its final preparations to bed down for the night. The night sky was barely visible through the thick canopy yet Ashton could sense its clarity and he could smell the freshness in the night air as he went over the occupation and withdrawal sequences in his mind one more time.

The first streaks of grey were beginning to filter through the jungle canopy when the patrol left its night position for the ambush site. The going was slow at first but improved as visibility became better. Each man had transferred three 'ambush meals' into his clothing in preparation for the occupation. Ambush meals consisted of anything that could be eaten cold and that did not give off a detectable odour when opened.

The previous evening had been encouraging for Ashton and his patrol. Further signal shots were heard from the direction of the enemy camp which indicated that a buildup of transit personnel was becoming more of a probability. There had been no activity along the track to their north which also indicated that any concentration was developing from the west.

They reached the ambush site at the time when a patrol would normally be moving out to the perimeter after a secure night. Ashton and Wilkins wasted no time in advising Collier and Dobel of their flank positions and responsibilities. The flank Claymores were laid, armed and camouflaged, and the initiating cable run to the flank positions, in under four minutes.

Ashton and Wilkins went to work immediately the flank protection was in and Dobel and Collier were physically covering the stretch along the track at either end of the site. The killing group mines went in easily in the loamy soil. With practised ease Ashton and Wilkins had the front mines laid, armed and camouflaged and firing cables deployed in less than ten minutes. Ashton gestured to each man to assume his position in the line behind the large log. From the inside of his shirt he withdrew the last of the ambush items he had carried there from their night location—the pair of M57 initiators, securely taped together with strong green canvas tape.

He removed the dust caps from the initiators and, one at a time, removed the dust caps from each firing cable. Finally, he connected the firing cables to the initiators, lay down comfortably behind the log and removed the safety bail from each initiator. His last action was to carefully remove the Konica camera from his pack, secure the pack's pocket and place the camera inside his shirt. The ambush had been set in just under fourteen minutes.

Ashton looked along the line of his patrol. Collier was lying at an oblique angle to the track and facing the approach to the right flank, with his left foot touching Ashton's right foot. Dobel was also lying oblique to the track but facing the approach to the left flank, with his right foot touching Wilkins' left foot. Ashton and Wilkins were in the middle of the pair and within a long arm's length of each other. Erickson lay sprawled behind the centre pair, facing toward the rear, with one foot touching each of them.

It was a good position: they had an effective killing zone of a little under fifty metres in length, with good views along the track in either direction. The cover from view provided by the fairly dense scrub gave the patrol a secure feeling. The log they lay behind provided protection from enemy fire while allowing the patrol an unrestricted view of any approach without placing pressure on their comfort.

While the scrub between the log and the track gave the patrol extremely good cover from visual detection by the enemy, it also restricted the patrol's view of the track to some degree. Only by concentrating on looking through the scrub at the track did the perspective increase markedly. There was no concern that the scrub would hinder the patrol when the action started because the blast and fragmentation from the mines would effectively clear most of the scrub from the front of the log.

There was little else for the patrol to do now but to stay alert, be very quiet and await the arrival of the enemy. Ashton allowed himself a small smile as he recalled a comic piece he'd heard on Armed Forces Radio one day. The one-liner had asked: 'What if they had a war . . . and nobody turned up.'

What if, indeed. Ashton thought.

14

The commander sensed a sudden change in the mood of the surrounding jungle. He remained very still, trying to comprehend the reason. Wilkins had noted it too and looked at his sergeant quizzically. Ashton smiled his 'enemy' smile and nodded. 'They're coming,' he whispered. The remainder of the patrol became fully alert at the sound of Ashton's voice, although none except Wilkins heard the words.

Each man examined his area of visual responsibility. Safety catches were checked; senses strained for a more positive indication that someone or something was approaching. Ashton eased back the sock top and glanced at his watch. It was almost 0950 hours.

Wilkins was the first to hear voices in the direction of the camp. Within seconds, all could hear the unmistakable approach of enemy soldiers. The odd voice above the slapping tread of Ho Chi Minh sandals, mixed in with the rattle of equipment, indicated beyond doubt that they were about to go into action.

Dobel, Wilkins and Ashton saw the enemy emerge from the denser jungle to the west. They were travelling at a medium pace for Vietnamese and it would not take long to cover the distance to the patrol. Wilkins immediately recognised the two at the front as the caretakers from the camp. They were dressed in the same black uniforms and carried the same weapons. Ashton quickly lost interest in them when he noticed that something was different about the enemy soldiers they were guiding out of the province.

Even from a distance Ashton could see that they were dressed in light grey or khaki blouses and trousers. As they drew closer, he noted that most of those he could see wore canvas boots while others wore classic Ho Chi Minh sandals. They were well equipped with bandoliers and chest webbing, and had belts which Ashton presumed carried their water bottle and rice sack.

Ashton breathed a small sigh of relief as he noted a gap beginning to grow between the group and the point at which the track emerged from the thicker jungle sixty metres away. Ashton tried to gauge the number in the group and decided there were upwards of twenty. They were closing quickly on the ambush site and he had to decide whether to hit them or to let them go, wait for the main group to pass and then ambush a later, smaller group. This was a common pattern of enemy travel.

It was a gamble to let anything go, and here was a group that was going to fit well into the killing zone. He noticed two men carrying a 57 millimetre recoilless rifle and there were a lot of RPGs and RPDs as well as a large mortar. The caretaker guides were now almost level with Ashton and Wilkins, and had ten or twelve metres to go before Ashton would have to initiate the Claymores.

Shit, thought Ashton, they're North Vietnamese Army regulars! Immediately there was a nagging doubt in the back of his mind. Here was a dedicated and well-disciplined group of soldiers. In two tours of South Vietnam he had never come up against a unit of NVA regulars and he had little first-hand knowledge of their tactics and likely reaction to specific situations. Should he allow this group to pass? No, that would only prolong the agony. The nagging doubt persisted, but he had made up his mind.

His whole body was trembling as the guides neared the initiation point. His mouth was dry and the blood pumped furiously in his temples. He breathed in slowly through his mouth and held it open. He stopped breathing momentarily and forced a half yawn to open his ear, nose and throat canal to equalise the internal pressure against the concussion that would come with the simultaneous detonation of six Claymore mines.

As the guides came into line with his predetermined initiation point, Ashton put the palm of his right hand on the dual M57 initiators and, with the left hand on top of the right, forced down hard on the plungers.

The ground beneath the patrol shook with the force of an almighty being striking the earth with a five tonne hammer. The detonation of four kilograms of high explosive C4 compound just two metres from the shielding log sent a shockwave through the patrol. The 4200 ball bearings from the six Claymore mines were sent hurtling across the ambush killing zone and beyond.

A vision of swirling, choking dust particles met Ashton as he raised his head above the log to examine the extent of the destruction. The explosive force in the direction of the killing zone ensured that most of the dust and debris was forward of the log that served to protect them from the danger of back blast.

Ashton quickly threw on his pack and picked up his weapon. The remainder of the patrol did likewise. In the brief time it took the dust and debris to settle, they were at one hundred per cent alert status. It was a critical period for the patrol, a period when even the slightest error of judgment or element of bad luck could mean the difference between success and failure of the ambush.

They scanned the area intently as the final particles of dust and debris settled, each man searching his area of responsibility for sign of survivors from the devastating effect of the mines. The jungle immediately to their front had changed remarkably. Where previously there was an entanglement of secondary growth that shielded them from the approaching enemy, it was now almost completely cleared.

Ashton had counted upwards of twenty enemy in the group. Under normal circumstances the patrol would not ambush an enemy in numbers exceeding eight or ten. Still, it was critical to determine exactly how many had entered the ambush so the numbers of dead or wounded could easily be confirmed after the dust and debris had cleared.

Many patrols in the past had moved on to a track, after the springing of an ambush, to search for items of intelligence value only to find themselves under fire from an enemy that had escaped both the head count and the lethal effect of the mines.

Ashton was conscious of this and many other potential dangers as he scanned the extent of the damage. It was difficult to achieve an accurate count from where he stood behind the log—there were bodies virtually everywhere. He now had a decision to make: go forward and search, or fade into the jungle behind the patrol and put as much distance between them and the ambush site as possible before a larger group came along.

Had the enemy been run of the mill Main or Local Force VC, Ashton might not have exposed the patrol to further danger by remaining longer than it took to photograph the area and confirm the numbers of dead. The situation here was more involved than that—this was quite a large group of NVA regulars. He knew the Task Force Commander would want to know as much as possible about them, and it was his duty to provide the information. There was little movement or noise from the track apart from small involuntary jerkings of arms, legs and heads and the noise of air escaping over the odd larynx.

'Flanks out!' the sergeant ordered in a raised whisper that could be heard by the patrol but was not loud enough to travel further. He slid over the log with Wilkins not far behind, while Collier made his way around the log to a position where he had a better view of the track to the right. Dobel moved forward hesitantly to cover the approach from the direction of the enemy camp.

The unmistakable smell that followed a successful Claymore ambush assailed their nostrils. It was a strange, even eerie, scent caused by the blending of odours of high explosive compound, disturbed earth, broken vegetation and released human plasma. Ashton had previously christened it 'the Claymore death smell' and Jim Collier referred to it as 'the sweet, sickly smell of death'.

Ashton moved to the right flank of the ambush, removing the camera from his shirt as he went. To get the best photograph of the entire killing zone—and back to the point where the track emerged from the wall of jungle—he moved to a position adjacent to where Collier was standing. Meanwhile, Wilkins busied himself with the counting of bodies, starting from the left flank and moving toward Collier's position.

'How many, Billy?' Ashton asked his scout as he made his way along the bodies on the track back toward Dobel's flank.

'Seventeen,' Wilkins answered without hesitation.

There were too many to do an effective search in the limited time they had so Ashton was prepared to be selective. He moved slowly past the scattered bodies until, halfway along the killing zone, he came to what appeared to be an officer with a document pouch over his shoulder. The enemy officer lay face down in a grassy area between the two tracks. The body of one of his comrades lay across the lower part of his torso. Ashton reached down and grasped the man's forearm in order to pull his body from the officer. His hand jerked in reflex revulsion. The arm felt like a roll of jelly wrapped in a sausage skin. The blast and pellets from the nearby mine had shattered the body tissue, causing it to lose much of its substance. Only stern experience kept Ashton's mind on the task.

He dragged the body clear and soon had the document pouch from the NVA officer in his hand. He opened it quickly and glanced inside. There were two maps, a notebook, a number of loose papers and a large roll of South Vietnamese currency secured with an elastic band. The denomination of the outer note was 500 dong, or about seven American dollars. Ashton removed the elastic band and rifled through the other notes; they all appeared to be 500 dong notes.

'Beaucoup tien,' Wilkins whispered, mixing a little French with his Vietnamese as the local South Vietnamese people appeared to do also.

Yes, thought Ashton, replacing the money, it certainly is a lot—not so much by our standards, but it could buy a lot of goods and services in any local village. Ashton slipped his right arm from his pack, threw the pouch strap over his head and locked the pouch to his body by replacing his pack. He quickly removed the officer's belt, withdrew a Tokarev K54 pistol from the holster and put it down his shirt. The pistol will be Collier's to make up for the one he missed out on from the first patrol, Ashton thought as he went through the officer's pockets, cramming everything from them down his shirt.

When he'd finished with the officer, he again moved along the line of bodies as Wilkins watched carefully. He was aware that they were running out of time. By the time they reached the end of the killing zone, Ashton had not found another body he felt warranted the time to search. They made their way back along the line toward Collier's flank and shortly after passing the dead officer came to what he believed to be the body of a non-commissioned officer. Ashton turned to Billy Wilkins and was about to indicate that a search of the NCO was in order when his whole body tensed.

'Click-click!' It was Dobel trying to attract their attention. Ashton looked in the area where Dobel was crouching beside the track, his left arm extended behind him with the thumb pointing toward the ground. Ashton's mouth went dry as he looked beyond Dobel and sighted a number of dark shapes moving about inside the treeline.

'Off the track quick, Billy,' Ashton said, loud enough for the patrol to hear. Wilkins was way ahead of his commander; he'd heard Dobel's warning and had spotted the enemy before Ashton did, and was moving quickly for the security of the ambush log even as the warning came. Ashton took two long, fast strides toward the log. He was yelling for Dobel and Collier to prepare to blow the flank Claymores when the enemy RPD opened up.

Crack! crack! crack! . . . Bump! bump! bump! . . .

Crack! crack! crack! crack! . . . Bump! bump! bump! bump!

The two bursts of fire from the Degtyarev light machine gun went directly along the track in line with where Ashton and Wilkins had been searching. The angry series of 'cracks' as the the 7.62mm bullets passed through the sound barrier adjacent to their position and the following 'bumps' caused by the slower moving sound from the discharging cartridges sent a chill through the two men. Fortunately for Collier, who had been standing in line with Ashton and the enemy's position, the aim of the machine-gunner was a little high.

With his back to the track, and furthest away on the right flank, Collier had been the last to be alerted by Dobel. As he turned to investigate the cause of the concern behind him, he saw his commander and Wilkins scurrying to get off the track. He crouched low as a reflex action just as the crack of the Soviet 7.62mm projectiles passed over his head. One struck the side of the tree by which he was crouched, tearing away the bark and showering him with the splintered debris.

'Blow the flanks!' Ashton screamed as he rose beside the log looking for a clear line of fire to engage the enemy. He could not fire because Dobel was still at his location near the track and between him and the enemy. He opened his mouth to shout at Dobel to get back to the flank initiator and blow his flank mine when he saw the stocky 2IC raise his weapon to its sighting position and press the firing button.

The weapon kicked in Dobel's hands as the golden-coloured HE projectile left the barrel of the launcher with a flat, hollow sound and flew in a graceful arc to detonate with a crump among the enemy just beyond the treeline.

'Get out of there, Gary!' Wilkins screamed from a new position near where Dobel's Claymore initiator was lying on the ground. The heavy sound of Wilkins' cutdown SLR, coming hard on the order for him to move, galvanised Dobel into action. In the two seconds before he moved, he fired all 28 rounds from his M16 magazine in one long burst into the treeline sixty metres away. Then he was moving across Ashton's front, changing his empty rifle magazine for a full one as he did. Immediately his line was clear, Ashton flicked up the brass leaf sight on the top of his M16 carrying handle, raised the weapon to his shoulder and released a 40mm HE projectile toward the enemy.

'I've got this,' Wilkins yelled as Dobel approached, indicating that he would take care of the left flank Claymore as soon as it was required. Dobel didn't argue and passed behind Wilkins to a position a few metres to the left of the scout. A large explosion from the right signified that Collier had fired the right flank Claymore. It was fast approaching time for them to withdraw.

As soon as the firing started, Erickson had moved to take up a position where he could still watch the rear and have a better chance of detecting any movement that might occur from an enemy flanking manoeuvre. He waited there, ever watchful. There was not much point in using his weapon as he had little idea where the enemy actually were.

'Stop!' Ashton called, shaking from the adrenalin rush. The patrol ceased firing and there was no sound from the direction of the enemy. Ashton thought it unlikely the enemy would wish to pursue a counter ambush option with much commitment after seeing most of a platoon's strength literally disappear in a puff of smoke before their eyes.

Still, it was a worrying time for Ashton. The clock had been running since he sprung the ambush. He was unsure how long that had been but remembered looking at his watch as the enemy had emerged from the thicker scrub. He glanced at his watch again—a minute before ten. It was less than ten minutes since he had blown the ambush but it felt like twice that time. Ashton slid over the log as he replaced the spent HE projectile in his XM148.

'Psssst!' Ashton attracted the attention of the patrol. With three distinct gestures, he quickly indicated that Dobel should replace

Wilkins at the initiator, Collier should join him by the log and Wilkins should head off in a southerly direction. The positions changed quickly and quietly and Wilkins began to move off toward the south when Erickson, who had been quietly kneeling and watching, suddenly sprang into action.

'Contact,' he screamed at the top of his voice, firing several short bursts from his M16 as he did so. 'Twenty metres away, they're trying to roll up this flank.'

'Blow it, Gary,' Ashton shouted, as two enemy guns opened up in support of their assaulting comrades.

The impact of the fire from the enemy machine guns was wide by at least ten metres to the east of their position. Ashton subconsciously noted that the machine guns were of different types as one had a slower rate of fire than the other and the probable cause of their lack of accuracy was the poor position from which they were supporting the assault. Collier located the position of the machine guns quickly and fired accurate, aimed, single shots into the area.

Ashton was quickly on to them as well and, although he had more potential problems to his immediate flank, he raised his weapon, sighted briefly and engaged the firing button with his left thumb. He watched the high explosive projectile impact into the area where one of Collier's bottom tracer rounds had struck and was happy with the result.

He was right, he reflected—if that was the supporting fire base for the assault, it was too oblique to the assaulters to give adequate support without endangering the left flank of the NVA assault formation, which was now starting to fire into the patrol's position as they came.

The left flank Claymore detonated with a sweet, merciful 'crump!' The 700 steel balls and the phosphorus compound from the WP34 grenade in front of the mine swept the enemy formation with devastating effect, completely breaking up the momentum of the assault.

'Let's go!' Ashton screamed, as he began firing his M16 at the assaulters in support of Erickson and Dobel.

'Go Gary!' he screamed again, hoping that Dobel would understand that he was trying to produce the embryo of a patrol rear-contact drill to extract them from their predicament. He knew that Collier and Erickson would understand immediately what he was trying to achieve.

Dobel came away from the position he occupied at a speed that would have surprised Ashton had he had time to notice. Before he went he fired the last rounds from the magazine on his weapon and, as he stood up, he fired the high explosive round from his launcher into the general area of the assaulting enemy. Ashton reloaded his launcher while Collier and Erickson covered Dobel away from the danger area.

'Go Jim!' he yelled at Collier, who was almost beside him. Collier slipped the change lever of his SLR fully forward to automatic and sent the last contents of his magazine toward the remaining enemy. As Collier moved to the rear, Ashton was grateful to hear Wilkins' voice behind him calling Dobel into break-contact formation. It's going to work, he thought with some relief.

'Go Bluey!' he called to Erickson and engaged the area to the flank where the enemy had been assaulting. He reduced his rate of fire when it became evident there was no longer any incoming fire from the enemy. Finally he ceased fire altogether. Wilkins opened up and called Ashton to go, but ceased fire also when he realised his commander had stopped firing and had ignored his call to leave. The area was silent now, apart from moaning and rustling sounds from the area of the assault. Ashton thought he could hear Vietnamese voices in the distance. He rose cautiously to his feet, aimed the XM148 in the general direction of the voices and released the high explosive round at the range at which he estimated the track and treeline to meet.

Ashton moved back toward Wilkins, quietly calling 'Hold fire' as he replaced the magazine on his M16. The patrol moved back through the security that the drill provided until Ashton was again in the position of being closest to where the contact had occurred. He raised his head and sniffed the breeze momentarily. There wasn't much of a breeze but what there was seemed to be across their front, almost from the west, north-west. He looked back at Wilkins with a question in his eyes. Wilkins held up two fingers to indicate twenty metres.

Ashton nodded and withdrew a 40mm projectile from a pouch on the left side of his belt. It was longer and more flat-nosed than a high explosive round and was grey in colour with a red

142

stripe around its circumference. He loaded the projectile, searched for a relatively clear line and fired the CS gas cartridge into the area just beyond the ambush position where the assault line had broken down. He loaded another gas cartridge and fired it into the general area of the ambush.

He turned toward the patrol, ejecting the second cartridge as he did so. When he reached the point where Wilkins crouched, he motioned the scout in front of him. The patrol soon formed naturally into its normal order of march and Ashton directed Wilkins to head south to look for an area of thick scrub that would provide security while he reported the contact to their Nui Dat headquarters.

They had gone over a hundred metres when Ashton halted the patrol. Under normal circumstances he would have broken a safe distance from the contact area, compiled a coded report and sent it without fear of compromise. This time he had an uneasy feeling about the situation. There had been enemy voices and movement to the north and to the west of them for as long as it had taken them to travel the last fifty metres.

His initial move south was designed to make directly for their pickup point and to advise Nui Dat when they were fifty to a hundred metres short of that location. The amount of enemy activity in the area since they broke from contact was most unusual and of great concern to Ashton. It made him wary of heading directly for the LZ where they had been inserted, as it was relatively close to the enemy camp and the only one in his AO.

He stopped the patrol to think the problem through and to advise headquarters of the potentially dangerous situation. No sooner had Erickson and Wilkins run the aerial than Ashton decided it was in their best interests to ask for an immediate extraction.

Simple three-letter codewords were available to alert headquarters to a variety of circumstances: when sighted by the enemy and deciding to remain in the area; when in occupation of an ambush position; or when they were being pressed by a numerically superior enemy and the patrol commander believed that the patrol was in serious jeopardy.

Ashton certainly believed that the latter was the case. It was obvious from the activity that the NVA were searching for them.

He did not know what the enemy strength had been in the camp but suspected that it was considerable. The little he knew about the NVA was that the 33rd NVA Regiment had its home in the provinces north of Phuoc Tuy but came down from time to time to bolster the flagging morale of Main Force, Local Force and Village guerrilla units. When it did so, it normally came in battalion strength.

It occurred to Ashton that there were some things the enemy could not possibly know and some that they were unlikely to have much idea about. He hated to give the Viet Cong credit for knowing too much when it came to a running firefight, but he was well aware that they knew a good deal about the topography and should not be sold short on that score.

There was no conceivable way the NVA could know that the LZ to their immediate south was the only one in Ashton's AO. If they had local VC with them, they might know that the LZ was the closest to the camp. But as far as Ashton knew, the local knowledge had died with the guides in the ambush. The possibility that the NVA had recruited other local guides last evening was one that could not be discounted.

Ashton thought it unlikely that the NVA would have maps of the area if they were just passing through. It was also unlikely that they would have the communications capacity to mount an effective, coordinated search. Going to the patrol's insertion LZ was preferable at this time than going through the painful process of getting an extension of the AO to include one of the larger landing zones to the south-east.

'Click-click!' It was Erickson wanting to know what message he was required to send. Ashton nodded and moved to where the signaller waited by his set. Nobody had sat down in the LUP; there was great tension in the group as they could hear Vietnamese voices continually to their north-west and west and, although the distance was hard to determine, they had no difficulty in distinguishing individual words.

'DUN,' the sergeant said as he squatted beside Erickson. DUN was the codeword for 'Require immediate extraction', and in Ashton's view immediate extraction *was* vital. He did not delude himself that the patrol could effectively sustain a running fight with the NVA for long. Much depended on their ammunition supplies and whether or not they managed to avoid casualties.

Ashton also knew that it was only a matter of time before the patrol's location was pinpointed by the numerically superior enemy force that appeared to be searching for them with great endeavour. How much time was a matter for fate to decide but he knew that, if ever the outcome came down to resolve, the NVA would need to be prepared to pay a high price for the scalps of Patrol Six-Six.

Erickson initiated communications with the base call sign and tapped out the codeword three times. The base station operator acknowledged receipt and advised Erickson to wait for a formal response. Erickson shifted the earpiece slightly in his ear for comfort and, as he did so, chanced to glance beyond the LUP to the west. He stiffened noticeably as he recognised the unmistakable shape of a human moving cautiously in a southerly direction about thirty metres distant.

The signaller glanced toward where Collier was kneeling and was gratified to see that the medic was also aware of the enemy presence. He slowly and quietly removed the earpiece and morse key from the radio set and put them in his pocket. He then switched off the set, released the aerial and closed the lid. The soft click of the vacuum catches attracted Ashton's attention. Their eyes met and Ashton was immediately aware of the impending danger.

Ashton scanned the area to the west while Erickson quietly closed and secured the top flap of his pack. He pulled firmly and constantly on the aerial until it released from the tree at the outer end. It came away without undue noise and Erickson quickly rewound the wire on to his fishing reel and put it down his shirt. He had reached for his pack to lift it on to his back when the discharge of Collier's cutdown SLR shattered the hard-worn quiet of the morning.

It was the unluckiest break the patrol had had all tour. The enemy were sweeping the area from north to south and the position of the extreme left flanking soldier in the formation was such that he all but walked on top of the LUP. Jim Collier watched the enemy soldier come through the scrub toward him. He wore no hat but was dressed as the NVA at the ambush site were. And he carried the standard infantry weapon of the NVA, a Simonov semi-automatic rifle, or SKS.

Collier judged the approaching soldier to be far from the most alert enemy he had encountered. Collier also caught the shadows of movement of other enemy in the line further to the west. As they swept south and came closer to the LUP, Collier's hand tightened on the pistol grip of his SLR and his body tensed as he held his breath and eased the change lever to 'R', for repetition, with his right thumb. He was not a religious man, but he prayed the enemy would not discover their location.

The enemy approached quietly. He appeared more intent on checking the whereabouts of the soldier to his immediate right as though he was concerned with being separated from the remainder of his unit. Collier knelt quietly; his weapon at the ready. The line the enemy was taking would bring him right to the spot where the medic waited.

There was less than two metres between them when the enemy soldier sensed that all was not well. He looked directly into Collier's face and his eyes widened in absolute astonishment and fear. He did not cry out but began to swing the SKS into a position of engagement when Collier squeezed the trigger once and shot him in the middle of the chest.

The heavy calibre bullet sent the NVA soldier cartwheeling backwards. Collier immediately engaged the area to the west where he believed the enemy's sweep line to be. Dobel and Ashton joined in with searching fire in the direction of Collier's engagement. Ashton was prepared to hold their position for as long as it took Erickson to shoulder his pack and be ready to move.

The enemy were caught in enfilade fire. A number of voices were screaming what sounded like structured commands in Vietnamese, but the lack of return fire from the enemy convinced Ashton that there was a degree of confusion in their ranks. He ordered the patrol to cease fire and they withdrew toward the east, then turned quickly north-east when the enemy eventually opened fire into the area where they had been.

Ashton pushed the patrol on toward the dry creek line that he and Wilkins had found on their ambush reconnaissance. They eventually found the creek at a point where the banks were too high for Ashton to consider a crossing to be safe. He turned them north and made a parallel course along the creek until they came to the crossing point discovered previously. The sound of enemy had long since faded in the distance and could no longer be heard.

Dobel, Erickson and Collier provided security for Ashton and Wilkins to cross the creek and check the other side for signs of recent enemy presence. Erickson and Collier crossed next. Dobel was last across and was responsible for erasing as many of the marks of their crossing as possible. On this occasion, it was a job that Dobel took time to do well.

Ashton moved the patrol into some thick bush almost thirty metres from the creek line and then turned south for a brief period before stopping the patrol in order to take a detailed look at his map. The patrol went into its LUP without the usual thoughts of settling down for a rest. No one removed a pack and Ashton did not concern himself with clearing the area to ensure it was secure for the stop. There was no real need, the adrenalin was running at peak levels and the patrol was ready to react to the slightest suspicion of danger.

Having checked their location, Ashton called the patrol members in and explained exactly where they were on the map, the direction to the LZ and the route he intended to take to get there. They were making for the north-eastern area of their insertion LZ and, now they were east of the creek, he hoped to keep the large bamboo clumps in that area between them and the enemy.

Because of their perilous situation Ashton made new patrol rendezvous points. The first one was just under a kilometre east of the eastern edge of their insertion LZ, in their patrol no-fire zone. It was at the north-east corner of a cleared area just a little larger than their insertion LZ. He made the second rendezvous point over two kilometres south, at the north-east corner of a huge cleared area shown on the pictographic map by one of Sticks Rawle's shaded map corrections. This area was three kilometres long and almost two kilometres wide. They studied the map in the commander's hand and compared the information with their own map until they were satisfied.

'Questions?' Ashton asked.

'Why don't we slip down the dry creekbed?' Dobel asked, a mixture of fear and confusion in his eyes. 'It's pretty clear in there and we could make . . .'

'Creek lines are out,' Ashton said emphatically, cutting across Dobel's comment. 'Any other questions?' Ashton had been impressed with his 2IC's performance in the firefight so far but a question like that, at this time, showed a complete lack of appreciation for tactical consequences. In the absence of further questions Ashton gestured to them to prepare to resume moving.

Dobel and Collier both moved away from the briefing shaking their heads. Dobel because he couldn't understand why Ashton had rejected his idea out of hand, and Collier because he couldn't believe that Dobel, who had done OK so far in the contacts, could ask such a cockhead question.

They moved slowly south. Ashton felt uncomfortable because it was park time and he was moving when his best instincts were telling him not to. They had not heard a thing from across the creek since the last contact with the enemy. They'd had no reply from the codeword message sent just before the contact over an hour ago. He knew that headquarters had received the message because they had given Erickson a 'Wait out' before they were forced to go off the air.

Ashton would have liked answers to his foremost questions. Where are the enemy and where are the helicopters? He could explain away the enemy's whereabouts logically by telling himself that they were either regrouping and licking their wounds or indulging in park time. It didn't seem right that Nui Dat had not sent an aircraft to see what was going on, especially since the patrol had gone off the air as soon as their emergency codeword was sent.

The ground on either side of them suggested they were approaching the point where the creek was joined by a smaller one coming in from the east. He decided to confirm his navigation at the junction before crossing the tributary to secure a place on the other side to find out what had happened to their extraction. Wilkins approached the junction with caution. They were thirty metres short of the junction and Ashton noticed that the countryside had changed to primary jungle without warning. It was cool and gloomy now under the canopy and the area across the tributary to the south looked perfect for what Ashton had in mind.

The slope of the ground here was odd and it intrigued Ashton the way it appeared to slope up to the main creek bank and away toward the tributary, almost as though the major creek was feeding the tributary. Wilkins was kneeling, motionless, and carefully scanning the opposite bank of the main creek through the gloom. His commander gestured to him to move closer to the main creek for a better view of the junction and he came upright in order to comply. Ashton was still pondering the unusual shape of the ground when a burst of fire from an RPD raked the area where Billy Wilkins was standing.

15

The sharp, whirling ring of the telephone slowly penetrated the cluttered and troubled mind of Colin Deane. In front of him was a formal directive from the Task Force Commander requiring him to reduce the use of Task Force air assets. Absently, he reached across the desk and picked up the handset.

'OC,' he said into the mouthpiece.

'Ops, sir,' Lieutenant Hanson identified himself. 'Could you please come down, sir? We think Ashton might be in trouble.'

'What sort of trouble, Peter?'

'He came up on air twenty-five minutes ago with his extraction codeword. Task Force Ops can't authorise an extraction and now the patrol has gone off the air.'

'OK, Peter, be with you shortly.' Deane replaced the handset, carefully picked the directive from among the papers on his desk, and made his way along the corridor to the operations room. As he walked, Deane pondered the implications of the directive. It said: 'Your patrols are to be made to remain in their AO after minor instances of contact with the enemy that are unlikely to seriously threaten a patrol's survivability.'

The major shook his head in disbelief. It was an ill-informed directive, no doubt drafted by a staff officer completely out of touch with the realities of operating in small groups well beyond the range of indirect fire support assets. He was still shaking his head when he walked into the operations room.

149

'Where's the OPSO, Sticks?' he fired at Sergeant Rawle as soon as it was evident that the operations officer was not in the room.

'Comcen, sir,' the sergeant replied, gesturing purposefully toward the door leading to the communications centre.

Peter Hanson and Harry Filer were discussing the probable causes of Ashton's failure to respond to their repeated calls. Deane looked around the room; there appeared to be a lot more people than there should have been and they all looked in his direction as he spoke.

'Anything new, Peter?'

'No, sir,' Hanson responded. Then, he realised that Deane was only vaguely aware of the latest developments. 'Ashton came up with his extraction codeword around thirty minutes ago. I spoke with Task Force Ops not long after that and was told that all available 9 Squadron helicopters are being used in support of a big battalion contact just south-east of the Courtenay rubber plantation.'

'*All* of them?'

'They're redeploying one of the companies from the battalion west of Thua Tich as a blocking force for the battalion in contact.'

'When will they be available to assist Ashton?' Deane needed more information, and he wanted it quickly.

'Not known, sir. Task Force Ops say they'll let us know. Is there some problem, sir?'

'Why do you ask?' Deane was looking past his operations officer at the four soldiers in the corner of the room.

'SO2 Ops at Task Force tells me it's unlikely that patrols in contact will be extracted in future. Is that really on this time, sir?'

Colin Deane handed the Task Force Commander's directive to Hanson and fixed the four soldiers in the corner with his gaze. 'What are all you men doing in here?' he asked, concentrating on Snowy Jacobs.

'Reggie Sigs, sir,' Jacobs replied, indicating by gesture that he and the soldier next to him were regimental signallers. It was common practice for regimental signallers to spend time in the communications centre when they were not on patrol. It sharpened their skills.

'Better get out of here,' Deane said to Jacobs, 'they're going to need the room in here shortly.' Jacobs nodded and went to

the bench to pick up his notebook. As he did he heard Deane
ask nobody in particular, 'Who are the stand-by patrols today?'

'We are, sir,' Jacobs said, as he made for the door. 'Patrol
Four-Five is stand-by one.'

'Who is the other one?' Deane looked at Harry Filer as he
spoke, noting that Hanson was still looking at the directive.

'Smithfield's patrol is stand-by two, sir,' Filer responded.

'Trooper Jacobs, isn't it?' Deane spoke to the snowy-headed
soldier as he opened the door of the communications centre to
leave.

'That's right, sir,' Jacobs said, pausing to hold the door fully
open to allow the other regimental signaller out.

'Round up both stand-by patrol commanders as soon as you
can, Trooper Jacobs,' the OC directed, 'and have them report to
me in the Ops Room immediately.'

'Yes, Sir!'

Jacobs was excited as he stepped onto the raised walkway
between the other ranks' mess hut and the shower block. As he
walked along it, the arc mesh rattled against the perforated steel
plate. He passed by his tent and walked toward the one occupied
by his patrol commander, Sergeant Bevan Willis.

'Bevan!' he called, 'OC wants to see you straight away.'

'What about?'

'The stand-by patrols are being stood by, I reckon.'

'Why's that?'

'Ashton could be in deep shit,' Jacobs suggested. 'Sent in his
extraction codeword nearly an hour ago and now the Sigs can't
raise him. The OC wants you and Smithfield in the Ops Room
five minutes ago.'

'OK,' Willis said. He fixed Jacobs with a thoughtful gaze.

'You get Keg Baker to round up the rest of our mob and
wait in the Troop lines until I get back,' he said as he moved
off toward the headquarters area.

'What about Smithfield, Bevan?' Jacobs asked urgently. 'The
OC said I was to fetch both of you.'

'OK,' Willis said again, changing direction toward Smithfield's
lines, 'I'll get Smithfield on the way through. You find Keg and
get the patrol squared away.'

Jacobs watched the back of his commander as he disappeared
between tents toward the lines further up the hill. He was excited

at the prospect of going to Ashton's assistance. Willis' patrol had not been in a firefight with the enemy in all the months they had been in country and it was becoming embarrassing not to have a story to tell in the boozer.

'Hey, Keg!' Jacobs yelled from the revetted wall of the corporal's tent. He knew Keg would be asleep. He was always asleep at this time of day. The hour or so before lunchtime and the hour or so after it seemed to be always taken in the horizontal position by the 2IC of Patrol Four-Five.

'Christ Almighty, Snow,' Baker said goodnaturedly, 'it's bloody park time don't you know.' He stretched. 'It'd better be bloody important.'

'Both stand-by patrols might be called out, Keg. Bevan and Nev Smithfield are just on their way to see the OC.' He entered the tent and fixed the corporal with a cheeky grin. 'Bevan said to tell you that you gotta hold our hands while the rest of us get stood by.'

Keg Baker swung his legs off the bed and sat up with a smile. There was not much in the way of preparation for a stand-by patrol to do. Most of it was done on a day to day basis. As far as he knew, everyone in the patrol had a full complement of ammunition, enough rations and water for at least one day and the myriad other items that went to make up the soldier's basic field requirements.

All that needed to be drawn was the communications equipment from the Signals store and the signals operating instructions from the Comcen. The equipment and instructions could not be drawn until the task was allocated. That was the patrol signaller's task, a fact that Jacobs was well aware of.

'I'm off to warn out the Sigs to get the comms gear ready, Keg,' Jacobs told his patrol 2IC as he made his way to the back entrance of the tent. 'Back in about ten.'

Corporal Baker looked at his watch. It was nearly lunchtime. Better go and warn the other blokes, he thought as he left the tent, and see if the bait layers in the kitchen will let us through the queue early.

'You wanted to see us, sir?' Bevan Willis inquired of his OC.

'That's right, Sergeant Willis,' Deane smiled, gesturing to both men to sit down. 'I don't know how much you've heard about the situation so far but suffice to say that I'm more than a little worried about Sergeant Ashton's patrol.' He nodded to Hanson. Neither of the sergeants spoke, as they could see Hanson moving toward the large map on the wall in order to brief them on Ashton's last known location and the reasons for Deane's concern.

Colin Deane moved to Hanson's desk where there were three telephones. One had a red stripe along the handset, another a yellow stripe and the third a green stripe. He selected the red handset which gave him a direct line to the Task Force CP, wound the handle three times and picked up the receiver.

'Ops!' the voice at the other end of the line said.

'That you, Bob?'

'That's right.'

'Colin Deane, Bob,' the major said with a long sigh. 'You know about the patrol we've got up near the Long Khanh border that we've lost contact with.' It was a statement, not a question.

'Yes, mate,' Major Bob Markea, the SO2 Operations, responded. 'Peter and I spoke before.'

'How are we looking regarding helicopters to get them out if we need to?'

'They're all up north redeploying troops. One of the battalions is in contact with elements of the 33rd NVA Regiment.'

'What about *gunships*?'

'They're all up there as well,' Markea replied, sensing that Deane was becoming frustrated or angry, perhaps both.

'Is the brigadier there?' Deane pressed the issue. 'I'll come down and have a word with him just as soon as I get a few things sorted out here.'

'He's at Fire Support Base Quail—a little closer to the action.'

'You mean that the "battalion plus" has artillery as well as gunships up there?'

'That's right,' Markea replied flatly, 'it's a big shit fight up there, Colin.'

'They must really be hurting for fire support then.' Deane's stinging sarcasm was not lost on the SO2.

'Be realistic, mate,' Markea said, a conciliarity note creeping into his voice, 'you've read the Commander's directive. It's unlikely you'll get helicopters until they've completed the task for the battalion.'

There was silence on the other end of the line.

'You still there, Col?' Markea inquired hesitantly.

'Yes,' Deane's voice boomed back. 'Listen, Bob, let's look at this objectively. Even if the task up north were to finish now, it would take the choppers twenty minutes to get back here, fifteen minutes to refuel and thirty minutes to get to Ashton's patrol.' He took a deep breath while he did some quick arithmetic. 'That's a little over an hour but we're more likely looking at ninety minutes.'

'That's right.'

'What about Yank gunships from Blackhorse?'

'That's a possibility,' Markea replied positively, 'I'll get on to that soonest.'

'Bob, I need to go up and speak to Ashton.' Deane spoke quietly into the mouthpiece. 'Can you get a recce chopper on my helipad in five minutes?'

'Yeah, we can do that. Might be a little longer than five, but you'll have it soon.'

'Thanks, Bob. I'll let you know if there's a problem at Ashton's end as soon as I can raise him.'

If I can raise him! The thought was in Deane's mind before he could stop it. He cradled the handset and rang off. It was not one of the best moments of the tour for Colin Deane. He shook his head violently to clear it, took a deep breath and turned his attention to the group, who were long finished with the briefing and had been watching and listening intently.

'You catch the drift of that?' Deane asked the group as Sticks Rawle came in with a roll of maps. 'It's clear to me that Ashton is probably in a good deal of trouble—everything that's happened points to it. But I don't want to cause a major panic over something that might have a simple solution, like a stuffed radio.' They all nodded. Each man had his own thoughts on the matter, but none believed that it was a simple matter like a faulty radio.

'Well, gents!' Deane looked at the two patrol commanders in front of him. 'I'm heading out to Ashton's area to get some answers.' He paused before continuing. 'I want both your patrols gunned up and on five minutes notice to move from'—he looked at his watch—'1345 hours.'

The two sergeants left the operations room, each with a roll of maps, and had only taken a few steps when they ran into Smithfield's 2IC.

'What's happening, Nev?' Corporal Bill Donovan flashed both men a smile of anticipation. 'Heard we might have a job on.'

'That's right, Bill,' Smithfield confirmed. 'Get the boys gunned up.' He knew there was no need to explain the reasons behind the 'job' as the bush telegraph worked at great speed on Nui Dat hill. 'No move before 1345, Bill, and five minutes notice to move from then.'

'Briefings?' Donovan asked simply.

Smithfield paused and looked at Willis. 'Want to do it together, mate?' he asked.

'OK. Let's do it in the squadron briefing hut at 1330 and hope we've got some updated information from the OC by then.'

'Set like a jelly then,' Smithfield said to no one in particular. 'Bill,' he continued, turning to Donovan, 'better get Swindler Crooks on to the signals gear post haste. And you'd better draw an M60 in case Ashton really needs to be dug out of this one.'

'Already done! Crooks is down there now with Snowy Jacobs. I'll get a gun and eight hundred rounds as soon as I can.'

The three men parted company. Donovan went in the direction of headquarters and the sergeants went to their respective tents to study the area around Ashton's last known location in as much detail as possible in the time available.

'Chopper inbound, sir.' Harry Filer spoke through the pigeonhole. 'Estimated time of arrival at Nadzab is three minutes.'

'Thanks Harry,' Deane acknowledged, 'I'd best get up to the pad.'

Colin Deane accepted the map Sticks Rawle handed to him and hurried down the corridor to his office. He removed the pistol belt and holster from the hatstand in the corner and strapped it around his waist. His gaze fell on the M16 rifle in the corner behind the hatstand. He thought briefly about it before he bent down and picked it up. He lifted a bandolier containing seven 20 round magazines from the hatstand and draped it across his chest. He let his gaze wander a final time before he picked up his bush hat from the top of a bookcase and stuffed it down his shirt as he headed for the door.

Deane's mind was so focused on Ashton's potential plight that he did not immediately notice that the helicopter awaiting his arrival at the Nadzab helipad was a new Bell 206 Kiowa. The realisation hit as he eased himself into the seat and the pilot leaned over to assist him with the intercom headset before introducing himself.

'Lieutenant Hal Monaghan, sir,' the young pilot said. 'Welcome to Flight Kiowa, the latest in 161 Recce Flight's efforts to stem the tide of communism.' Deane smiled. Monaghan obviously knew the brief detail of the situation with Ashton and his patrol and he appreciated the effort to make light of the situation.

Deane pressed the transmit switch with his foot. 'Thanks, Hal,' he said. 'Nice to get new equipment now and again.'

'Sure is,' Monaghan said. 'This one's quite a lot different to the old Bell 47, and a lot faster. You want to go somewhere east of the Nui Hot, is that right, sir?'

'That's right,' Deane confirmed, checking the map, 'with best possible speed.'

'Roger that!' Monaghan lifted the helicopter from the helipad on top of the Nui Dat hill. They made a sweeping left-hand turn that took them across the top of the Luscombe Bowl, where many of the entertainment groups played from time to time, before climbing to 1500 feet and levelling out on a north-east track that would eventually take them into the Xuyen Moc district, across the top of Thua Tich and into Ashton's area.

'How come you get to play with the new toy, Hal?' Deane asked. Discussion was the best form of distraction in Deane's view and he felt, at that moment, that he was badly in need of distraction.

'I've only been in country two months, sir,' Monaghan replied with a chuckle, 'but I did a conversion to the Kiowa back in Australia.'

There seemed to be a fundamental and unspoken problem with time in country, a problem that appeared to transcend rank, age and maturity. The moment Lieutenant Monaghan mentioned that he'd been in country for only two months Colin Deane found himself thinking, 'nobody has ten months left in this shithole'.

Deane's mood changed when he looked out the open doorway and saw a flight of four Iroquois helicopters north of the Binh Ba rubber plantation and heading south toward Nui Dat. The sight of the Iroquois returning lifted his morale and he gave a silent prayer that they had finished their task with the battalions and would be retasked to support Ashton as soon as they'd refuelled. He chuckled to himself and looked at the pilot while his foot gently depressed the intercom switch. 'Nobody's got that much time left in country, Hal,' he taunted.

Hal Monaghan burst out laughing. A thousand people had said the same thing to him in the past two months.

16

Even before Wilkins cried out in pain Ashton knew that the scout had been hit by at least one of the bullets from the light machine gun. It had taken brief seconds for the eight round burst from the RPD to sweep the area and for Ashton to instinctively seek cover below the crest between Wilkins and himself. Amid the angry 'cracks' and 'bumps' as the bullets passed close by, he'd detected the familiar dull 'thwack' of a bullet striking flesh and bone.

Wilkins was spun almost two full turns by the impact and landed a little over a metre forward and two metres to the right from where his commander lay. The scout was on the lip of the crest formed by the strange topography that had intrigued Ashton earlier.

'Billy's hit!' Ashton screamed as he crawled toward the crest for a clear view of what was happening. 'Roll this way, Billy!' he yelled, hoping Wilkins would hear and attempt to help himself to the safe ground on Ashton's side of the crest.

Wilkins began to roll as Ashton's head, shoulders and weapon cleared the crest sufficiently for him to see the muzzle flashes from the RPD across the creek as it fired a long second burst. Much of the burst swept harmlessly overhead but two of the bullets struck the ground near Wilkins as he rolled, and one struck him in the back of the left leg just below the knee joint.

Instinctively, Ashton fired a 40mm HE projectile and watched it detonate a metre to the left of the muzzle flash. He followed the high explosive impact with several carefully aimed single shots from the M16 into the area where he assessed the enemy gunner to be.

'Bluey!' Ashton screamed again, firing several more single shots into the area, 'get Billy out of here.' As he did so, an AK47 opened up from a point four or five metres north of the RPD. One of its bullets from the burst struck the ground in front of Ashton, spraying him with dirt.

The sound of Collier's SLR was music to Ashton's ears. The well-placed rounds impacted in the area where the AK47 was and the assault rifle did not fire again. Ashton ceased fire and carefully scanned the jungle across the creek. He could detect no sign of movement through the gloom. He thought it odd that there were only two enemy in the position. If the enemy were seriously looking to annihilate them, they would need to be in larger groups to be effective. A chill went through him when he realised it was likely that the enemy across the creek were there merely to locate the patrol—as part of a larger plan to encircle and destroy them piecemeal.

Ashton shook such thoughts from his mind and attempted to focus on the immediate problem. It occurred to him that they would be silhouetted critically against the lighter, sparser scrub to the east and that any movement near the crest would need to be kept as low to the ground as possible. He was unaware of Erickson dragging Wilkins away from the crest and of Erickson and Dobel then taking an end each and moving the wounded scout quickly to the rear.

'Get out of there, Rowan,' Jim Collier screamed at Ashton from his selected vantage point higher up on the crest toward the north. 'They've got Billy.'

Ashton crawled backwards a full metre and, hampered severely by his pack, rolled awkwardly for several more metres before getting to his feet to follow Dobel and Erickson, who were struggling awkwardly with Wilkins. He ran a few steps, reloading the launcher as he went. He stopped and turned toward the contact area to survey the scene. He was in the lowest part of the ground to the east of the crest and in no position to provide accurate direct fire support for Collier. Still, he raised the weapon and aimed a 40mm HE projectile to clear the crest and detonate somewhere in the trees across the creek.

His judgment was poor and the projectile struck the apex of the crest. It did not detonate, as the round had to make a number of revolutions for the fuse to become armed and there was insufficient distance between himself and the crest for that to occur. Instead, the projectile ricocheted off the crest and spun away to detonate uselessly high up in the canopy south of the enemy's position.

'Go on the next one, Jimmy,' he yelled at Collier as he reloaded. There was no time to dwell on his sighting error. They were in big trouble now with a wounded man to contend with and no sign of a response to their call for assistance. Collier fired several more single shots into the area until the hollow 'thunk' of Ashton's discharging weapon galvanised him into action.

Collier extracted himself by the same method that Ashton used. A short backward crawl, followed by a downhill roll before executing a controlled movement that brought him to his feet in a position well below the crest and facing the contact area. There had been no firing from the enemy since the AK47 had been silenced by Collier's SLR.

Ashton reloaded the launcher with another HE round. He found it difficult with his shaking hands to chamber the projectile. He glanced rearward to see Dobel effortlessly lift Wilkins on to his back in a fireman's carry and start off in an easterly direction with Erickson leading. He caught Collier's attention and motioned for him to move but Collier hesitated and gestured at something lying on the ground in front of Ashton.

Ashton failed to understand what he was trying to tell him and again motioned for him to withdraw. Instead of moving to the rear, Collier moved forward toward the crest where Wilkins had lain after being shot. Keeping as low to the ground as possible, he reached over the crest and dragged in the object. It was Wilkins' SLR. Ashton realised that the movement must have been detected by any enemy still across the creek, but there was no firing and the doubts came back. Were there only two enemy? Did we get them both? How many more enemy were on their way to throw a large net around the patrol?

He fought to shake off these thoughts and hissed at Collier to get the hell out. Collier responded by moving quickly back past Ashton with the hint of a smile on his face. Wilkins' SLR was unique among the cutdown rifles in the squadron and the enemy were not going to be allowed to capture such a prize so easily. Besides, if Wilkins' wounds were serious enough for him to be sent home, Collier figured that he might have first claim on the weapon.

The patrol withdrew east from the contact area, with Ashton leading. Next in line was Erickson followed by Dobel, who had the additional burden of the wounded Wilkins. Collier brought up the rear, and in this situation was responsible to be on the alert for an enemy approach from either flank as well as from the rear.

Ashton was aware that Wilkins' wounds would need attention as soon as possible. He turned south after forty metres and crossed the small creek that ran from east to west into the larger watercourse where the last contact had occurred. The presence of a number of pools of water in the creek reminded him that they would all be low on water by the end of the day. Sooner, even, he thought, if we keep having contacts. Contacts caused excessive water loss due to the additional perspiration created when the body was overcome by the adrenalin rush of excitement, anticipation and fear.

They crossed the creek at a point where Ashton felt that much of the disturbance left by their crossing could readily be obliterated or restored by Collier. He turned south-east as soon as Collier had completed the task and halted the patrol after they'd travelled a further sixty metres.

He appointed Erickson to a position just ahead of where they halted. He motioned Dobel toward him and indicated a small, clear area several metres away where he could lay the injured Wilkins down, and quickly checked Wilkins as the pair went by. The ash grey colour of the scout's face was noticeable in spite of the layers of camouflage paint that had built up over the four days since their insertion. The piece of sweatcloth that Wilkins normally wore around his head as a band was now in his mouth. He was obviously conscious as the pain he was feeling showed in the grimace on his face and the tightly screwed closure of his eyes.

Ashton assisted Dobel to place Wilkins on the ground as gently as possible. He cried out briefly with the pain of movement but managed to muffle much of the scream by clenching his teeth against the sweatcloth. The scout's almost empty backpack was restricting him and aggravating his wounded right shoulder. The sergeant quickly unbuckled the right shoulder strap and eased the pack from his scout.

It was the first opportunity for anyone to examine the extent of Wilkins' injuries. The bullet from the initial burst had struck him in the fleshy part of the shoulder below the clavicle and exited at the back above the area where the top of the arm joined the body. The wound started to bleed profusely now that the pack strap was removed. Fortunately for Wilkins, the pack strap had restricted the flow of blood and much blood loss had been averted.

Collier arrived with his medical kit and Ashton motioned Dobel to a position on their back track. Collier unbuckled the web belt that supported Wilkins' ammunition and utility pouches and, with Ashton's assistance, removed the belt and harness before making a quick examination of the wounds. He assessed the leg wound to be the last priority as the round appeared to have gone through the top of the calf muscle, completely missing the major artery and the bones.

Jim Collier quickly drew the razor-sharp 'Baby Kabar' from its sheath on his harness and cut the tape that held a large field or 'shell' dressing on Wilkins' harness. The dressing came away in his hand and he passed it to Ashton without a word. He put his hand inside the front of Billy's shirt and withdrew the green cord that held his friend's dogtags and two fifteen milligram ampoules of morphine. Carefully he cut one of the ampoules free of the tape that held it to the cord.

While Ashton separated the field dressing from its waterproof cover, Collier inserted the razor-sharp knife into Wilkins' American camouflage trousers just above the wound in the left leg and slit the material from the knee to the top of the thigh. He began to remove the ampoule from its hard plastic outer shell when Wilkins opened his eyes and focused painfully on what his comrades were doing.

'We're in deep shit now,' he whispered hoarsely, 'aren't we?'

'You could say that, Billy,' Ashton replied. 'About as deep as we've ever been in.'

'I didn't see 'em, Rowan.' The pain showed in his eyes. 'I let you blokes down, and now we're in deep shit because of it.'

'For fuck's sake, Wilkins!' Collier interjected with a low hiss. Ashton and Wilkins looked at Collier but his head was down as he concentrated on preparing the ampoule. The tone surprised Ashton. It was a tone he'd not heard Collier use before—a cross between anger and banter.

'You used to be OK,' Collier continued without looking up, 'but now you're wounded you've turned into a real whining prick.'

Wilkins smiled; he had heard that tone before. It was the feigned anger and despair that usually accompanied a bout of Collier's black humour. Wilkins was still smiling when Collier threw the short needle into his thigh like a dart and squeezed the morphine from the tube into his patient.

'There!' he exclaimed with another hiss. 'That ought to stop your fuckin' whining for a while. Another couple of minutes and you'll be able to float to the LZ.'

Ashton squatted close to Wilkins with the large wound dressing held loosely in his hand. He glanced at Collier and could see tears welling in the medic's eyes as he reached for the dressing.

'Get that other dressing from his water bottle,' Collier said with authority, 'while I look after this dopey prick's shoulder.'

Ashton moved quickly to comply. Collier's reaction to Wilkins' plight was certainly a lot different from his reaction when Allen Cunningham was wounded. This time there was real fear and frustration and Collier was hiding it behind a brash and authoritative exterior. Ashton was more than happy to let the medic order him around and to assist in any way possible. This time Collier had many more reasons to be afraid. The patrol's situation was desperate and the potential for it to end in disaster in a short period of time was very real. Ashton also was afraid, but ultimately the patrol members would look to him to come up with a plan for their salvation.

There's no plan, Ashton thought as he cut the tape that secured Wilkins second shell dressing. 'There's only luck now, and nerve.'

He knew he was right, of course. All he had to do was to decide which way to go. If the NVA concentrated their search effort in the area where he decided to go, the patrol would be in a whole lot more trouble. Training, experience, a little good luck and steady nerve had saved patrols in the past. That was why they were required to undergo the intense training regimen they did, and that is why they underwent a searching selection process to determine if they had the right mental attitude and other qualities for the job.

It was vastly different being in a rifle company of an infantry battalion with almost instant communications and artillery or mortars on call to break up an enemy assault or probe. And there were the numbers to hold ground while the wounded were being attended to.

There was no such luxury here on an SAS patrol. One man wounded meant a twenty per cent casualty rate and a much more than twenty per cent reduction in effectiveness—a fair slice out of any unit's fighting capability, not to mention the additional strain that the reduced support placed on the other members.

'I'm going to need a hand to sit him up.' The sound of Collier's voice and the tug on his hand as the medic snatched the shell dressing from it brought the patrol commander back to the present.

'OK,' he said, moving to take hold of Wilkins' good arm. He admonished himself briefly for losing track of what was going on. Keep your mind on the job, he thought, we've got to get Billy fixed up and away from here as soon as possible.

Ashton looked at Collier's medical handiwork and gave thanks that he had such an able and dedicated patrol medic. Wilkins was already showing signs that the morphine was working by helping them as they got him leaning against a tree. Collier immediately went to work on the damage to the left leg, cutting away more of the trouser to do so. The effect of the morphine could be seen in Wilkins' eyes but it had not yet affected his voice.

'If I lose my leg, Ashton,' he smiled up at his commander, 'my old man is gonna be pretty pissed off with you.'

'Don't be fuckin' stupid, Billy,' Collier ripped into him jokingly. 'You're more likely to lose your arm at the shoulder than your leg.'

'He'll be pretty pissed off with that as well! I won't be much help around the property then.' He smiled sadly but brightened as he thought of something humorous. 'And wallpaper hanging will be out!'

The three men smiled. It was bullshit bravado and they knew it, but it was the sort of comic relief that had kept them going on many occasions when they were up against the odds or when the way ahead became difficult. Ashton patted Wilkins on his good shoulder as he picked up his rifle and moved quietly across to where Dobel was kneeling beside a tree.

'How's it going, Gary?' Dobel looked him in the eye and Ashton could see the raw fear.

'Where the fuck are they, Rowan?'

'I don't know, Gary. If I knew that, I'd know which way to go to avoid them.'

'Not the Nogs,' Dobel had a look of disbelief that his commander had misunderstood the question. 'The choppers . . . where the fuck are the choppers?'

'I don't know that either, Gary,' Ashton said, with more calm than he felt. 'I'd feel a lot better if I did.'

All the indicators that Dobel was coming apart were there and the problem was of immediate concern to Ashton. He knew precisely what Dobel was going through, he'd had similar feelings during his first tour when they were in trouble that none of them had experienced before. It was the same now, only this time he was the leader, and he wasn't absolutely sure that he wouldn't come apart himself. It was now a matter of nerve.

The sum total of the events of the day was building inside Dobel and there needed to be a release. Ashton was more than aware that it was Dobel's first time in a contact of this type. The remainder of the patrol had been in a similar position previously, albeit not as desperate, and had survived. All Dobel had to compare it to was the contacts he'd had while he was with an infantry battalion—with its greater numbers, firepower and priority support system.

'We're in deep shit, Gary,' Ashton said quietly to his 2IC. 'We've got a number of problems that I'd prefer we didn't have.' He looked directly into Dobel's eyes. *'And I really don't need any more.'*

Dobel stared back at his commander and Ashton was at a loss to know what might be going on in his mind. He needed to make the corporal let go the things that were obviously troubling him. SAS training didn't cover this. And Ashton knew that some soldiers got through the selection system who really didn't have what it took and he wondered if Dobel was one of them. He even began to wonder if he himself had what it took to get through the hardship that must certainly lie ahead.

Ashton was happy with the way Dobel had handled himself during and since the ambush. He had used his weapon when required, he had not frozen on the contact drill when Wilkins was hit and, apart from wanting to go down the creek to save time, he had yet to take a wrong option or make a wrong move. Still, Ashton was a long way from convinced that his 2IC could take over the patrol and run it with any degree of confidence if something were to happen to himself.

'The choppers are not our main problem at the moment, Gary,' Ashton said quietly. 'The location and strength of the enemy and Billy's wounds are our immediate major problems—and in that order.'

Dobel nodded his head and Ashton could only hope that he did understand and would forget about the helicopters until they turned up. 'There is nothing we can do about the extraction at this time,' he said. 'They acknowledged our codeword before we went off the air and that should be enough to fire them up.'

'It's been an *hour* since we sent the codeword.'

'More like an hour and a half,' Ashton agreed, trying to get off the subject. Then he said, 'Do you think you can run the patrol if something happens to me, Gary?'

The directness of the question seemed to confuse Dobel. He looked blankly at Ashton as though he hadn't heard. Ashton knew it was something that must have occupied Dobel's conscious thought. It certainly had for him when he was the 2IC of a patrol. Ashton took his hesitancy to represent a negative response.

'Do you want me to delegate responsibility for command to Erickson?' Ashton asked and watched closely as Dobel considered what he'd said. There was no expression on his face. You would at least expect some expression, Ashton thought, the man must have lost it completely.

'No,' Dobel responded after a pause, 'I'll be OK.' He looked directly at Ashton and saw the doubt in his eyes. 'Really, Rowan,' he said with as much conviction as Ashton had ever heard, 'I'll be OK.'

'All right,' Ashton said, not sure that he was convinced. He removed the map from the side pocket of his trousers and held it in front of Dobel. 'We'll leave here as soon as Collier finishes patching Billy up.'

Dobel nodded as Ashton explained that they would move south and try to link up with the eastern or north-eastern edge of their insertion LZ. If the enemy pressured them there, they would move east to the other likely LZ in their no-fire zone or, as a last resort, to the large cleared area to the south. Ashton was pleased when Dobel produced his own map and confirmed the general direction and destination. He stood up to leave but bent forward slightly toward Dobel before he did.

'How do you feel about giving your 148 to Erickson, Gary? You're going to be busy lumping Billy around, and I'd like to retain the capability of having both launchers readily available.' Ashton had already determined that Dobel was best suited to carry Wilkins all the way, should it be required.

Dobel looked up at his commander and nodded. It made sense, he thought, he was the strongest in the patrol and the best choice to do any carrying that was required. He could hardly operate his weapon freely while carrying Wilkins and the 40mm HE rounds were a great deterrent in a contact even if it was more for their noise value than any damage they were likely to inflict.

'I'll let Erickson know,' Ashton said as he turned to go. 'You can sort out the transfer before we get under way.'

'Chopper!' the wounded scout whispered hoarsely.

Ashton stood up quickly, listening intently. For several seconds he heard nothing. Then the unmistakable noise of a helicopter emerged in the distance. As it grew louder, something seemed to be wrong. It's not an Iroquois, Ashton thought, and it's not a Bell 47. These were the helicopters the patrol was familiar with. If it isn't one of those, his mind told him, it must be a Yank chopper. Ashton moved toward Erickson as he reached for the PRC 68 unit in the pouch on his belt. The aircraft was getting closer, louder.

'Get out your mirror, Bluey,' he ordered as he raised the aerial on the small radio transceiver and turned it on. The radio was already set on the patrol's allocated VHF frequency but, because of the unfamiliar sound of the engine, Ashton believed the aircraft was not an Australian one. He changed to the emergency UHF frequency that all aircraft in the country monitored and turned on the distress beacon for a full four seconds.

He disengaged the beacon and waited. His body shook with apprehension. Suddenly, relief flooded through him when he heard an unmistakably Australian voice boom through the static crackle and rush of helicopter noise.

'Roger,' the voice said clearly and calmly, 'this is Possum Five. I have your beacon, please come up on voice.'

17

Rowan Ashton quickly changed to the primary ground/air frequency. His whole body relaxed with relief. He glanced toward Wilkins propped against the tree, his eyes closed. The morphine had obviously done its job and he looked at peace with the world. All except Wilkins knew that they were now in contact with someone who could relay messages to their Nui Dat base and Ashton sensed the mood change to one of expectation. He raised the small radio so that his mouth was close to the microphone and pushed the PTT button.

'Possum Five,' Ashton spoke softly and clearly into the mouthpiece, 'this is Bravo Nine Sierra Six-Six, do you read? . . . Over.' Ashton released the button and waited. He was elated to hear the familiar sound of Colin Deane's voice come through the small receiver.

'Call sign Six-Six,' Deane said calmly, 'this is Sunray, Bravo Nine Sierra, on board Possum Five. 'What is your situation? . . . Over.'

With communications established, Ashton dropped the formality of using call signs to identify himself. He had a lot to say and the longer he stayed at their present location to say it the more chance there was that the searching NVA would find them. The appearance of the unarmed reconnaissance helicopter from 161 Helicopter Squadron meant absolutely nothing so far as patrol security was concerned. They were aware that all could die here on the ground and there was nothing the men in the helicopter could do to help them.

'We ambushed a big mob around ten hundred hours this morning,' Ashton responded, trying for as much brevity as possible, 'and got seventeen confirmed KIA.' He thought before he spoke again. 'Only got one body searched before they were into us.' He paused again. 'We've had two contacts since that time and I've got a man wounded.' He released the PTT button.

'How bad?' There was obvious concern in the major's voice.

'Not good. Right shoulder and left leg—can't walk and should be a stretcher case.'

'OK. Any idea what you're up against?'

'NVA.' Ashton was annoyed with the way the conversation was going. He was more interested in how long it might be before they were extracted. Still he added, 'A company at least, perhaps more.'

'NVA confirmed?'

Fuck's sake, thought Ashton, what am I doing here if I don't know the difference between NVA and the local yarpers?

'They're NVA, all right. A large force moved into the camp yesterday and into last night and we ambushed the advance party as they left this morning. We were forced into a contact to avoid a sweep search and one of my blokes was wounded when we had another contact with what I believe was a small cut-off party.'

'What size force?'

'Hard to say,' Ashton responded wearily. He had already told Deane there was more than a company and he was becoming increasingly frustrated. 'More than a company and less than a battalion . . . how long before we see the extraction helicopters?'

'The assets are not available at this time.' Ashton detected a hard edge in Deane's voice. 'Ops is trying to get you a Yank gun team from Blackhorse.'

The news was devastating. Momentarily, a feeling of hopelessness overcame him but he regained his composure quickly. 'Look,' he said into the microphone, 'we're only a hundred metres from where we had the last contact and we have to move from here before they get on to us.'

'I need to pinpoint your location,' Deane said. 'Show us a mirror or panel.'

'You're too far to our south-west to see either,' Ashton replied, nodding and pointing to Erickson to show the mirror as soon as the aircraft was visible. 'We don't have you visual as yet and you'll need to move to your north-east before we can show you some light.'

The helicopter slowly came nearer to the patrol's location and, by the time Ashton could see it through the sparser canopy out to the south-west, he had an uneasy feeling that the aircraft was descending as it came closer. It was after 1300 hours and the sun was in perfect position for signalling with mirrors, but because of the canopy the aircraft would need to be within a 45 degree angle overhead for the mirror to be seen.

To Ashton's relatively inexperienced eye the helicopter appeared to be below 1500 feet and descending. Erickson began working the mirror to bring the bright orange dot that appeared in the mirror's sighting aperture on to the pilot's compartment. As he did so, they heard the slow, deep thumping of a heavy machine gun away to the north-west. First there were three thumps, then a pause, followed by four thumps. Ashton realised immediately what its significance was.

'We have your mirror,' Deane said, as the pilot adjusted the aircraft heading and began to track in their direction.

'Possum,' Ashton cried into the small radio, 'you need to get some height quickly! You're under fire from a twelve point seven machine gun.'

As he spoke, Ashton heard another series of five thumps, followed by five more. There was an incredibly loud sound which signified a hit by one of the large calibre bullets on the helicopter. He watched in disbelief as the chopper slewed violently to the right as though some massive hammer had struck its left side with enormous force. The tail boom came around almost 90 degrees with the force. Momentarily the helicopter appeared motionless and in an impossible flying position, then descended quickly from the sky in a violent, leftward banking manoeuvre before dropping out of sight.

No sooner had Deane and Hal Monaghan heard Ashton's warning than the inside forward part of the right-hand skid was struck with massive force by a projectile from the enemy's HMG.

Monaghan swore as the aircraft lurched upward to the right. He made a correction and the nose of the aircraft dipped and slewed more to the right, bringing the tail boom lurching around over 90 degrees to the left. He reduced power and the aircraft hung motionless in the air for the briefest of moments before dropping gracefully from the sky.

Still fighting for control, Monaghan increased power slightly and turned the aircraft left toward the area where the machine gun fire had come from. The Kiowa descended quickly as the pilot fought the controls. He hoped that the lower he got the faster he would descend from the enemy gunner's view, and would then have to take his chances with small arms fire from any enemy directly below. Soon he was satisfied that he had things under control, the blood pounding in his temples now that the initial instinctive reaction was completed and the adrenalin rush began to take over.

He allowed the helicopter to descend a little further before easing the controls to straighten the aircraft's flightpath and executing a right-hand turn that washed off excess airspeed and brought the Kiowa on to a southerly course two hundred feet above the jungle's canopy. Monaghan allowed the machine to lose more height until it settled thirty feet above the treetops.

Neither man spoke for several minutes as they tracked south and approached a large clearing almost two thousand metres across. They passed across the treeline on the northern fringe of the clearing and Monaghan let the helicopter settle closer to the ground for four hundred metres and gain airspeed before easing it upward steadily so that, by the time they reached the other side of the cleared area, they were flying at two thousand feet.

'That was a near thing, Hal,' Colin Deane observed with more calm than he felt. His mouth was dry and his whole body was shaking from the aftershock.

'Don't need them every day, sir,' the pilot agreed. The concentration required to fly the helicopter had long since over-ridden his delayed shock. 'What now, sir, back to the patrol?'

'I think so,' Deane confirmed, 'but stay up here in the clouds this time.' Then, as an afterthought, he said, 'Can you get my Comcen? I'd like to speak to my OPSO.'

While Monaghan switched to the required VHF channel to call Nui Dat, Deane studied the map on his knees and tried to recall how the mirror flash from Ashton's position related to his location on the map. But it didn't fit, at least Deane couldn't make it fit. Things had happened so fast after he sighted the mirror that there had been little time for anything other than to hang on tight. He finally gave up trying to plot Ashton's position when he recognised Peter Hanson's voice coming through his head set. He squeezed the PTT button that allowed him to speak on the external frequency.

'Seagull . . . Sunray here.' He dispensed with the formalities of call sign identification and spoke into the small microphone. 'Please update me on the situation back there.'

'There's a gunnie team cranking up at Blackhorse at the moment,' Hanson said. 'They say'—there was a pause as the operations officer checked his watch—'time on station about forty-five minutes from now.'

'What about our own choppers?'

'They're waiting at Kangaroo for word to pick up stand-by one in time to link up with the Yanks. They should be at our pad inside fifteen minutes.'

'Better get both stand-by patrols airborne with those choppers. It's quite a lot more desperate up here than I care to think about.'

'Not possible,' Hanson said, resisting the urge to question his commander on the patrol's situation. 'There are only four choppers available, the remainder are still involved up north.'

Deane did some calculations. One chopper to fly Zero-One, one to fly Zero-Two and pick up Ashton's patrol, two to carry the stand-by patrols, and one spare for emergencies. That made five. He wrestled a little longer with the problem as they slowly approached the area where he'd contacted the patrol previously.

'Seagull . . . Sunray.' Deane reopened communications. 'Get on to higher and tell them that the patrol up here is in contact with a large NVA force that has pursued them since they ambushed and killed a fair number this morning.' He paused briefly to think about the remainder of the message. 'It has had two further contacts with the enemy since that time and one of the patrol members is wounded and unable to walk.'

'What size force?'

'Patrol Six-Six advises more than a company and less than a battalion.'

'OK,' Hanson said, 'I'll get on to higher as soon . . . ' His voice trailed off. 'Wait.' There was a long pause while Hanson examined the message Sergeant Rawle had handed him. 'Message just in from higher,' Hanson continued. 'Seems like the enemy has broken contact up north and there were not as many as first thought.'

'It looks increasingly like Patrol Six-Six has the NVA battalion up here,' Deane responded, unable to keep the excitement out of his voice, 'and the enemy group north of you are merely a delaying force to make sure the bulk of the battalion got a good headstart into Long Khanh Province.'

'Do you want me to offer that theory to higher?' Hanson smiled as he asked the question, knowing that the Task Force signallers were already monitoring their transmission.

'Why not?' Colin Deane responded, thinking a similar thing. 'Might as well go on the record as having said it.'

'One more thing,' Hanson offered, 'our gunship teams are on their way back to rearm and refuel. Do you want them on station?'

'Most definitely, and get stand-by two airborne as soon as there's an available chopper.'

'Roger that.'

'Oh, and Seagull,' Deane said as an afterthought, 'also advise higher that we have a badly damaged right skid on this helicopter due to being struck by ground fire from an enemy twelve point seven machine gun.'

'Roger.' Hanson sensed that they had nothing more to communicate.

'Sunray . . . Out.' Deane closed the transmission and turned to Monaghan. 'OK, Hal,' he said with a smile, 'let's go and find my patrol.'

The devastation Ashton felt at the instant the helicopter lurched, slewed and appeared to fall out of the sky turned quickly to fear, the type of fear that induces panic. But the sound of the aircraft's turbine engine recovering and continuing to operate calmed him and the fear quickly subsided. He listened intently to the engine noise and tracked it in his mind as it headed south at low level. Within minutes the sound faded and eventually he could no longer hear it.

'Click-click.' He caught everyone's attention and held up his hand with all five digits spread. One by one the patrol members acknowledged. He turned off the radio, stored the aerial and put the unit down his shirt. He knew Deane would be back if it was humanly possible. He was concerned, though, that neither the pilot nor Deane had contacted him since the aircraft had been hit. He sat down and took the green plastic cigarette case from his shirt pocket and studied it absently.

He removed one of the cigarettes from the packet as Jim Collier knelt down in front of him. Ignoring the medic, he lit the cigarette and drew deeply. He waited for the hacking cough but it didn't come. He looked up at Collier and questioned him with his eyes.

'Give us a Durrie, mate,' Collier pleaded.

'I gave you a cigarette two days ago, Jimmy,' Ashton said, pokerfaced. 'What did you do with it?'

For the briefest second Collier was stunned, but his face broke into a broad smile when he realised the humour behind the words. 'I gave it to Billy,' he said without hesitation. 'Bedside manner, you know.'

Both men smiled as Ashton offered the open end of the cigarette packet, the seriousness of the situation momentarily forgotten in the humour of the exchange. Collier withdrew a cigarette and lit it from the burning end of Ashton's.

'How *is* Billy?' Ashton asked the medic before he could move away.

'He's resting OK. I don't think he'll be able to walk—someone will have to carry him.'

'Gary will do that.'

'Short distances to start with, Rowan. I need to check the wound often to make sure the bleeding doesn't get too severe before we notice it.'

Ashton nodded and Collier stood up to make his way to where Wilkins sat propped against the tree. Normally the commander would have admonished Collier for walking across the LUP with a cigarette in his hand, but he couldn't be bothered. He smiled to himself. The more desperate the situation, he thought, the more lenient I get.

Jim Collier was in the process of constructing a double sling to carry Wilkins' rifle on his back when he heard the faint sound of the returning helicopter in the distance. He looked up to see Ashton forcing his cigarette butt into the ground and was about to attract his attention to the approaching aircraft when Ashton sat upright, listening.

Within seconds, all had heard it. Even Wilkins opened his eyes but remained silent. He looked at Collier as he slung the SLR down on his back and then at Ashton in time to see him remove the PRC 68 from his shirt front. Dobel and Erickson hardly moved a muscle at the sound of the aircraft but both could feel their energy returning.

'. . . Possum Five . . . Over,' Ashton heard as he switched on the radio. It wasn't Deane's voice and he missed the first part of the transmission but there was little doubt that it was meant for him.

'Six-Six . . . Over.'

'Sunray.' Deane's voice came on air. 'Sorry to lose you for a bit but we had a minor problem to attend to.' There was a hint of dryness in his voice. 'What is your situation now?'

'I'm about to move shortly,' Ashton replied, as the helicopter came into view, high up and several hundred metres to the east of their location. 'We haven't heard anything of the enemy since the last contact and that concerns me.'

'I need another fix on your position, I didn't quite get the last one.'

'OK,' Ashton replied, smiling to himself and holding up his cupped hand to Erickson and wiggling it to signify that he should work the mirror again. 'Stand by.' Erickson quickly worked the orange dot on to the helicopter with practised ease.

'I have you!' Deane's voice betrayed the discomfort caused by the flash of light. 'Thank you.'

The helicopter circled to the right and further away from their position before Colin Deane spoke again.

'Six-Six, this is Sunray,' he said, 'what are your immediate plans? . . . Over.'

Piss off, Ashton thought, I can't tell you my plans in clear. Ashton was concerned that the NVA had a transceiver capability and to divulge his intentions on an open frequency might place the patrol at greater risk. He took a deep breath before he spoke.

'I am concerned that the enemy may have the means to monitor this transmission,' he said, knowing that Deane would understand immediately, 'but I did hope that my immediate plans included an extraction.'

'Extraction agency inbound as we speak.' Deane's voice betrayed the amusement he felt at Ashton's comment on extraction. 'Estimate their time of arrival in this area in four zero minutes.'

Ashton's face cracked into a wide smile; so did Erickson's. He was several feet away and watching his arc of responsibility while hanging on every word of the conversation. It occurred to Ashton that the two landing zones he had designated as emergency rendezvous were outside the patrol's area of operations, and that operational clearance to use them was required to avoid unnecessary clashes with friendly forces.

'Sunray, this is Six-Six . . . Over.'

'Sunray . . . Over.'

'Do you have a comprehensive marked map of my AO?'

'Affirmative,' Deane replied, glancing down at the map Rawle had given him. It detailed all the information relating to Ashton's patrol.

'You have my insertion LZ and no-fire zone marked?'

'Affirmative,' Deane confirmed after a brief pause.

'I need clearance to move into the no-fire zone if I'm compromised at my planned extraction LZ,' Ashton said, concentrating on the plan that was milling around inside his head. 'And I may need to go beyond that, toward the south for a couple of klicks, if it really turns to shit.'

'Am I to understand that you intend to come out where you went in?'

'Affirmative, but at the eastern end.'

'Roger,' Deane said flatly. 'Then your alternate is the area about a kilometre to the east of that point?'

'That's correct, and my next best bet is a long way to the south at a large open area that will give me plenty of options for an extraction point.'

'Roger.' Deane's tone was matter of fact. 'We've been down there shaking the bugs out of this aircraft. We'll leave you to it for now.' He glanced at his watch and wondered where the time had gone. 'The extraction agency should be with you in about three seven minutes.' There was a pause before Deane concluded with the only words he could bring to mind. 'Good luck!'

'Six-Six,' Ashton said finally. 'Roger . . . Out.'

Ashton watched mournfully as the most dependable link they had with the outside world turned south to head toward Nui Dat. He swallowed hard, switched off the small radio, stowed the aerial and returned the unit to its carry pouch. A feeling of utter loneliness descended upon him and he felt very, very vulnerable.

Sergeant Ashton calculated that the north-eastern edge of their insertion LZ was a little under three hundred metres away. He led the patrol south, knowing that he was now pushing against the clock to reach the area before or at the same time as the extraction agency.

Three hundred metres in thirty minutes seemed a reasonable task but, with a man wounded and an enemy force of unknown numbers and disposition searching for them, Ashton realised he had to balance speed and security.

Ashton assessed that the twelve point seven millimetre heavy machine gun sounded about a klick to the north-west from the approximate location of the enemy bunker system. It was unlikely that the gun had engaged the helicopter from the bunker system because the jungle canopy around that area was too thick to allow the gunner a good sight of the aircraft. Ashton decided that the gunner must have had a suitable vantage point near the camp or that the weapon was firing from a much closer position than he thought. He hoped it meant the enemy's heavy weapons were still in or near the camp.

They patrolled south with as much speed as Ashton dared. The undergrowth was sparse and the going was good for everybody except Dobel, who had the additional weight and hindrance of the wounded Wilkins on his back. Their heading took them east of a number of large bamboo clumps that became larger the further south they went. Ashton decided that the bamboo here was an extension of the clumps he'd sighted just after their insertion—which now seemed weeks ago.

Dobel struggled on without complaint until Ashton called a halt at the completion of one hundred metres worth of Erickson's paces. He moved the patrol into the shelter of one of the larger overhanging clumps of bamboo. It was clear under the umbrella of thick leaves and thorny stalks and while visibility varied, Ashton thought they would be relatively safe there.

Bamboo had great advantages and few disadvantages for a small patrol. It was totally impossible for a large formation of soldiers to assault through and yet a small group could move quickly and quietly through a large area of the taller species, provided it was prepared to accept the many direction changes that would be required to maintain a general line of march.

With assistance from Jim Collier, Dobel thankfully lay Wilkins on the thick mat of fallen leaves and withdrew several metres to take up a position on the perimeter where he could see through the overhanging branches at the lighter area beyond. He was tired and his back was aching from carrying Wilkins. It had been a day like none he had even remotely experienced before. There was a permanent knot of fear in his stomach that threatened to burst out through his rib cage. He took a long drink of water and felt better. He remembered that he hadn't eaten at all that day so he reached into a pocket and pulled out a small packet of biscuits from his unused ambush meals.

Wilkins winced as his two comrades lay him on the ground. Collier looked at his right shoulder and could see the unusually large blood stain that indicated that his wound had opened up and was bleeding heavily from the jolting ride on Dobel's back. The grimace on Wilkins' face was sufficient warning that the morphine was wearing off. The medic removed a bottle of codeine phosphate from his pocket and a water bottle from its carrier, then leaned forward and shook Wilkins gently.

'Billy,' he said softly, watching closely for a response. Wilkins opened his eyes slowly and looked into the troubled face of his friend.

'I feel like shit, mate,' he croaked, coughing as he spoke.

'I know,' Collier lied, having no idea what such wounds would feel like. 'Can you get these into you?' he urged, offering the tablets to Wilkins. 'I need to get another couple of dressings on to your shoulder.' Wilkins took the tablets with his left hand, threw them awkwardly into his mouth and forced himself to chew into them before reaching out to take the water bottle.

Collier immediately busied himself with taking the waterproof covers off both large field dressings. He attempted to exert more pressure on the wound from both front and back in an effort to stop the flow of blood. He could see it was causing Wilkins some distress as the pain-killing effect of the codeine had not yet started.

When Collier completed the task he sat back on his heels and took the water bottle from Wilkins' hand to take a long drink himself. He raised the water bottle to his lips and from the corner of his eye he detected movement to the side, in the direction of the creek.

He turned his head sharply to the right in time to see a North Vietnamese soldier aiming an AK47 assault rifle directly at him. At that moment Jim Collier knew the true fear of death and, as he opened his mouth to scream a warning, the enemy was struck in the head and chest by a five round burst of 5.56mm fire from Gary Dobel's M16.

18

'And that's as much as we know at this time.' Sergeant Bevan Willis glanced at his watch as he concluded the briefing of both stand-by patrols. 'My patrol has just over eight minutes to get up to the chopper pad,' he reminded them. 'Patrol Six-Two is on five minutes notice to move from now.' He looked to Smithfield for his nod of confirmation. 'The ops officer will update the situation as soon as the OC calls in. For my blokes, that may mean we have to be briefed after we're airborne.'

The ten men began to drift toward the open door to the briefing hut and the piles of individual webbing and weapons just outside. All were heavily smeared with camouflage paint and moved with purpose. As the first man neared the door, the familiar form of Peter Hanson appeared in the doorway.

'We have news from the front,' he said without humour, a stern expression on his face, 'and none of it good.'

The patrol members muttered as they eased back from the door to let him pass, and crowded forward with him as he made his way to the large pictographic map of Phuoc Tuy and adjoining provinces that covered the far wall. He picked up the short, remodelled pool cue that the operations staff used as a pointer, studied the map for a few seconds, and pointed to where Colin Deane had recently reported Ashton's position.

'Ashton is here,' he said, 'about three hundred metres from the LZ where he went in.' He looked at the faces in the room and felt the tension building. He moved the pointer to the north and tapped the map.

181

'Patrol Six-Six ambushed and killed seventeen NVA at this approximate location just before ten hundred hours this morning'—he paused to let the information sink in—'and has been pursued by a large NVA force of over company strength since that time.'

'Wheeeew!' The long, loud, half whistle came from Snowy Jacobs. The nervous laugh that followed caused several heads to turn in his direction. 'Good move, Ashton,' Jacobs said with a forced smile, 'coax them all down into one area, surround 'em, then shoot the shit out of 'em.'

There was genuine laughter from most in the room. It was typical of the bravado-based humour that prevailed in the squadron when things were not going as well as they might. Peter Hanson did not laugh and the exaggerated noise from his false throat-clearing brought the attention of everyone back to the briefing. The serious expression on his face caused them to settle quickly.

'Patrol Six-Six has had two contacts since the ambush,' he continued, looking from face to face. 'Enemy casualties not known,' he paused again briefly, 'but Ashton has a man wounded.' There was absolute silence in the room, broken only by the occasional shuffle of boots on the concrete floor. Hanson allowed the gravity of the news to sink in.

Fuck you, Ashton, Bevan Willis thought, shaking his head in wonder, my first contact as a patrol commander and we're going into action against half the North Vietnamese Army.

'Who's wounded?' Jacobs fired at the operations officer. 'And how bad?' He was not a person who was going to die wondering if he should have asked a question or not.

'We don't know who's wounded,' Hanson answered the question seriously, 'but he has a wound to the right shoulder and the left leg.' He looked intently at Jacobs to confirm that the soldier was happy with the answer. Jacobs was nodding; there wasn't much left to say on the issue.

'I have to tell you that the situation up there may become even more serious,' Hanson continued. 'The OC's chopper was almost shot down by a twelve point seven near Ashton's location.' He could see by the expressions that this was one piece of information they would have preferred him to keep to himself.

'You know the plot with the American light fire team from Blackhorse'—he looked directly at Willis. 'Your choppers will RV with them over the Nui Hot.' His gaze passed from Willis to Smithfield. 'Latest word is that the chopper taking your mob is inbound with our Bushranger gunships.' Smithfield nodded as Hanson continued. 'You will be about ten or fifteen minutes behind Willis and the Bushrangers will join you as soon as they rearm and refuel.'

Bevan Willis and his patrol began to file out of the briefing hut leaving Peter Hanson and Smithfield's patrol in speculative discussion over Ashton's predicament. They quickly slipped into their equipment. It was a different equipment load than was carried on normal patrol operations and was even different from what was carried on a pure ten man ambush task.

Most patrols deployed with full, heavy packs with enough food and water to last at least five days. Most stand-by patrols travelled light as they were designed to provide short-term assistance to downed aircrew or to patrols who ran into difficulties—as Patrol Six-Six had done. Each member of the stand-by patrols carried only enough food for one day, water for two days and almost a double load of ammunition.

Willis had a thought about the state of Ashton's ammunition holdings. He converted the thought to an order.

'Keg,' he said to Russell Baker, 'slip down to Squadron Headquarters, find Charlie King, and get four or five bandoliers of 5.56 and 7.62mm ammo and a heap of 40mm HE bombs.'

Keg Baker acknowledged the order as he picked up his SLR and hurried off to find King.

That's a fair idea, thought Snowy Jacobs, if Ashton is in deep shit, he could be low on ammo. He shouldered the small, light pack that carried an AN/PRC 25 VHF radio, and silently congratulated Willis for his thoughtfulness.

'Need a hand, Keg?' Roy Kent, the patrol scout, called after Baker.

'OK,' the 2IC called back. There was going to be a fair bit of ammo to pick up.

Roy Kent hoisted his M16 and followed him toward the headquarters building while Bevan Willis, Snowy Jacobs and Keith Grenville, the patrol medic, made their way up the dusty track that led to the units' helicopter landing pad.

Colin Deane was quietly thoughtful as the helicopter made its way toward Nui Dat. Hal Monaghan was also quiet, keeping a watchful eye on the damaged right skid of his aircraft. The constant vibration had caused it to deteriorate considerably. He feared the skid was going to part company from the forward strut area and he thought it might ultimately affect his landing.

Fifteen minutes flying time from Nui Dat, Monaghan noticed the flight of four Iroquois helicopters several hundred feet below and off to their right. They were tracking a little north of north-east. The small, white-painted sections on the rotor blades made distinctive circles against the dark green jungle canopy below.

'There go the cavalry,' Monaghan said as he activated the intercom and pointed.

Deane looked in the direction indicated but could only make out the rotor signature of the rear two choppers. He smiled thinly and with great relief. It was the helicopters with one of the stand-by patrols on board. The plan was starting to come together and, if Ashton had any luck at all in avoiding the enemy until he could be extracted, the whole thing might still be brought to a successful conclusion.

Monaghan made several frequency changes and spoke briefly with the helicopters, his flight headquarters and the Nui Dat tactical artillery before satisfying himself that he was clear all the way into Nui Dat. He turned to the Envoy frequency to hear a 9 Squadron helicopter speaking with the SAS Comcen. Monaghan looked over at Colin Deane and realised that he was preoccupied with thoughts and had not heard the transmission.

'Seems like you're going to have a visitor, sir.'

'Is that so, Hal?' the major responded, his mind tuning quickly to the present. 'And who might that be?'

'Hardrock himself. Seems he must have come back from the fire support base on the Iroquois that's picking up your other stand-by patrol.'

'Really?' Major Deane responded with raised eyebrows and a nod. It was a statement more than a question. Brigadier Bill McCreadie was relatively new in country and the combined battalion operations that had just concluded to the east of the Courtenay rubber plantation were the first under his direction since assuming command three weeks previously.

There was silence in the aircraft cabin for several minutes before Monaghan called the air traffic control agency at Nui Dat to clear his aircraft for final approach and began to descend slowly. As he did, he noted the rotor disc signature of an RAAF Iroquois landing at Nadzab. He leaned forward and pointed toward the hill. 'That'll be him landing now.'

They were still a kilometre from Nadzab and could barely make out the activity on the ground. By the time they reached the eastern end of the Task Force airfield, the RAAF helicopter started to ascend and move off toward the east before turning north-east to pass fifty metres away on Deane's side of the Army chopper. Deane noted the familiar figures of Smithfield seated on the seat near the open left-hand door, Trooper Kevin Simmons, his patrol scout, seated cross-legged on the floor facing the open doorway with his medic, Jack Gardiner, just visible.

Deane and Smithfield exchanged sombre waves of acknow-ledgment. The moment passed and Deane concentrated his attention on the figures standing at the back of the helicopter pad. As the Kiowa slowly approached, he thought he could identify two of the figures as Peter Hanson and the brigadier.

Bill McCreadie was a tall and powerfully built man who dominated any situation merely by his presence. Deane knew that McCreadie was well liked and respected by his staff because he displayed a willingness to seek advice from as many avenues as possible before deciding a policy issue that drove the day to day operations of the Task Force machine. Deane's mind focused briefly on the recent directive he'd received on the future use of helicopter hours by his squadron and wondered bitterly where the informed advice for that decision had come from.

His attention was suddenly attracted to an area beyond the western side of the hill and his mood changed markedly as he watched first one, then two, and finally a third Australian helicopter gunship come into view. They were flying low between the old Provincial Route 2 and the 'ring' road that provided civilian by-pass of the Australian Task Force base. As he watched, they came around on to a north-east heading and began to gain height until they disappeared from his view.

'I'm going to have to hover to let you out, sir,' Monaghan's voice cut across his thoughts as they made their final approach to the pad. 'This right skid could collapse under the full weight.'

'That's fine, Hal.' Deane smiled and looked at the pilot as he spoke. 'I expect you have to fill out a damage report when you get back.'

'That's right, sir,' Monaghan replied with a nervous laugh, thinking of how he was going to explain being as low as he was when they were hit. 'That should be a lot of fun.'

'It's a good thing there was an operational reason for us to be at the height we were.' Deane looked meaningfully at Monaghan, leaving the pilot in no doubt that he would support any fair explanation.

'Hello, Colin,' McCreadie said as Deane approached the group on the pad. The Task Force Commander took half a pace toward him and held out his right hand.

'Sir!' Deane replied and forced his body into the erect military posture used to greet one's superior officer when saluting is not appropriate. He then stepped forward to grasp the proffered hand.

'You're ops officer has pretty well brought me up to date in the few minutes I've been here,' the Brigadier said softly, 'but I'd like to hear your thoughts on the situation. And perhaps we can discuss some matters of policy while we wait this thing out.'

'Very well, sir,' Deane responded cautiously. He found the brigadier's affable approach a little unsettling, 'Shall we go down to my office?' He gestured to the Land Rover that stood in the shade of the overhanging bamboo at the edge of the pad.

'Let the rest go in the vehicle, Colin,' McCreadie said, 'we might use a less bumpy means.'

'Very well, sir.' Deane smiled and indicated with a nod to Hanson that he should take the remainder of the visitors ahead in the Land Rover.

'Sergeant Cross has put aside your lunch, sir,' Hanson advised his commander as he moved toward the vehicle.

'Lunch, sir?' Deane asked the brigadier as the two men commenced walking down the hill toward the Squadron Head-quarters area.

'Just coffee would be fine,' McCreadie said appreciatively. 'Your OPSO tells me you have a theory that it's the main NVA force that's on to your patrol. I that so?'

'All indications point to that being the case, sir.'

'How so?' The brigadier nudged a small stone with the toe of his boot.

'Several days ago,' Deane began cautiously, unsure of how much of the story McCreadie already knew, 'Patrol Six-Six found a bunker system occupied by a large enemy force. Before they had an opportunity to check the camp, the enemy moved out during the night, taking the best part of all night to do so.'

'So?'

'Over the next two days, Sergeant Ashton—that's the patrol commander—went in and looked around the camp and found evidence that the unit was 274 VC Regiment.'

'Why wasn't I aware of this?' McCreadie's brow furrowed.

'I phoned it down to your Ops immediately, sir, but it was only speculative information—because Ashton never actually saw the enemy heading up the track to Long Khanh.'

'Very well.' The brigadier was satisfied with this explanation. 'Where do the NVA come into it?'

'When Ashton finished the camp recce he was tasked to ambush the track leading out of our province. He noted a buildup of enemy forces at the camp all day yesterday while he was making his ambush preparations and into last night.' Deane sighed heavily. 'And this morning he ambushed the first group out of the camp.'

'All right then, Colin,' McCreadie acknowledged, 'what's your theory?'

'I believe the VC somehow got on to the fact that your current battalion operations were specifically targeting 274 VC Regiment and whatever elements there were of 33 NVA Regiment in the province,' Deane said openly, 'and the VC infrastructure chiefs of Military Region Seven decided to move those units out to avoid a confrontation that might damage them greatly.'

'And that would be why my eastern battalion found next to nothing,' McCreadie mused, 'and the battalion at Courtenay was held up.'

'274 VC Regiment got out first,' Colin Deane suggested. 'They were closest to the escape route and that's why the eastern battalion found very little.' He paused briefly before continuing. 'The NVA were further west and either not in a position for a quick exit or received late notice of the plan to get out.'

'Hence the delaying force?' McCreadie acknowledged the feasibility of the theory.

'That would be my guess, sir.'

With coffee poured, Deane gestured to the Brigadier to have a seat in one of the comfortably padded cane chairs. He was keen to discuss the only directive the new Task Force Commander had yet sent to any unit and was equally keen to find out why he hadn't been consulted before the decision was made and the directive issued.

'This directive, sir'—Deane started the question warily, choosing his words carefully—'the one on the use of air assets. I'm not sure that it won't cost us lives eventually.'

'I'm sure it would, Colin,' the brigadier said gravely. 'That's why I'll be looking at it more closely in the light of what has happened to your patrol today.'

'That's good, sir!'

'Yes,' the brigadier went on, 'I had it in mind to enforce the directive today, and staff advice from some areas strongly supported that course of action.'

Damn, thought Colin Deane, without a case in the brigadier's eyes for the opposition to argue, there's no way I'm going to find out who my enemies in court are.

'I think the patrol commander on the ground is best placed to make the decision on the seriousness of his situation,' he offered.

'That's sound logic, of course,' McCreadie agreed, 'but isn't it possible the patrol commander might overstate the seriousness of the situation?'

'I don't believe that's an issue, sir,' Deane said defensively. 'What is at issue here is the individual's perception of the threat.'

'Explain!'

'Well, sir,' Deane said slowly, trying to recall a conversation he'd had with Ashton on that very subject earlier in the year, 'individual patrol commanders have a different perception of the threat, and what might appear to be a quite serious situation to one patrol commander may not appear so to another.'

The brigadier indicated by the slight nod of his head that he understood but Deane knew he wasn't totally convinced.

'I expect it all comes down to nerve,' Colin Deane said, 'and confidence in the team you've got.' He looked at the Task Force Commander. 'That's why we have selection . . . and of course every extraction conducted as a result of enemy pressure has to be justified on return.'

'On what do we gauge the justification?' the question surprised Deane.

'Service experience is all we've got, sir,' Deane said wearily. 'My patrol commanders are in no doubt that if I suspect something is amiss the patrol will go back in the next day—or, in the case of extremely poor judgment on the part of the commander, a job will be found for him in another part of the Army.'

The telephone on Deane's desk rang three times. The brigadier was still smiling faintly as Deane got up to answer.

'OC . . . *What*?' he said, shocked by the news conveyed by his operations officer. 'That must have only just happened.' Deane listened as Hanson explained. 'Yes, very well,' the major said, 'deploy stand-by one to look after it.' As he listened intently to Hanson's closing words he noticed the brigadier begin to take an interest in the call. 'No, Peter,' he said softly, 'the brigadier and I will be up shortly.'

Bill McCreadie watched intently as Deane flopped wearily into the chair behind his desk. Absently he put an elbow on the desk and held the handpiece across the upturned palm of his left hand, contemplating what he had just heard. Finally, he placed the handset in its cradle and looked across at the brigadier.

'That was from Albatross Zero-One, sir,' he said, his face a mixture of concern and worry. 'One of the Yank gunships in support of Ashton's patrol has been shot down.'

19

The slight movement beneath the bamboo toward the creek distracted Dobel from his meagre meal of biscuits and water. At first he was unsure what it was. As the shadow came closer, it materialised into the unmistakable form of a NVA soldier, moving from the creek toward the area of the LUP occupied by Collier and the wounded Wilkins.

The enemy moved silently, an AK47 held directly in front of his body, ready for action. In an instant, Dobel noted the enemy wore no hat and his grey, khaki/green uniform was dark from perspiration. He wore standard NVA canvas boots and chest webbing and there was a small rice sack on the left side of his belt.

Fear gripped Gary Dobel. He felt the blood drain from his body and begin to pound in his temples. The back of his throat was dry in spite of the long drink of water he had just taken. A huge knot of fear built quickly in his stomach and his body began to tremble slightly.

Erickson's M16 lay across his lap, the barrel facing the direction of the approaching enemy. He dared not move for fear it would alert the enemy to his presence. He felt an involuntary movement as his right hand reached cautiously for the pistol grip. He still held the water bottle loosely in his left hand, its base resting on the ground beside him. He released the water bottle and inched his left hand slowly toward the foregrip of the weapon.

Dobel felt a little better with the M16 in his hands. He raised it slightly, moving the change lever to the automatic fire position.

His mouth was open and his breath shallow and rasping. The noise of his breathing was like a crescendo in his ears—he was sure the enemy soldier must certainly hear it.

He watched the NVA soldier closely. He wanted to look beyond the enemy and his mind screamed frantically: Look behind him and find out where his mates are. But he dared not shift his eyes in case he could not locate the enemy again. He waited trembling as the enemy approached. The M16 felt strange and uncomfortably light in his hands. It was a standard M16 and it lacked the weight his XM148 had in its forward end.

The NVA soldier moved across Dobel's front and the possibility of him missing the LUP altogether became a real one. A movement from the medic to sit back on his heels and drink from his water bottle caused the enemy to see him. The NVA soldier was behind and to the right of Collier and stopped immediately. Not taking his eyes from Collier's back, he raised the AK47 and sighted the weapon directly at him.

What the fuck's he doing? The thought flashed quickly through Dobel's mind as he raised the M16. Doesn't he realise there must be more of us? The M16 came smoothly to his shoulder. Instinctively he took a sight picture on the enemy's chest, and squeezed the trigger. Two of the 5.56mm bullets struck the NVA soldier in the chest and another struck him in the head.

Jim Collier dropped the water bottle and reached frantically for the SLR beside his body. The fear was gone now, replaced by the instinct for survival. He rolled a metre or two and came smoothly into an upright crouch, the SLR pointing toward the place where the enemy had fallen. He scanned the area for further danger, but there was no sign of immediate threat.

Collier licked his lips and remembered the water bottle. He cast a quick glance around the area where he had been kneeling near Wilkins. It wasn't there. He looked in Ashton's direction; his commander wasn't at the position he'd occupied when they stopped. The medic glanced quickly around the LUP and saw him beside Dobel. He felt the tension continue to build as the four fit members of the patrol scanned the bamboo thoroughly for further sign of the enemy. There was none.

'Click-click.' Ashton got everyone's attention quickly. He made a sign to indicate that they were to get out of the area as quickly as possible. The LUP became a hive of activity as they prepared to move. Ashton went to assist Collier with his equipment and to prepare the wounded Wilkins for travel. As he approached, he saw Collier intently searching the area around where Wilkins lay.

'You lookin' for this, Jimmy?' Wilkins held up a water bottle. Collier took the bottle and shook it gently, embarrassment and anger in his face.

'Why didn't you let me know you had it? You seen me looking for the fuckin' thing.'

'You can't just throw our water away like you just did, Jimmy,' Wilkins smiled in mock admonishment, 'it's getting pretty low.'

Collier smiled, his anger spent. He screwed the cap on to the bottle, replaced it in its cover and started to quickly repack the medical kit. The remaining members, including Wilkins, were tense and alert for a reaction to the contact. Ashton was concerned by the situation—not by the contact but by the fact that a lone enemy was scouting on his own. What does it mean? he asked himself before his attention was demanded by Wilkins' persistent tugging at his sleeve.

'They're scouting us, Rowan,' Wilkins said urgently. 'They're scouting us singly, to pinpoint our location.'

Good theory, Ashton thought, how *valid* is another matter. He considered the situation from the enemy's perspective. They know generally where we've been so far by the contacts, he thought. First we ambush a big mob, then a section or so in an extended sweep is looking for us. His brow creased as Wilkins' theory became more feasible. A two man cutoff group next, and now single scouts.

Rowan Ashton looked at his wounded scout and dearly wished him better. Wilkins was likely right, he conceded, the area was so big that the enemy commander must need to send them out in singles to cover it.

'But why?' he said aloud, without realising he had spoken.

'Why what?' Collier fired at him as he finished securing his pack.

'Why is the enemy putting so much effort into looking for us?' Ashton asked both men. 'If the NVA are looking to get out of the province rather than fight, why are they spending so much time looking for us?'

'They probably want their money back, Rowan,' Wilkins offered with a smile. Ashton looked sharply at him and then remembered the satchel taken from the dead NVA officer. It was a good point made in jest. Ashton was anxious to get out of the immediate area but he felt that what they were discussing could be vital to their survival.

'Not the money, Billy,' he replied soberly. 'There can't be more than fifty thousand dong in the bag, and although it'll buy a few luxuries for them in the villages it's not enough to sacrifice the security of a battalion over.'

'What fifty thousand dong?' Collier queried, his curiosity roused.

'There has to be something else in that satchel.' Ashton directed his speculative remark at Wilkins, ignoring Collier completely. 'There's no time to ferret about in the bag now,' he added thoughtfully, 'and even if we did, we wouldn't understand what we were reading anyway.'

'What money, Rowan?' Collier persisted. 'What satchel?'

'This satchel.' Ashton turned his right side to Collier and patted the plain leather satchel that hung there. 'We took it off an officer in the ambush.' He patted again and felt the hardness of something against his shirt. Pulling out the K54 pistol, he offered it to the wide-eyed Collier.

'What's this?' the medic asked with some curiosity, eyeing the pistol avariciously.

'It's yours,' Ashton said with a slight smile, knowing it would take Collier's mind off the money. 'To make up for the one you reckon I diddled you out of on the first patrol.' Collier's eyes opened even wider as he took the pistol from his commander and put it down his own shirt. For once Collier was speechless, but both Ashton and Wilkins noticed the gratitude in his eyes.

'Let's get going,' Ashton ordered, as he caught the attention of Dobel and Erickson and gave the signal to move immediately. 'This place could be crawling with Nogs at any time.' He thought briefly about that and knew he didn't believe it. The Nogs are not going to come looking for us, he told himself, my bet is they'll be waiting for us somewhere up ahead.

Dobel went across the LUP to pick up Wilkins, who was standing on his right leg and grasping a large bamboo stalk with his left hand. He knew it was not possible to walk but he wanted to make the move on to Dobel's shoulder as painless as possible for both of them. Collier gave Wilkins a friendly tap on his good shoulder before moving past Dobel.

'Thanks, Gary,' he said as they crossed. There was a strange note in Collier's voice that Dobel had not heard before and the look in the medic's eye made the corporal feel uncomfortable, even a little embarrassed. A nod was all Dobel could muster.

He saved my life! The thought drifted in and out of Collier's mind. Of all people, *Dobel* saved my life! Jim Collier knew he would be indebted to Dobel for the rest of his life. He hated the thought of it, but whatever happened between them from now on was of no consequence. Even if he saved Dobel's life ten times in return, it was a debt you could never repay. 'Why Dobel?' Collier asked himself repeatedly, 'why?'

Ashton forced a fair but safe pace from the LUP in the bamboo clump. Movement away from the bamboo belt was good; they made little noise apart from that generated by Dobel as he struggled under the weight of Wilkins. They needed to move fairly quickly in Ashton's estimation because he had a bad feeling that, by this time, the enemy commander might have worked out where they were heading. If that *was* the case, he wanted to be there on the ground so the patrol would have prior warning when the enemy were moving in.

Ashton halted his men on the edge of a cleared area which, according to his calculations, should not have been there. They had come just over a hundred and fifty metres by Erickson's paces and the presence of the clearing took him by surprise. He checked carefully, unsure that it was the LZ even though most indications were that it was. They had come out almost on the point of the north-east corner. The straggly clumps of thorny bamboo were less than twenty metres away.

The clumps grew right up to the edge of the clearing before they stopped and this pleased Ashton. The clumps here were smaller and more spread out and did not have the proximity that caused the stems to mat above the ground. Instead of being open and clear beneath matted stems, the extremities in this area hung down and created the nearest thing to a barbed wire entanglement that Ashton could have hoped for.

It meant that the area of bamboo and beyond was of little tactical significance and would remain so unless the enemy already had troops in secure positions there. Ashton doubted that this was the case, as it would have been irresistible for anyone in that area not to engage them as they approached, unless there were other good reasons not to.

That will have to be cleared, Ashton convinced himself, the enemy could be in there waiting to provide fire support for an assault against them, or even to be the assault force themselves.

Ashton and Collier made a closer examination of the area and confirmed there was no one lurking in the bamboo. Ashton identified the large dead tree he'd used to confirm the LZ during the insertion. The tree was more difficult to locate from the ground than it had been from the air. The trunk was situated inside the treeline almost at the point where the patrol emerged and he was able to locate it only by looking through the canopy above.

Another large tree lay along the edge of the LZ where it had fallen not long ago. The trunk was almost a metre in diameter and its presence gave Ashton a secure feeling. Its bulk could be used as protection to fight from should that be required, but there were still a number of areas of concern for Ashton. The enemy could still get at him from three sides, including the rear.

A slow follow-up and assault from the east, covered by supporting fire from their rear, was absolutely the worst scenario imaginable to Ashton. This would force him to either go on to the LZ or attempt to escape along its edge to the south. In the latter case, if the enemy had positioned cutoff parties to the south, the patrol would face annihilation.

Ashton shuddered and quickly put the thought out of his mind. He looked around the area quickly, assessing his next move. The large fallen tree was just inside the treeline and the width of the LZ at that point was a little over seventy metres. He gestured to Dobel to put Wilkins down close to the fallen tree. He looked carefully at the wounded scout's face as they passed and saw that he was in great pain.

'Jimmy,' he said softly, yet loud enough for all to hear, 'get another dose of morphine or something into Billy and have another look at the bleeding.' It was an order that he didn't have to give but it broke the silence of the long haul from the last stop.

'Bluey,' he spoke again, 'you and I will watch the front and flanks.' He paused, head to one side, listening hard for a familiar sound. 'Gary, you keep an eye on the rear.'

Ashton moved in behind the log and peered across the stretch of open ground at the treeline on the other side of the LZ. He thought it odd that the bamboo just stopped at the clearing and he remembered from his prepatrol air recce that the deep creek continued across the LZ some forty metres to the west. He decided it was an old cultivation that used water from the creek.

Collier finished injecting the 15 milligrams of morphine into Wilkins and reached under the top flap of his pack for two 'shell' dressings. The blood from Wilkins' wound had not begun to show through the outer dressing to any extent, so he put the fresh dressings down his shirt and fastened his pack. He was just slipping his pack on when he detected the faint, dull downbeat of helicopter rotors.

'Choppers,' he said excitedly, 'no risk!'

The spirits of the patrol rose at the sound. Ashton looked briefly at Wilkins; he was either asleep or unconscious. He unclipped the pouch containing his PRC 68, withdrew the small radio, raised the aerial and turned it on. He placed the radio on the ground beside him and leaned the aerial against the log.

He looked back across the LZ, scanning the area carefully, his whole body tensed. The feeling of elation left him as he strained to confirm a movement he thought he detected on the other side. The noise of the approaching helicopters was becoming more distinct.

The enemy obviously had not heard it. A number of automatic weapons opened up on the patrol from across the clearing.

'Bravo Nine Sierra Six-Six, this is Albatross Zero-One, do you read? . . . Over.' The voice of Squadron Leader Kevin Green, the lead helicopter pilot, was barely audible above the noise of the patrol's weapons as they returned fire at the enemy on the opposite side of the LZ.

The patrol was in contact with the enemy across the clearing for a full minute before the radio beside Ashton burst into voice. He fired a 40mm HE projectile which detonated in the area where most of the enemy fire appeared to be originating and reached down for the radio.

'Albatross,' Ashton screamed into the microphone, 'this is call sign Six-Six. I'm in a dick-dragger of a contact down here. How long before we can have some suppressive fire?'

'This is Albatross,' Green's voice responded calmly. 'We need you to mark friendlies and give some target identification and description . . . Over.'

'Roger,' Ashton said. 'The first smoke you see will be the enemy's location, wait out.' He quickly loaded a smoke projectile into his launcher, sighted the weapon on the enemy's position through the lower aperture and engaged the firing button with his left thumb.

'Get ready to throw smoke here, Jimmy,' Ashton screamed above the noise, as he watched the projectile speed across the clearing and land on the edge just inside the treeline. In a few moments smoke began to billow from the point of impact.

'I see white smoke on the southern side of the clearing,' the Albatross leader said calmly. 'Please confirm: white smoke?'

'White smoke confirmed, that's the enemy's location,' Ashton responded. The Albatross lead aircraft was now less than a kilometre from the LZ and flying at over 2000 feet. The remaining aircraft could not be seen but Ashton was aware they were loitering somewhere in the vicinity. He ejected the spent smoke cartridge from his 148 and loaded his second last CS gas cartridge. This also would make white smoke, as well as tickling their eyes and exposed skin.

'Please mark your position, Six-Six,' the lead pilot ordered, 'I have the gun team standing by.'

'Roger . . . Wait.' Ashton yelled at the medic, 'Smoke.'

Collier threw the No 83 smoke grenade almost ten metres diagonally toward the edge of the clearing to their south. The single 'crack' as the striker lever initiated the primer almost assured them that the grenade was good. Collier watched the smoke billow from the base of the grenade and rise slowly for a short distance before being taken away to the south-east on the prevailing breeze.

'I see yellow smoke.' The pilot's voice sounded again as Ashton fired the CS gas cartridge into the enemy area. 'Confirm: yellow smoke?'

'Yellow smoke confirmed.' Ashton reloaded the launcher with a HE cartridge. It occurred to him that the enemy across the clearing had stopped firing. He smiled ruefully; it was not surprising, no doubt they knew they were about to come under fire from the air.

'Six-Six.' It was the lead pilot. 'We have Gunslinger rolling at this time, passing to you.'

'Six-Six, this is Gunslinger Two-Three.' The American drawl cut across the transmission. 'Thanks for the invite to your shootout, man, we're twenty seconds from the target area. What have you got down there for us?' Ashton had worked with American gunships on his previous tour but still took a full second to understand what was said.

'We're in contact with an unknown number of NVA—company strength, may be more, and they have heavy weapons.'

'That's as good as we get anywhere in country!' There was a happy inflection to the drawl. 'Where do you all want this goddamn ordnance, man?'

Ashton could see and hear the gunships clearly, but they were still a long way off and he realised they must not have received a full briefing from the Albatross lead pilot.

'Roger. The friendlies are located on the north-east corner of the pad and designated by yellow smoke. The bad guys are on the southern side of the pad and marked by white smoke.' As he spoke, the question of the heavy weapons came into his mind. 'Stay on the south side of the pad, we're not sure where their heavy weapons are located.'

'Roger. Got all that, man,' the voice drawled. 'This is Gunslinger Two-Three rollin' in live this time.'

'Keep your eyes peeled out the back, Gary,' Ashton threw at Dobel when he noticed that his attention was drawn to the imminent happenings in front of them. The American light fire team were just under half a kilometre from the target, two abreast, when they fired the first salvo of 2.75 inch HE rockets.

Ashton and his patrol had seen a gunship strike many times before but it never ceased to entertain while you were on the right side of it. The two puffs of smoke from the rear of each gunship signified the release of the rockets. They appeared to drop away from the helicopter slightly before being propelled forward in a fishtail motion, leaving a wispy smoke trail as they went, to finally impact into the enemy area.

The detonation of the high explosive rockets was followed immediately by a loud, deep, four second roar from the onboard miniguns in each helicopter. They spewed their 7.62mm death over the enemy at the rate of one hundred rounds per second from each minigun.

The Gunslingers broke left and right, gaining altitude as they did so. The left-hand attack aircraft came around in a tight, banking turn shortly after passing the patrol and Ashton experienced an instant adrenalin surge as he saw green lights drift beneath the chopper as it banked just over a hundred metres beyond the LZ.

Ashton calculated, from the trajectory of the green tracer, that the enemy gunner was somewhere near the opposite corner of the pad. The noise subsided quickly and Ashton fired a 40mm HE projectile into the opposite corner of the clearing and reloaded with a white smoke cartridge, ready for the next pass.

'Get another smoke ready, Jimmy,' Ashton said as the radio crackled again.

'Six-Six, this is Albatross Zero-One,' the calm voice said, 'how is your situation on the ground now?'

'The enemy appear to have stopped firing at us,' Ashton replied without formalities, 'but the gunnie that broke left after the last pass was fired on as he banked. My problem at the moment is that my wounded man has lost consciousness.' He looked down quickly to confirm, expecting to see Wilkins still unconscious. Instead, he found himself staring into the grimacing face of his scout, who stared back in disbelief that his commander had misled the lead aircraft pilot.

'Roger Six-Six,' the pilot replied, 'how do you read the situation?'

'I don't like it,' Ashton replied truthfully. 'I think these blokes down here are getting set up for something. I think we've got some captured documents from the ambush this morning that they want pretty bad.'

'Roger, Six-Six,' Green came back, 'we'll go with another gunship pass and see if we can get Zero-Two in close behind it.' There was a pause. 'Stand by to mark your position.'

'Six-Six,' Ashton said absently into the microphone. He was becoming uneasy about the way the enemy were reacting or, more precisely, how they were not reacting. They had ceased fire on the patrol position since the smoke and gas were fired into them and had shot at just the one gunship they could see as it broke left. The sergeant was beginning to feel more comfortable with the idea of bolting for the LZ a kilometre to the east, using the Gunslinger gunship team to shepherd the move. He raised the small radio to his face to offer the suggestion when a crackling rush of noise burst from the receiver.

'Six-Six, throw smoke now,' the lead pilot said.

'Roger,' Ashton replied, instantly caught up in the excitement of it all. 'Jimmy,' he yelled to Collier without explanation. Collier heard the pilot's request and threw the second yellow smoke grenade into the same general vicinity as the first. At the same time Ashton raised the launcher to his shoulder and fired the white smoke cartridge into the area between where he had landed the first cartridge and where he believed the enemy anti–air gunner to be.

'Gunships inbound,' was all Ashton heard from the radio to signify the coming of the second pass.

Ashton watched as the Gunslingers came in again from the west, two abreast. They were at a hundred feet or a little higher, he judged. From four or five hundred metres out, each crew released a pair of rockets within a heartbeat of the other. There was a full second's pause and another two rockets were fired; a further second later two more rockets sped toward the enemy on the ground. The 'rrrrrrrrrr' of the minigun fire was longer on this pass and designed to cover more of the occupied area.

The attack aircraft again banked left and right. Ashton held his breath as the left-hand aircraft climbed steadily, followed by five or six floating green lights. The lights passed above and below the forward tailboom area and he thought it must have been hit. The aircraft had climbed to almost two hundred feet above the trees when there was a hissing, whistling noise and the gunship appeared to lose power.

All in view of the action watched as a wisp of smoke emerged from the gunship and the pilot fought for power against a failing engine. The aircraft moved off sluggishly toward the east. The hissing and whistling persisted until the aircraft was lost to sight beyond the canopy of trees in that direction.

'Got him!' Bluey Erickson cried, raising and firing his borrowed launcher. The gold-coloured HE round impacted on the other side of the clearing. 'That's where the prick is!' Ashton realised that Erickson must be talking about the enemy gunner and raised his 148 to fire also, but it didn't discharge. He squeezed the locking latch, forced the small handgrip down and slid the tube forward. A spent white smoke cartridge fell out.

There was no time for embarrassment, but Ashton hid whatever he felt by sliding a HE projectile into the chamber and firing into the area that Erickson had engaged. He'd reloaded the weapon with another gold-coloured projectile when the radio began to crackle again.

'Six-Six,' Kevin Green opened, with less calm in his voice. 'We're holding Zero-Two until a Bushranger team arrives. We have a stand-by patrol on board Zero-Four,' he continued. 'Do you require assistance on the ground?'

'Negative,' Ashton replied with a dry laugh. 'I think this position will be untenable very soon. Can we have the gunship that's left suppress the area while we make a dash for the LZ to the east?'

'Not at this time. Gunslinger Two-Four is no longer supporting this task. He's left the area for the LZ to the east where Gunslinger Two-Three finally went down.'

'Roger.' It made sense that the second gunship pilot would want to provide protection for his mate until assistance arrived. 'Gunslinger Two-Three went down at the pad to the east of here, is that correct?' Ashton added, a plan of sorts developing in his mind.

'That's affirmative.'

Ashton came back immediately: 'Can you put the stand-by patrol into that pad? That way they can secure the Yank gunnie and provide support for us when we arrive.'

'I'll clear that through Envoy,' the pilot said.

As far as the lead pilot was concerned it seemed the best plan. There was no way they were able to get the stand-by in to support Patrol Six-Six and its commander knew it. The second stand-by patrol could join Bravo Nine Sierra Four-Five at the downed Gunslinger's location and the Bushrangers could cover Patrol Six-Six in its break for the eastern LZ. He asked his co-pilot to secure the necessary clearance to deploy the stand-by patrols to protect the downed aircraft.

Ashton put the radio down his shirt and turned back toward the clearing, searching the treeline opposite for any movement. He couldn't remember when he'd been so afraid for his life. They *had* to break away from this place or they would die here. The log they were sheltering behind was a godsend. It was in a perfect position to protect them from the enemy's small arms fire from across the clearing. It was also large enough for all the patrol to fit behind and still be within speaking distance now that the need for whispering was gone. Without the log, they would have either been dead or been forced to leave the area before the gunships arrived.

'We'll move from here as soon as our own gunships turn up,' Ashton advised his patrol members. 'Be prepared to move east as fast as we can when the first rockets hit the treeline over there.' He paused a while and gathered his thoughts.

'You got any 40 millimetre gas, Bluey?'

'No mate,' Erickson replied, 'I only got HE off Gary.'

'I've got two CS and two smoke,' Dobel offered, 'and a couple of canister.'

'Give them here,' Ashton ordered. 'That'll give me three CS and four smoke and seven HE left,' he tallied quickly. 'I hope those stand-by pricks have brought some more ammo.'

As he spoke, the sudden rushing noise of incoming rocket-propelled grenades took them by surprise. One detonated harmlessly between them and the nearest bamboo clumps, the second burst in the trees on the edge of the clearing directly in front of them. They ducked instinctively and Ashton felt a burning numbness in his left side just below the waist line. He knew he'd been hit by shrapnel.

'I'm hit, Jimmy.' Ashton's voice was strangely casual. He remembered the radio in his shirt as he grabbed at his side with his left hand. He slid his right hand inside his shirt and withdrew the PRC 68. There was no longer a carrier wave, the radio was dead. He examined it carefully and found that shrapnel had sliced a good way through the radio before ricocheting from the unit into his side.

'We'd better swap radios, Gary. This one must be yours'—he gave a cracked smile—'it's fucked.'

The automatic weapons across the creek began firing again as Collier reached Ashton to render medical assistance. None of the angry 'cracks' were close enough to the patrol to cause much grief. Two more RPG rounds burst in the trees near them, the grenadier who put the first grenade almost into the bamboo had improved, his tree burst was a lot closer. Collier undid Ashton's shirt and pulled it and his undershirt out in order to look at the wound.

'It's fuck-all,' was Collier's verdict as he pulled one of the shell dressings he was keeping for Wilkins from inside his shirt. 'My mate's dog got a worse cut than this when he jumped the barbed wire fence.' The shrapnel had sliced clean through the fleshy area above the hip bone and torn a large hole in the lower back area of Ashton's shirt. He had been saved from serious injury by the radio. Surprisingly, the bleeding was not bad.

The bursts of fire coming from beyond the LZ became more sporadic but no more effective. Another B41 rocket from an RPG launcher burst in the trees off to their right without troubling them. The second one in the salvo got through the trees and hit the dead LZ marker tree right in the middle, completely shattering the trunk and sending it crashing down behind the patrol.

Ashton began to smile in delight that the NVA had inadvertently made additional cover for the patrol, when Collier squirted half a bottle of iodine directly on to his wound. He writhed in agony as the iodine contacted the open wound, giving him more pain than the shrapnel had. The medic bound it quickly with the large wound dressing and ragged him for being a bloody sook.

Ashton extended the aerial of Dobel's radio and turned it on. The channel opened with the familiar rush of helicopter noise.

'Bravo Nine Sierra Six-Six, this is Bushranger Seven-One.' The classic Australian voice brought instant hope to the men huddled behind the log. 'What's occurring? . . . Over.'

20

Rowan Ashton recognised the friendly voice of Squadron Leader Brian Gilmore. He and Gilmore had forged a firm friendship through a series of events that spanned two tours of South Vietnam. Gilmore was a junior Squadron Leader who flew the troop carrying slicks with No 9 Squadron when Ashton was a private on his first tour in Vietnam. He and Gilmore shared many an experience in the bars at Vung Tau as well as during the insertion and extraction periods of the patrol cycle.

On a number of occasions, Gilmore had sneaked Ashton into the RAAF Vung Tau officers' mess and, on all but one occasion, he was discovered and evicted by the alert President of the Mess Committee. There was no castigation for Ashton over any of those incidents and if any reprimand ever befell Gilmore, he never mentioned it.

Gilmore was now a senior Squadron Leader and Flight Commander of Australia's own 'Bushranger' gunship teams. They had not 'done the town' in Vung Tau during this tour, but preferred to share each other's company in the quiet and friendly atmosphere of either the 'Peter Badcoe' all ranks services club on the Vung Tau base or in the officers' and sergeants' mess on Ashton's SAS hill.

'Bushranger Seven-One,' Ashton said clearly into the microphone. 'This is call sign Six-Six, I have the potential for a major disaster down here. And I need suppressive fire for a long period while I bolt for the east.'

'Roger that,' Gilmore replied. 'You have a heavy fire team in support today. Stand by to mark your position while I line up my birds.'

'Roger that. Standing by.'

Ashton slipped the radio into the front of his shirt, freed a smoke grenade from his belt and threw it to Collier. He opened his launcher carefully and caught the gold-coloured HE projectile and replaced it with a smoke cartridge.

Erickson raised himself up behind the log to gain easier access to the smoke grenade on his belt when several rounds from a long burst of automatic fire from across the clearing struck the log in front of him. One of the bullets tore large hardwood splinters from the log and sent them flying in all directions. Several of the flying splinters embedded in Erickson's left cheek and neck. He spun sideways and slipped backwards, flopping down heavily behind the protection of the log, the largest of the splinters protruding from his cheek.

Dobel was shocked, he thought the signaller was seriously wounded. Collier also saw Erickson flop behind the log and immediately went to his aid. The largest splinter, several inches long, had embedded itself under the skin and along the jaw line in the fleshy part of Erickson's cheek. The sharp, jagged, pointed end was protruding a full inch from where it had entered.

Erickson wore a stunned expression. Collier reached him quickly, grasped the longest stem of the splinter on the entry side of the wound and pulled fast and hard. The splinter came out without resistance but not without pain. The jolt brought Erickson out of his shock.

'What happened?' He asked Collier, still a little dazed.

'You got some splinters in your face,' Collier replied quickly, 'nothing to whinge about.' Erickson nodded and wiped the side of his face with his hand. There was blood—a lot of blood—but there was no time to worry about it.

'Call sign Six-Six.' Ashton heard the muffled voice of Brian Gilmore coming from inside his shirt. 'Throw smoke now.'

'OK Jimmy,' Ashton yelled, not bothering to answer the radio, 'get ready to throw your smoke.' He raised the 148 to his shoulder, sent a smoke cartridge across the clearing and quickly fished the radio from inside his shirt.

'Bushranger, this is Six-Six. The first colour smoke you'll see will mark the enemy.'

'Roger, Six-Six,' Gilmore's voice eventually came through the receiver after a long pause. The smoke began to billow across the clearing. 'I see white smoke.'

'That's affirmative.' Ashton confirmed.

'Roger Six-Six, mark your position and get ready to bolt.' He advised. 'We're rolling on the target in one-five seconds.'

'Throw that smoke, Jimmy,' Ashton ordered. 'And get ready to leave.' He looked at Dobel and gestured in Wilkins' direction. 'We've got fifteen seconds.'

Ashton watched the gunships approach from the west at maximum attack height and speed. They appeared to be in a loose, staggered, line-astern formation several hundred metres apart. The lead and rear helicopters were set on one course and the middle one slightly out of the line and to the right and as they approached. Ashton's fear soared momentarily when he saw several green lights float in between and below the lead and second gunships.

The sound of automatic firing coming from the west told Ashton that the NVA had set up a machine gun several hundred metres beyond the bamboo clumps. Another three green lights appeared between the second and third gunships until, suddenly, he realised that the lead gunship had fired his first two rockets. It was time to go.

'OK!' Ashton yelled a cautionary command. 'Let's get the fuck out of here.'

Sergeant Willis led his stand-by patrol off their helicopter, which had just settled alongside the twisted wreckage of the American gunship at the landing zone to the east of Ashhton's group. The remaining member of the American light fire team cruised over-head, checking the jungle continually for signs of approaching enemy.

Bevan Willis urged Roy Kent toward the rear of the crashed gunship, beckoning him to go behind it and into the jungle beyond. The gunship was crumpled badly and the left skid was torn off. It seemed there would not have been much damage at all if it hadn't hit the stand-alone tree that grew just eight metres from the main treeline. There was a heavy smell of JP4 aviation fuel in the area and he wondered why the whole thing hadn't blown up on impact.

The gunship had come in low across the trees and, suddenly confronted by a cleared area, the pilot had made a snap decision to make an emergency landing. With little clearway, he flew his helicopter solidly on to the LZ in a running landing just metres from the treeline. The gunship hit the ground hard, bounced, and struck the tree almost a metre above the ground, snapping it completely. The aircraft then tipped slightly toward the left before settling on the ground with the left-hand pilot compartment crushed against the stump.

'Hey, man!' The nasal drawl of the right hand crewman startled the patrol. 'Help us, would ya?'

'Into the trees just to the rear of the tail, Roy,' Willis ordered his scout. 'Keg,' he called quietly to his 2IC, and indicated he should take up a position in the trees forward of the aircraft's cabin.

With security addressed as best he could, Willis and his medic approached the aircraft with less regard for the possible presence of enemy. It was most likely that any enemy in the area were involved in the contact to the west and, even if they weren't, Willis knew he didn't have enough manpower to secure the area properly.

The helicopter noise to the west had increased a good deal and, above the sound of the gunships in support of Ashton, Snowy Jacobs heard the noise of a helicopter on short final approach to their clearing. 'Another chopper coming in, Bevan,' he called across to his patrol commander as he made his way to the right-hand pilot's door. 'Could be Smithfield's mob.'

I hope so, thought Willis, as they reached the twisted wreckage, we could do with a bit more security here.

Jacobs pulled down on the door handle and wrenched the door open. He noted that the pilot on this side was still strapped in. He raised himself on to his toes, craned his neck, and found himself looking down the bore of a .45 calibre service pistol.

'You should put that away, mate,' Jacobs said drily, after a startled jerk, 'you could kill someone really good-looking.'

'Aussies!' The pilot's drawl was accompanied by a painful grimace that was meant to pass as a smile, but he relaxed the grip on the .45. Jacobs looked past him at the other pilot. The wreckage looked much worse from the inside of the helicopter. The front was crumpled but the left side had absorbed the brunt of the impact and was reduced to less than one-third of its normal size.

'I think my buddy's dead, man,' the pilot said, 'he hasn't moved since we went in.' He wriggled painfully in the seat. 'My legs are stuck in here.' Jacobs agreed with both points as he unplugged the intercom jack and removed the American's helmet.

The helicopter with Smithfield's stand-by patrol on board was just landing. Jacobs stepped back from the wrecked gunship, unhooked the AN/PRC 25 radio handset from his harness and waited until the helicopter was airborne and moving away before he activated the talk switch.

'Albatross aircraft just departing downed gunship,' he opened the transmission. 'This is Bravo Nine Sierra Four-Five. We've got wounded people down here and we'll need Dustoff as soon as possible.'

'This is Albatross Zero-Five,' a voice replied. 'Roger, we'll check that for you.'

'Bravo Nine Sierra Four-Five?' The American drawl came through Jacobs' earpiece. 'Is that your call sign, buddy?'

'Roger that.'

'This is Gunslinger Two-Four,' the voice said. 'I've got Dustoff and a couple of gun teams inbound for this area from Blackhorse right now.' There was a brief pause. 'I expect them any time in the next quarter hour.'

'Roger . . . Out.' Jacobs terminated the transmission. There was no need to concern himself further with Dustoff requirements. He turned to look for Bevan Willis and saw him with Smithfield near the tail of the helicopter. Their discussion broke up quickly and Smithfield beckoned his patrol to him and briefed them. Meanwhile, there was a lot of interesting chatter on Jacobs' radio. Albatross Zero-One was talking to Ashton about his break from the LZ but he could only hear the Albatross side of the conversation.

Kevin Simmons, Smithfield's scout, headed toward Keg Baker's position and Bill Donovan hefted his M60 and moved toward Roy Kent. Jack Gardiner and Joe Crooks headed straight for Jacobs near the cabin of the helicopter.

'Anyone alive in there?' Gardiner asked the question as though he didn't expect a positive answer.

'You bet there's someone alive in there!' The American drawl nudged Gardiner's medical instincts and he stepped past Jacobs to the open door of the helicopter.

'Where does it hurt most?'

'My legs, goddamn it. I already told your goddamn buddy.'

'His legs are jammed in,' Jacobs said. 'We'll need something to get him out.'

Gardiner looked across at the other pilot. He shuddered when he saw the crushed body and he knew instantly that the man was dead.

The crewman in the right-hand rear compartment had been removed by Smithfield and Grenville and laid out on the ground beside the aircraft. He had a number of broken ribs, a broken left arm and severe concussion.

The crewman from the left side of the helicopter was dead. It appeared that he had been thrown forward and out of the aircraft when it struck the ground. The strap of the monkey belt he was wearing had restrained him from being thrown completely clear and he'd been crushed to death when the chopper slid sideways, pinning him beneath the airframe.

'Swindler!' Smithfield hailed his signaller and motioned toward the pinned body. 'We need a long pole or two to get this bloke out.'

Smithfield and Crooks went off toward the treeline for poles while Grenville worked on the other crewman's injuries. Gardiner and Jacobs prized the surviving pilot from his seat with a strong, short stick. He was in remarkably good shape—minor cuts and bruises mostly, and a badly damaged left knee. Wounds were dressed and painkillers administered by the medics and by the time Smithfield and Crooks returned both men were resting easy.

'They're about to winch Ashton's wounded man out,' Jacobs advised Willis. 'Don't know from where.'

'Give a hand here,' Smithfield ordered everyone within earshot. 'Let's see if we can lift this thing up high enough to get these blokes out.'

Smithfield slid the two poles under the aircraft and, with two men on each pole, they lifted the airframe sufficiently for Gardiner to pull the dead crewman free. He was a terrible mess that no one wanted anything more to do with, so they left him beside the chopper, still in his monkey belt, for the Dustoff crew to recover. There was no hope of them trying to get the dead pilot out—it was obvious that jacks, pulleys and large metal cutters would be required to remove that body.

When the medics had done what they could for the living, Willis ordered them out to the treeline nearest the aircraft, while the two commanders and their signallers remained near the injured aircrew to await the arrival of the Dustoff team from Blackhorse. They listened to the chatter that indicated that Ashton's wounded man was being winched to safety until it concluded and the helicopter headed back to Nui Dat.

That left each man alone with his thoughts, some wondering what was happening with Ashton, wondering if the enemy would continue to pursue him all the way to this LZ—hoping, if so, that the LZ would be clear of all friendly forces before the NVA arrived. Jacobs spent a lot of time wondering how Dustoff were going to get the body of the dead pilot out of the helicopter. He'd heard they used high pressure fire hoses at Long Binh to remove bodies from badly damaged aircraft.

'Call sign Four-Five.' The American drawl came through both radio sets. 'The clearance team will be on station shortly and I'll be heading back to my house.' There was a pause. 'How many of my buddies down there made it?'

'Roger, Gunslinger,' Jacobs answered. 'Two of your mates will be OK, but the left-hand pilot and crewman didn't make it . . . Sorry.'

'Hell, man, that's downright disappointin'. But that's war for ya.'

'That's right,' Jacobs said, subdued. 'Thanks for hanging around.'

'You're welcome! Thank you guys for goin' down there and lookin' after my buddies.'

The transmission finished and the brief silence was broken by the sound of a large flight of helicopters. The patrols identified the markings as American as the gunship teams flew in crisscross patterns along and around the LZ.

Then two helicopters came in low over the trees and settled on the pad. One had the Red Cross markings of the Dustoff team. Both helicopters landed but the rotors continued to turn slowly. Three men from the Dustoff chopper headed for Willis and his group, and the four green-clad men who alighted from the second aircraft headed directly for the damaged gunship.

After a brief explanation by Smithfield, a captain who looked and behaved like a doctor ordered the group away from the gunship. The doctor quickly examined the surviving pilot and crewman before going to the other side of the gunship to check what was there. While he did this, one of the doctor's party headed back to the Dustoff chopper and returned with another man, two stretchers and a bundle of something that no one in Willis' group could identify.

As the patrol groups watched, one of the medics unclipped the monkey belt's strap from its ring on the floor, and with the assistance of another man unceremoniously manoeuvred the dead crewman's body into a large green bag and zipped it up. They loaded the bag on one of the stretchers, carried it to the Dustoff helicopter and tipped it on to the floor. The survivors were then stretchered to the waiting chopper, which immediately increased power and lifted out of the pad, heading east. It banked steeply into a 180 degree turn as it gained height and finally straightened on a westerly heading before disappearing from view.

While all this was going on, the group from the second helicopter laid long slings on the ground in front of the damaged gunship. There was a huge noise as the largest of helicopters, the Sikorsky Sky Crane, moved slowly across the LZ like a giant grasshopper until it hovered above the gunship and lowered a large hook.

One of the ground crew secured the hook to the upper portion of the gunship and the powerful 'Grasshopper' lifted the gunship a few metres forward and lowered it on to the slings. Another crewman drew the slings around the gunship and secured them to the hook. The 'Grasshopper' powered directly up and out of the LZ, inching slowly forward as it did until it gained sufficient height to turn toward the west. It finally disappeared from view, taking with it the underslung load of the gunship with the crushed pilot still in the left front seat.

The recovery ground crew quickly returned to their aircraft and the SAS patrols watched as the pilot increased power, eased up on the collective pitch and the helicopter lifted out of the pad, banked to the left and disappeared toward the west. The whole operation seemed to take less than ten minutes.

As the noise of the rotors slowly subsided, an eerie stillness descended over the immediate area. The scenario played out in front of the Australians had been completed with almost mystic grace and it left them with a sense of disbelief. The silence lasted for several minutes before the spell broke and the local jungle creatures discovered the courage to resume their activities as nature intended.

For the SAS stand-by patrols left on the ground, the uncertain fate of Ashton's patrol was now inextricably linked to their own.

21

Squadron Leader Brian Gilmore lined Bushranger Seven-One up on the white smoke he'd called for from Ashton. It was billowing just inside the treeline several hundred metres distant. He sighted a little short of the smoke and fired one rocket from the pod of seven on either side of the Huey gunship. Immediately, he adjusted for aim and fired another rocket from each side at the point of origin of the smoke.

He watched the rockets fishtail away from the Huey to detonate among the trees in the general vicinity of his aim point. The rockets were seldom accurate against a pinpoint target and to achieve a degree of accuracy from a vibrating helicopter platform was very difficult. The best that could be expected was to keep the enemy's head down and spray a little shrapnel about. Subconsciously, Gilmore noted several green lights float across in front of and below his gunship as he lined up for the minigun run on the enemy position.

'Incoming fire from the north,' he automatically alerted all Bushranger call signs as he aimed through the sighting system and released a four second stream of 7.62mm death from the rapid-firing weapons on either side of the gunship.

'Sighted,' Aircraftsman Clive Grant yelled into the intercom and fired a long burst from the twin M60s mounted in his crewman's compartment. He watched the red tracer rounds strike the ground near where the enemy fire had come from. He tried to 'walk' the fire from his guns on to the area but the chopper's airspeed quickly put the target out of his gun's left arc of fire and he knew that he'd missed.

'Mark it,' Gilmore ordered. He pushed gently on the pedals and manipulated the cyclic and collective controls to break right across the treetops and, staying low, continued to manipulate the controls through a 180 degree turn until he levelled the gunship out facing west and headed for the roll-in point for the second pass.

'Near the clearing at the north-west corner of the LZ, Greg,' Grant yelled excitedly as he tried to direct Corporal Greg Horton's attention to the target area.

'Not sighted,' the senior crewman on the right-hand side of the Huey responded. Soon they came level with Bushranger Seven-Five, the last gunship in the attack formation, as he released the first of his rockets. The enemy position was shielded from Horton's view by the treetops on the southern edge of the LZ and all the senior crewman could see was the tracer from the left-hand door guns of Bushranger Seven-Five, as the crewman aboard engaged the area across the LZ.

'Seven-Three,' Gilmore's voice crackled across the airwaves, 'we need to straddle the pad next pass.' Bushranger Seven-Three had already completed his pass and broken right when Gilmore's directive reached him.

'Roger, Seven-One,' Flying Officer Rick Devlin said. He brought Bushranger Seven-Three around in a tight, right-hand turn to form up inside Bushranger Seven-One, who made a slower, more sweeping turn at the top of the attack run to line up on the area where the enemy ground fire had come from.

'Seven-Five,' Gilmore directed the trailing gunship, 'Seven-Three and Seven-One will straddle the LZ line abreast for this pass while I look for the machine-gunner down there.' He paused. 'You line up on the same attack run this time.'

'Roger, Seven-One,' Flying Officer Mick Whatling replied as he executed a tight, right-hand turn to come into line several hundred metres astern of Bushranger Seven-Three.

The two leading gunships set themselves for their second attack on the enemy. The smoke that Ashton's patrol had provided on the enemy's position had long since expired but the target area was fixed in their minds now and the active effect of billowing smoke was no longer required.

'Stand by to release rockets.' Gilmore gave the cautionary command as he sighted into the area north of the LZ and west of the creek. Devlin focused Bushranger Seven-Three's sight at the area of the main enemy concentration and waited.

'Release!' Gilmore's order was followed almost immediately by the puffs of smoke that signified the release of his rockets. Devlin waited until he was almost abreast of the enemy air gunner's position before he released the first pair of rockets in his second pass. There was no return fire from the enemy machine gun to the north of the LZ.

Gilmore's rocket and minigun attack, or possibly the engagement of the area by the door gunners on the first pass, had silenced the threat. Nick Devlin pressed the attack by Bushranger Seven-Three past the south-east corner of the clearing and broke right at the same time that Gilmore broke left toward the north. Within seconds of the break, the first 2.75 inch rockets from Bushranger Seven-Five's second pass struck the enemy's position.

'One more for lucky,' Gilmore instructed his team, using Vietnamese bar talk to ease the tension. 'Same formation as the first pass.'

'Seven-Three,' Devlin responded.

'Seven-Five,' Whatling's voice said.

Gilmore flew Bushranger Seven-One very low and fast over the area to the north of the LZ to get into position to lead the third pass. He was wary as it was from this area that the Kiowa Recce helicopter carrying Colin Deane had been engaged and hit by the enemy heavy machine gun earlier in the day.

The three helicopter gunships lined up on the target area in the same 'staggered line-astern' formation they had employed on the first pass. Gilmore looked through the sighting system and noted an explosion in the treetops where Ashton's patrol had been earlier. He smiled thinly as he realised the plan was working so far. The NVA were still bombarding Ashton's old position and he hoped the Bushranger activity had given Ashton a clean break from the enemy and a good headstart toward the LZ to the east.

With the third rocket and minigun pass completed, the Bushrangers had expended almost half their ammunition payload and Gilmore decided to break off the attack to conserve ammunition for the extraction he hoped would occur soon. He gave a silent prayer that Ashton made good time to the eastern LZ. A shortage of ammunition was not likely to become a factor in the extraction. A shortage of fuel, though, would be another matter.

By the time the first rockets from Bushranger Seven-One impacted in the trees above the NVA position, Gary Dobel had the wounded Wilkins on his back and was ready to head east. Ashton fired a 40mm HE projectile into the south-east corner of the LZ.

'Come on,' he ordered hoarsely, as he led the laden Dobel quickly away, reloading his launcher as he went. Erickson was next to leave. He also fired a HE projectile from his launcher into the area across the clearing where the enemy were under fire from the gunships. Collier followed closely, checking the area across the clearing continually for any sign that the enemy had noticed their departure.

Ashton set a pace that Dobel found difficult to maintain. The sergeant was feeling good about the extent of their break from the enemy. The going was easy through the sparse secondary growth and the patrol had travelled almost three hundred and fifty metres when they encountered an area of extensive bomb damage. The wall of twisted logs and debris in front of them sent morale plummeting; it was a setback they didn't need. They had been almost running before reaching this point and now Ashton's elation turned to frustration.

They encountered the fringe of an old bunker system shortly after entering the bombed area. The system had obviously been the target for the general purpose bombs that caused the destruction. Ashton tried to maintain as fast a pace as possible but the difficult passage through the fallen tree obstacles was becoming too much for Dobel. Although the 2IC did his best to maintain the pace and still protect Wilkins, the continual battering and snagging by the deadfall was causing the wounded man great discomfort.

They travelled almost a hundred metres through the damaged area. Ashton finally halted the patrol on the edge of a large bomb crater. He was conscious of the time constraints of the helicopters holding somewhere to the south and awaiting his arrival at the new LZ location. He was also conscious that the patrol was in fearful flight and any pretence of security was lost from the moment they'd entered the damaged area. To continue in this way was neither sensible or sustainable.

He quickly went to the assistance of Dobel and between them they carefully lay Wilkins on the ground. Ashton checked the condition of his scout and was distressed to find him in great pain The wound in his shoulder had opened from the buffeting and was bleeding again. He motioned to Dobel to relieve Collier as rear protection and beckoned to Collier. Erickson went forward as an automatic action and took up a defensive posture just beyond the lip of the crater.

'Get some more painkillers into him, Jimmy,' Ashton ordered the medic, 'and see what you can do with the bleeding.'

'He's lost a lot of blood from the shoulder, Rowan,' Collier said as he made a quick but detailed inspection of Wilkins.

'I know,' Ashton responded, reaching inside his shirt for the PRC 68 set. 'I'm going to try to get him winched out.'

'You can't do that, Rowan,' Collier pleaded, 'the horse collar under the arm will kill him.'

'I realise that.' Ashton raised the aerial and turned on the small ground/air radio. 'I'm hoping we can tie him to a jungle penetrator.'

Collier didn't answer. That should work, he thought, if I dope him up enough. The jungle penetrator was like a folding anchor with four prongs or arms that were fluked at the ends. It was designed to penetrate the jungle canopy where the standard 'horse collar' sling was not be able to. The flukes were just broad enough to sit on, uncomfortably, and Collier could visualise Wilkins secured to the penetrator, with a sling around his back to keep him upright.

'Albatross Zero-One,' Ashton said softly into the small microphone, 'this is Six-Six, do you read? . . . Over.'

'Zero-One.'

'We're on the edge of a bomb crater almost five hundred metres east of our old location.' Ashton spoke with more calm than he felt. 'I'd like to winch out my wounded man.' While he waited for a response he watched Collier attend to the scout.

'Roger, Six-Six,' Kevin Green acknowledged. 'Be aware that we only have forty minutes of loiter time remaining before we have to return to Nui Dat for fuel.'

'How long is that liable to be?'

'You'll be without top cover for approximately ninety minutes.'

'Roger that. We're in a large bombed-out area and the movement is causing my man a lot of grief. It will be better for everyone if we can get him out.'

'OK. We'll try and get you *all* out on the winch. You'll need to mark your position.'

'Roger . . . Wait.' Ashton felt heartened by the possibility of them all being picked up from the edge of the crater. 'You'll need a penetrator to get my man out—his wounds won't cope with the horse collar and he'll have to go up on his own. Stand by.' He paused as he looked around the position for the most likely member to release the smoke.

'Bluey,' he called quietly to Erickson, 'turf a smoke grenade into the crater.' He knew that Erickson had one No 83 smoke grenade left.

'Standing by to throw smoke,' Ashton said into the microphone. The moments ticked by as he waited, expectantly.

'Roger. Throw smoke now,' Green eventually said through the background noise of the rotors.

Erickson responded immediately he heard the pilot's order and threw the grenade into the dry crater. In a few seconds, red smoke began to billow up from the large hole in the ground.

'I see red smoke?' the lead pilot queried.

'Red smoke confirmed,' Ashton said as he began to shake the pack from his back.

'Roger. Zero-Five will be with you in one minute.'

Ashton acknowledged this. 'I'm going to send up the NVA document satchel with my wounded man. Can you drop it at Task Force on the way to the hospital at Vung Tau?'

'Right, we'll see what we can do.'

Ashton slipped the radio into his shirt without turning it off, removed the satchel from his shoulder and unclipped the side pocket of his pack. He rummaged deep into the pocket and withdrew a 6 metre roll of flat nylon tape and quickly tied an overhand knot in one end to form a 15 centimetre loop. The sound of helicopters became louder as Zero-Five positioned himself to effect the extraction, while the Bushranger gunships flew a racetrack pattern around the site to shepherd all those involved in the operation.

Albatross Zero-Five came in low and slow from the south-east into what little breeze there was. The jungle penetrator was already halfway to the ground as the Huey positioned itself above the edge of the crater and steadied to commence the winching operation. Ashton replaced his pack with some effort and moved to assist Collier with the weight of the almost unconscious scout.

The penetrator came down just over a metre from Ashton and Collier. Ashton moved toward it and allowed it to touch the ground to earth any static electricity that might have built up from its deployment. He quickly pulled down three of the prongs and moved back to help Collier get Wilkins seated.

It was a difficult task trying to get the scout on to the unweighted and unstable penetrator. Ashton had to signal the crewman to raise the penetrator slightly to make seating of Wilkins a little easier. They lifted him on to the prongs with Collier grasping the back of Wilkins' shirt on his badly damaged right side in order to ease any discomfort.

With the scout slumped on the penetrator and steadied by Collier, Ashton slipped the loop in the nylon tape over one of the prongs supporting his legs. He then passed the tape over both legs and under the second prong, pulled it firmly tight and tied it off with two half hitches. With that completed, he put the NVA satchel strap across Wilkins' good shoulder and tied the scout's upper torso to the penetrator's vertical column by wrapping the tape twice around both and lashing the area between the two with a clove hitch and an extra hitch for security. Then Ashton stood back and gave the thumbs-up signal to the crewman to start the winch recovery procedure.

As Wilkins began to rise through the air, Ashton and Collier heard the unmistakable sound of machine gun fire from above and to the south. A feeling of extreme vulnerability passed over them. Both men scrambled for the weapons they'd left near the edge of the crater, where Collier had treated Wilkins.

Ashton swooped on his weapon and scanned the immediate area in search of the source of the firing. He saw nothing. He then looked up in time to see Zero-Five start to gain height and move off toward the north-east. The tracer coming from the left-hand door gun told him that the crewman was engaging a target on the ground to the south of their position. The senior crewman's head was still protruding from the right-hand cargo doorway and the concern on his face was evident as he continued to winch up the semi-conscious Wilkins, who dangled on the penetrator several metres below the aircraft.

The noise from the departing Huey subsided and the vibrations inside Ashton's shirt alerted him that someone was speaking on the PRC 68. He withdrew the radio and listened.

'Six-Six, this is Zero-One.' It was Green's anxious voice. 'Do you read? . . . Over.' It was obvious he had been trying to contact the patrol for some time. Ashton quickly pressed the PTT button.

'Six-Six,' he said, a feeling of freedom suddenly coming over him. Without the burden of the wounded Wilkins they were a fully mobile unit again.

Green's voice returned. 'Bushranger Seven-Three has sighted enemy one hundred and fifty metres south of your location just outside the bomb-damaged area.'

'Roger that.' One hundred and fifty metres in this terrain was a very long way.

'I'm afraid winch extraction of the rest of you from your present location is no longer an option.'

'Roger,' Ashton said again, without disappointment. 'I'm happier now that my wounded bloke is out.' He paused briefly. 'Please confirm whether the LZ to the east has been secured.'

'That's affirmative. Two stand-by patrols are in place.'

'OK, we'll bolt for the LZ now and hope to get there before you blokes have to leave.'

The lead pilot's voice answered, 'You've got just over thirty minutes to be there and inboard before we have to return to Nui Dat. Good luck!'

'Six-Six, out.' Ashton switched off the radio and returned it to its pouch as he looked around at his men.

'Click-click.' Attracting their attention, the commander made several gestures to indicate they were to head for the LZ at the fastest pace possible and that Collier would scout the way. Each nodded and Ashton moved toward where Collier stood, waiting for the word to go. Ashton shook his head as he reached his newly appointed scout.

'Come on Jimmy,' he said with a half smile, 'what's the matter with you, for fuck's sake? Billy would have been halfway to the LZ by now.'

'There's a hell of a lot going on up there, sir,' Peter Hanson said to his commander as Colin Deane and Bill McCreadie walked into the crowded operations room. It was some time since Hanson had advised his Squadron Commander and the brigadier of the fate of the American gunship.

'Feel free to brief us, Peter,' Deane said, and motioned the Task Force Commander to the chair facing the operations map.

'Since we spoke earlier, sir,' Hanson started, 'Ashton has broken contact with the NVA and is heading east to the LZ—where the American gunship went down.'

Deane thought that a briefing like this at such an early stage of the brigadier's tour was of great benefit to the squadron. Particularly when it was given by someone as competent as Hanson.

'Both stand-by patrols have been inserted into that LZ,' Hanson continued, pointing to it on the map. 'The partner gunship stayed loitering in the vicinity to cover the patrols and the grounded aircrew. Then a recovery team from Blackhorse went in and removed the casualties and the wreckage.'

'Very good, Peter,' Deane acknowledged. 'What is Ashton's situation at the moment?'

'Zero-One relayed a request from Ashton. It was a very firm request to winch out his wounded patrol member and some documents or something in a satchel.'

'Document satchel?' The brigadier sat erect, his interest heightened.

'That's correct, sir. It seems that Ashton captured a bag or satchel full of documents and other items in the ambush this morning.'

'What other items?'

'Not known, sir, but Ashton believes the NVA are only pursuing him so persistently because of whatever it is.' The brigadier nodded.

'I authorised the winch operation on the basis that winching one man would be a fairly fast exercise,' Hanson went on quickly,

222

'and that assuming Ashton was right we should get the satchel to the Intelligence Staff as soon as possible.'

'Good!' the brigadier said emphatically.

'The wounded man,' Colin Deane looked sternly at Hanson as he spoke, 'has a severe wound to one of his shoulders. Wasn't a winching operation going to cause him severe trauma?'

'I don't know the answer to that, sir, but I was prepared to back Ashton's judgment.' Deane nodded. No doubt Ashton would have considered all the factors before making such a request.

'It seems a fair decision to me, Colin.' McCreadie's words cut across the major's thoughts, defending Hanson's stand. 'This Ashton appears to have his shit together.' Deane nodded his head.

'Sir!' A hand holding a page of message paper appeared through the pigeonhole between the operations room and the Comcen. Hanson stepped across the room and read the message carefully before looking up.

'It's from Zero-One, sir,' he said happily. 'Albatross Zero-Five has picked up Ashton's wounded bloke and the satchel and is inbound for the Task Force pad now.' He placed the sheet of paper on a nearby desk. 'Touch and go only—a request that Intelligence Staff meet the chopper.' The six men in the operations room smiled with relief. All knew it must have been a tricky task. Deane rose to his feet and looked at Hanson.

'Thank you, Peter,' he said with feeling, knowing that he might not have authorised the winching operation had he been consulted. 'You are right, of course, Ashton does have impeccable judgment.'

'Or luck, sir.'

'And that too,' Deane agreed as he turned to the brigadier. 'Will you be wanting to meet the helicopter, sir?'

'Thank you, yes,' McCreadie replied absently, his thoughts already focused on the satchel and its contents.

'I'll have the Ops driver take you,' Deane told his commander. The two men left the room.

'Your squadron has done good work so far today, Colin,' McCreadie said as they walked toward the vehicle.

'Thank you, sir,' Deane replied proudly. 'And so have the RAAF mob.'

'Yes they have, but we should save our congratulations until they're all back safe and sound.' McCreadie grasped Deane's hand warmly. 'Good luck for the rest of the day, and we'll see about that matter of air assets.'

'Major Deane!' Hanson's cry diverted their attention. 'Word has just come from Zero-One, sir,' he called out, hurrying toward them. He stopped at the end of the vehicle and looked uncomfortably at his superiors. Deane nodded to him to continue.

'The RAAF extraction agency is fuel-critical, sir, and if Ashton doesn't make the LZ in the next twenty minutes or so, all three patrols could be without any form of support for up to an hour and a half.'

22

When they finally broke free of the matted scrub leading away from the bomb crater, Ashton calculated that they had less than three hundred metres to the relative security provided by the stand-by patrols. He propped his men momentarily after emerging from the damaged area and took a full minute to check his map against the distance that Erickson had paced on the ground. It was also an opportunity for the patrol members to listen as best they could to the surrounding jungle through the constant, if faint, noise of the distant helicopters.

'Let me know when we've gone two hundred metres from here,' Ashton directed Erickson, before moving quietly to the side of his new scout.

'We've been coming a little north of our bearing, Jimmy,' he confided as they were about to move off, 'so we'll need to bend a little south of east to make sure we don't miss the LZ.'

'OK,' Collier said, checking his wrist compass to confirm the direction. 'I'll get going then.' Ashton nodded and followed immediately behind.

The patrol moved cautiously now because of the enemy sighted near the winch point. Jim Collier scouted well through the more open secondary jungle. Ashton was pleased that he looked so capable, as he knew in his heart that Wilkins would not take part in another patrol on this tour. If Collier proved his worth as a scout he would be the preferred choice to take over the role if he wanted it. Ashton believed scouting was a job that only one in ten could do really well and being comfortable with the task was the fundamental ingredient of success.

Bluey Erickson attracted Ashton's attention with a brief wave of his hand to signify that they had travelled the two hundred metres. Ashton halted the patrol and removed the PRC 68 from his belt. He calculated that it was a hundred metres to the LZ and he needed to alert both the stand-by patrols and the extraction agency of his proximity.

'Albatross Zero-One,' he spoke softly into the microphone, 'this is call sign Six-Six. I reckon we're one hundred metres from the LZ and estimate we'll be there in around five minutes.'

'This is Albatross Zero-One.' The relief in the lead pilot's voice was evident. 'Roger that, Six-Six. I'll start to position my slicks for your extraction.'

'Six-Six, out.' Ashton returned the set to its pouch. He turned toward Collier but was immobilised when he noticed his scout in a defensive crouch, facing back toward the west. The arm across his body at shoulder height with the thumb down told a story that Ashton preferred not to hear.

Fuck, no! Ashton thought as he turned to face the threat. The adrenalin began to pump through his body, his mouth became instantly dry and a knot of fear gripped him. He raised his weapon and eased the change lever to automatic as he tried to pinpoint the precise location of the enemy. He sensed that Erickson and Dobel had also gone into a defensive posture and was relieved that, as a patrol, they were as ready as could be to meet the threat.

It took several seconds for Ashton to see the enemy—over twenty metres away and emerging from the shadows. They were heading quickly toward the LZ in an oblique direction that would have them pass almost through the patrol. It was difficult to determine their number but it appeared to be at least a dozen. The patrol held their fire and waited, hoping the enemy would pass across their front without noticing them.

Ashton said a silent prayer of thanks that the timing had been so fortunate. A few minutes earlier and the enemy would have appeared while he was on the radio to the extraction agency. He made a swift appreciation of his options as he watched the enemy approach. They were definitely NVA, there was no doubt. In the leading group of six Ashton noted a PPSH and several AK47s, with an RPD carried by the third soldier in line.

Persistent little pricks, he thought. He allowed himself a brief smile as he recalled the sight of Billy Wilkins disappearing under Albatross Zero-Five with the satchel of documents and money hanging around his neck. The leading group was within ten metres and Ashton now realised the enemy would pass them completely by. This didn't lessen his concern as it would put the enemy between his men and the stand-by patrols at the LZ. There was no option but to initiate a contact and use the momentum of the contact drill to propel them toward the LZ in advance of the enemy. He aimed his combined weapon at the NVA soldier with the RPD and squeezed the trigger of the M16.

The first burst struck its target, the second burst raked the three soldiers following. Ashton fired the 40mm HE projectile from his XM148 into the following group. The rest of the patrol engaged the first group immediately after Ashton initiated the contact, raking the area with sustained automatic weapon fire.

The leading enemy did not return fire and Ashton had no time to assess the results of the encounter. He quickly emptied the remainder of his M16 magazine into the area where the following group had deployed to return fire at the patrol. As the bolt locked open on the empty magazine, Ashton pressed the magazine release catch, dropped the empty magazine on the ground, withdrew a full magazine from a front pouch and placed it on the weapon.

'Gary!' he screamed, as he hit the catch on the side of the weapon that released the bolt forward to pick up the top round in the new magazine and ram it into the chamber. 'Take Bluey and go.'

There was no answer from the rear of the patrol but the sound of both weapons unloading the remainder of the rounds from their magazines told Ashton that his order was being acted on. Ashton and Collier began to fire selective bursts of two or three rounds into the second group's area and Dobel released a 40mm HE projectile into the same area before quickly following Erickson away from the approaching enemy.

'Go!' Dobel ordered Ashton and Collier as he and Erickson engaged the enemy from their new position ten metres away.

Ashton and Collier raked the area with whatever ammunition was left in their magazines before they ran, reloading as they went, to a position more than ten metres beyond Dobel and Erickson. Ashton realised they were heading toward the north, away from the LZ, and that to continue to do so would cause a major problem in the not too distant future.

'Go, Gary!' he screamed again as he changed to semi-automatic and began selective engagement of the area with single, aimed shots. 'Head more east,' he shouted, taking a second to point. 'Behind us!'

Dobel and Erickson went past the spot where Ashton and Collier were covering the move before crossing over behind the commander and the scout to take up a position east of them. The enemy had fired very little, if at all, during the encounter. The aggressive savagery of the patrol's engagement, the speed of their withdrawal and the virtual annihilation of the forward group had stunned the enemy into inactivity. Ashton knew it could not last—the NVA were professional soldiers and professional soldiers were never long in deciding a course of action.

'Go, Rowan!' Dobel's words were drowned in the fire from his and Erickson's M16s.

Ashton and Collier withdrew past, then behind, the other two, and in doing so swung the direction of the withdrawal toward the south-east. Ashton calculated the contact drill had taken them fifty or sixty metres but he was not sure precisely where they were in relation to the LZ. He decided that his best option was to continue a little east of south-east and hope to hit the LZ before he was forced to search for it.

'Cease!' he ordered. Dobel and Erickson looked in his direction and Ashton beckoned them silently to join Collier and himself while the scout carefully scanned the area for enemy presence. As soon as Dobel and Erickson came up, he checked that everyone was OK—they were. With weapons reloaded, the patrol headed in the general direction of the LZ in what Ashton would later describe as a state of controlled panic.

At the LZ, Willis and Smithfield listened intently to the firefight as it developed and had little trouble following Ashton's progress from the direction of the voices and the gunfire. It was evident that the last call, 'Cease!,' was only forty or so metres from the corner of the LZ occupied by Willis and a little to the north-west. There was no way of determining the nature and result of the contact and the only option for the stand-by patrols was to wait and expect anything.

There was one positive aspect for those waiting. The initial outburst of firing and the subsequent movements of the patrol had given them a reasonable idea of where the enemy had been when contact was initiated. It was now simply a matter of time before either Ashton or the enemy showed up.

Bill Donovan joined a 100 round belt to the fifty rounds already on his weapon. He folded the belts neatly in concertina fashion close to the gun to reduce drag at the feed port. He then lay behind the M60 and watched the area to his front intently. He had read the signs and was convinced that any visit from the enemy would be from his front. He was patient and calm, with just a hint of excited anticipation running gently through his body like a small electric current.

Bevan Willis strained every one of his body's senses almost to breaking point trying to maintain a fix on the movement of Ashton's patrol from the noises to their front. He hoped Ashton would come up on the radio so they could get some idea of where the patrol was in case they were forced to engage the enemy. Willis was concerned for more than one reason. This could well be his first real contact in which command responsibility was vested in him.

Willis hoped Ashton would arrive before the enemy did. The commander on the ground was in overall command in situations where a stand-by patrol was deployed to support a patrol in trouble and the presence of Ashton would relieve him of that responsibility. He was aware of movement out to his right front and figured that it had to be Ashton's patrol. Whatever was making the noise was moving from west to east a short distance to the north of the clearing. He was about to alert Baker and Grenville when Jacobs' hoarse whisper caught his attention.

'Dobel!' Jacobs excitedly pointed in the direction that Willis had been looking.

'What?'

'Gary Dobel. Over there, twenty or so metres.' Jacobs pointed again. 'I'd know that dumb prick's walk in any jungle, anywhere.'

'Click-click.' Willis made the clicking of his tongue as loud as he could. The movement to the north ceased but there was no response. Willis was about to click his tongue again but held back as he remembered a whistling signal used by the patrol he and Ashton had belonged to on their previous tour. He pursed his lips and forced the whistling sound in the direction where the movement had been. There was a brief pause before the sound was imitated from the north.

The tension immediately ran out of Willis and he reproduced the sound to confirm its validity and his location. There was another brief pause before the return whistle reached him and movement again commenced from out toward the north. This time there was no doubt that the sounds were heading in their direction.

Within seconds, Jim Collier came into view. He recognised Keg Baker immediately and the broad grin on his face provided a window to his feelings. Ashton followed several paces behind. He was trying to advise Albatross Zero-One of their marry-up with the stand-by patrols but the PRC 68 wouldn't transmit. Finally, he was directed by Baker to where Willis was positioned. Ashton motioned to his patrol members to take up positions among Willis' men for the time being, while he assessed the situation.

'Bevan!' Ashton nodded a greeting as he approached. 'We've got a bunch of NVA on our arse. What's your disposition here?'

Willis quickly outlined the positions that his and Smithfield's patrols occupied on the corner of the LZ. He made a point of Bill Donovan's location with the M60 and advised Ashton that Keg Baker had their resupply of ammunition.

'What do you want us to do now, Rowan?' Willis gladly offered the overall command to Ashton, who looked carefully around the position before he spoke.

'You take two of my blokes, Dobel and Collier,' he said, assuming command easily. 'Have Dobel give all the SLR ammo to Collier and split the rest between the remaining three of us.' He paused. 'Bluey and I will join Smithfield's mob. I'll head over there now and let Albatross know we've arrived.' It was natural for Ashton to want to seek Smithfield's patrol location as both sergeants were from the same Troop.

Willis nodded and moved off to pass the word to Ashton's patrol and to detail the ammunition breakup. Ashton made his way toward Smithfield's patrol to use the radio that he knew Joe Crooks would have. He was abreast of Bill Donovan's position when the corner of his eye caught movement out to the front and a little to their left.

He carefully went to ground on the left side of Donovan, who did not even glance in his direction. Donovan had also noticed movement to the front and was concentrating hard on it. Ashton raised himself slightly and looked along the line of Smithfield's patrol. Everyone was watching the area to their front intently. It told him they had been attracted by the movement and were ready for what was about to happen. There could be no doubt in anyone's mind that the movement to the front was enemy.

'When you're ready, Bill,' Ashton quietly advised Smithfield's 2IC as he lay rock steady behind the machine gun. Donovan barely moved, his nod was so slight.

Ashton looked back at Willis' patrol and was happy to note that they too had sensed the presence of enemy and were concentrating on the area to the immediate west of the LZ. Donovan and Ashton watched as the movement materialised into human forms moving cautiously in a line across the front of the combined patrols. They were moving from the south-west toward the north-east, obviously sweeping the area without realising that their right flanking man was only twenty metres from the clearing.

Ashton found it incredible that the enemy had not detected the movement made by his patrol near the edge of the LZ. They were sweeping directly across the front; soon they would be in line with Donovan's M60. It was a situation machine-gunners dream about, a line of enemy in enfilade to their gun. Donovan waited for just the right moment, aimed the gun at the centre base in the middle of the line as he saw it, and squeezed and held the trigger.

A twenty round burst from the M60 swept along the line of enemy soldiers, tracer rounds indicated the grazing fire that Donovan achieved. No sooner had the M60 opened up than most of the rifles and 40mm launchers in the group joined the battle. With the long burst of twenty rounds expended, Donovan concentrated on firing short bursts of three to five rounds at selected targets until he had expended almost eighty rounds.

'Cease firing!' Ashton screamed to be heard above the din. He moved then, for time was short, and went directly to the position where he had seen Joe Crooks. The cries and groans from the area to the front indicated that a number of enemy had been wounded in the effective, if impromptu, ambush. There was only sporadic return fire from the enemy, most of which was ineffectively high, and when the patrols ceased fire at Ashton's command the enemy appeared to stop firing also.

'Nev,' Ashton said to Smithfield as he went by on the way to Crooks' position, 'have your blokes ready to work the extraction.' Smithfield nodded, pleased that Ashton had arrived. The weary and wounded commander reached Crooks and indicated that he was to follow him to the edge of the LZ. Crooks knew immediately what was required and he quickly adjusted the pack that held the radio, handed the handset to Ashton and followed him to the LZ.

'Better get your mirror out, Joey,' Ashton said as he lifted the handset to speak. 'I expect Zero-One will want to see something of us.

'Albatross Zero-One, this is Bravo Nine Sierra Six-Six,' he said slowly and softly into the mouthpiece, 'we're with call sign Four-Five now and have been in contact with an unknown size enemy force here at the LZ since our arrival.'

'Roger, Six-Six.' Kevin Green's normally calm voice showed a little excitement. 'I have two American gun teams standing by as well as Bushranger to assist with your extraction . . . Please show me some light and advise details of the enemy situation.'

'Roger. Wait out,' Ashton acknowledged. 'Mirror!' he called softly to Crooks. Within seconds Joe Crooks had his mirror trained on the helicopter out to the south.

'I have your mirror,' Green confirmed. 'Where are the enemy in relation to you?

'I'm not sure where the main enemy concentration is, but the last contact was with a group on the western side of the LZ thirty to fifty metres from our position.' Ashton paused for breath. 'They could be anywhere around the LZ by now and I suggest you give the whole area a workover if you have three gun teams.'

'What are your numbers on the ground?' The lead pilot queried, ignoring Ashton's advice on the employment of the Huey gunships.

'We're in two groups of seven at this time, and only three in each group has a pack.'

'Roger, Six-Six, we'll go with two slicks for the extraction—seven in each.' It was an easy ask for a Huey with very little fuel on board to pick up seven men.

Ashton scarcely cared about the choppers' load, but he did know that this was not a good place from which to extract the patrols. They needed to be further down the LZ so that the pilots could land the two Hueys, one behind the other, with enough room to get out of the pad safely.

'Zero-One,' Ashton said quickly, knowing that Bevan Willis would be monitoring the transmissions, 'I'm going to move call sign Four-Five further down the pad to the south. We're a little squashed into the corner here.' He signalled to Willis to take his group down past the position that Smithfield presently occupied.

'Roger, Six-Six,' Green replied, 'please complete the move quickly. The gunships will be in position shortly.'

Ashton closed the transmission and watched Willis' patrol with Dobel and Collier among them move swiftly down the side of the LZ as directed. Willis himself held a smoke grenade in his left hand ready to activate as soon as it was called for.

'Ten metres,' Ashton called to Willis as he went past. Willis nodded and smiled now that he understood why Ashton had decided to move his patrol.

Dobel broke away from the Willis patrol and moved to where Ashton and Crooks were crouching on the edge of the clearing. He removed a bandolier of 5.56mm ammunition in clip form and two bandoliers of 40mm HE projectiles from around his neck and handed them to his commander without a word.

'Thanks, Gary.' Ashton watched him disappear into the treeline with another two bandoliers of M16 ammunition, in search of Erickson. Ashton shook his head in wonder. Dobel really had come of age as a soldier in the past hours and there was now a serious chance that he would make a first class patrol 2IC.

Ashton was concerned that the enemy had not shown themselves since their sweep line had suffered badly at the hands of Donovan's M60 and the patrol's intense rifle fire. He knew that the sudden appearance of so much firepower would make any commander consider the value of pressing an attack further—particularly in view of the number of casualties his subunits had suffered already.

There must really be something important in that satchel, he thought, as he watched Willis move his seven man group into position near the edge of the clearing, with five of the seven members facing toward the area of likely threat.

'Zero-One,' Ashton said into the mouthpiece. 'Call sign Four-Five is in position now. No sign of the enemy since our initial contact here at the LZ.'

'Roger, Six-Six.' Green's voice reverberated through the hand-set. 'Stand by to throw smoke at both patrol locations.'

'Six-Six,' Ashton responded happily, hoping that this was the last act in what seemed a very long and tiring play.

23

'You guys from Blackhorse still with us?' Squadron Leader Kevin Green asked over the helicopter chatter frequency.

'Crossbow One-One . . . affirm.' The drawling American accent came through the headsets.

'Playboy Three-One . . .' another drawl followed. 'We're stoogin' around two clicks west of you.'

'We have a show about to start here,' Green advised the Americans. 'If you want a part, you'd better line up with Bushranger near the base of the May Tao.'

'Crossbow rollin' for May Tao now,' the Crossbow leader replied.

'Playboy will be with you ASAP,' the Playboy leader added.

'Crossbow, Playboy,' Green said, mindful that the Americans had been engaging targets to the north and north-west, 'what ordnance do you guys have left?'

'Crossbow has over half a complement of rockets, minigun and 40 mike mike,' the Crossbow leader offered. 'We got enough ordnance to light up that LZee like a goddamn Christmas tree.'

'We got seventy-five per cent ammo holdings,' the Playboy leader said, 'but this team don't carry no 40 mike mike.'

'Roger,' Green acknowledged, thinking of the Gunslinger team that had had two of its aircrew killed on this LZ. 'Bushranger only has enough time for two passes at the LZ at most. Would you guys like to lead the first pass?'

'Crossbow . . . that's affirmative,' the team leader responded enthusiastically. 'We got a score or two to settle with them gooks down there.'

The Playboy call sign did not answer but Kevin Green could see both American teams converging on the area where Brian Gilmore's Bushrangers were holding near the base of the May Tao. He worked the controls of Albatross Zero-One and turned south to be in the best position to control the attack formations.

Green manoeuvred his lead helicopter through a left-hand turn at 2000 feet a little to the south of Gilmore's Bushrangers and straightened up until he could see the extraction LZ in the distance, directly in front. The American gun teams were joining Gilmore as he did so. He briefly checked his instrument panel and was ready launch the first pass.

'Crossbow,' Green directed the American team leader, 'come to a heading of zero one zero degrees at 80 knots and I'll adjust as required.'

'Turning zero one zero,' the Crossbow leader obliged, 'and 80 knots.' Green watched the American light fire team turn toward the LZ at low speed.

'Playboy,' Green instructed the second team, 'turn zero one zero also and line up three hundred metres to the east of Crossbow.'

'Comin' round now,' the Playboy leader acknowledged.

'Bushranger,' Green said to Gilmore, 'you trail Crossbow on the first pass. I want you to spread your pass out so that we have continuous fire on the western side of the LZ for as long as possible and Crossbow has time to tack on to your last bird for his second pass.'

It was a simple plan as far as Kevin Green was concerned. He would put the Americans down either side of the clearing on the first pass to see where the enemy might bob up. Gilmore's Bushrangers would spread the attack to allow time for Crossbow and Playboy to line up for a second pass on the side of the LZ where the enemy were most likely to be. The slicks, Albatross Zero-Two and Albatross Zero-Three, would slip in and pick up the patrols while Bushranger made its second run with miniguns only.

'Crossbow,' Green directed 'you're two hundred metres too far west. Can you adjust, please?' The two American teams began to move accordingly.

'Two minutes to target,' Green advised all call signs. 'Calling for smoke now.' The lead pilot flicked the switch on his centre console, allowing him to transmit on the Fox Mike frequency.

'Bravo Nine Sierra Six-Six, this is Albatross Zero-One. Throw smoke now . . . Over.'

'Roger . . . Stand by,' Ashton responded.

Kevin Green watched the area intently for the smoke to appear. Within thirty seconds it began to billow from two places on the western side of the clearing. The breeze on the ground had died a little and the smoke went directly upward, allowing the gunships lower down near the ground a good indication of their target heading. The American gun teams had both assisted in the extraction of SAS patrols previously and adjusted their attack direction as soon as the smoke became visible.

'I see one red and one yellow smoke?' the lead pilot said.

'Confirm one red and one yellow,' Ashton replied.

'Roger, Six-Six, keep the smoke going until I indicate otherwise.' Green paused briefly to assess the time on target of the Crossbows. 'The gunships will be with you in one minute.'

'Six-Six.' There was a degree of relief in Ashton's voice as he acknowledged the advice.

Green quickly switched to the UHF chatter frequency as he checked the approach of the gunships. The Crossbow team were directly on heading with the billowing smoke to assist them but the Playboy gunships were too close to the Crossbow leader to strike the treeline on the eastern edge of the LZ.

'Turn right, Playboy,' Green directed the Playboy leader. 'You're fifty metres too close to Crossbow to hit the eastern treeline.' The two gunships rolled slightly right for several seconds and straightened. They had corrected to half the distance required.

'Same again, Playboy. That will bring you on to attack heading.' Again the Playboy gunship turned right for several seconds and straightened up.

'Perfect, Playboy, hold on attack heading.' Green looked through the lower chin window plexiglass beneath the tail rotor pedals to see Bushranger Seven-One following the Crossbow team toward the target area.

'Last call on the enemy,' Green told all call signs, 'is that the patrol had a contact less than five minutes ago at the north-western corner of the pad.' He paused to let that sink in. 'But there are no guarantees they won't bob up anywhere around the LZ. The safest break is probably still right after the pad . . . Copy?'

'Crossbow . . . copy.'

'Playboy . . . copy.'

'Copy that,' Gilmore also acknowledged, as the Bushrangers sped toward the target astern of the American team.

.'Crossbow,' Kevin Green opened his final transmission before the attack commenced, 'your target area is twenty to thirty metres from the smoke inside the western treeline.'

There was a long pause. 'Got that, Zero-One,' the Crossbow leader said. 'Going hot this instant.'

Green saw the puffs of smoke from the rear of the lead Crossbow and watched as the two rockets sped toward the trees. Almost immediately, two rockets sped from the second Crossbow gunship. Alternately, they fired two more rockets apiece before the puffs of discharge from the front of the lead Huey signified the firing of his 40mm high explosive ordnance at 120 rounds per minute.

The Playboy team were simultaneously engaging the eastern side of the LZ with 2.75 inch rockets and minigun fire. They broke right at the end of their run and came around to the south in a tight 180 degree turn. The Crossbow gunships also broke right after pressing their attack a long way past the northern treeline and fell into a line astern of the Playboy team.

'Playboy!' Green could see a problem if the teams remained with the approach headings as briefed. 'Stay in front of Crossbow and run your next pass on the western side of the LZ—twenty to thirty metres from the smoke.'

'Playboy . . . Coming round on the Bushranger's tail.'

'Roger, that,' Green acknowledged. 'Crossbow,' he added, seeing that team halfway down the eastern side of the LZ, 'follow Playboy in and I'll tag my slicks on to your tail.'

'Crossbow.'

'Zero-Two and Zero-Three!' Green summoned the slicks allocated to pick up the patrols. 'Better line up behind the next pass from Crossbow. Make your run right behind them and Bushranger will cover you with a minigun pass.'

'Zero-Two.'

'Zero-Three.'

Kevin Green made several checks and watched the Playboy team run at the target area. The lighter slicks fell quickly in behind the Crossbow team as Brian Gilmore brought Bushranger around for a second pass. The lack of enemy ground fire led him to hope that the NVA had called off the pressure on Ashton for some reason.

'Six-Six.' The voice of the lead pilot broke into Gilmore's thoughts. 'The slicks will be with you in three zero seconds.'

'Roger . . . Out!' The tone of Ashton's voice betrayed his desire to get aboard the incoming slicks at any cost.

Rowan Ashton gave the handset back to Swindler Crooks. He knew Willis would have heard the transmission and know that the slicks would be with them soon. He made his way to the treeline as one of the Playboy gunships made its second minigun pass. The noise was deafening, but Ashton hoped it would continue that way right to the time they were extracted.

'Slicks in thirty seconds,' he yelled at Smithfield. The other sergeant nodded and got his patrol to the edge of the treeline, ready to dash for the helicopters as soon as they landed. Each man still scanned the jungle to his front for any sudden appearance of enemy. Ashton knew that Willis and his patrol would be doing the same.

'Any order on, Nev,' Ashton shouted, loud enough for all of Smithfield's patrol to hear over the sound of the Crossbow leader's second pass. 'I'll keep Crooks with me for last on.'

Smithfield nodded his agreement without hesitation. It was fairly standard practice in most patrols that the commander and signaller were last aboard the extraction agency so that, in a case where a patrol was split during an extraction and the extraction aborted, the commander would have his signaller with him to communicate with their headquarters.

The unmistakable slower and deeper sounding beat of the rotors heralded the approach of the slicks behind the second Crossbow gunship. Ashton made his way back to where Crooks crouched in the open, several metres from the treeline. Willis was about to activate another smoke grenade and Ashton noted that their last one was about to expire. He had had no call from

Zero-One to terminate smoke but he decided not to bother wasting any more.

Ten pairs of eyes carefully watched the jungle beyond the treeline until the slicks were almost on the ground. Only Ashton and Crooks watched the opposite side of the LZ for their group, while Willis and Jacobs did likewise for theirs.

'GO! GO!' Ashton and Willis screamed almost simultaneously as the pair of Hueys began their short final approach. The patrols dashed for the settling helicopters with all the speed they could muster. Weapons were slid across the floor as the eager passengers literally dived through the cargo doorways.

Kevin Simmons, the first of Smithfield's patrol aboard Albatross Zero-Two, almost lost his rifle as it skidded across the checker plate floor of the Huey and only a desperate lunge on his part saved it from slipping over the door sill on the other side and on to the ground. The men piled in behind Simmons like cattle anxious to get down the race in advance of the prod.

At Albatross Zero-Three, Roy Kent and Gary Dobel were first aboard and fought to balance themselves in order to be able to fire from the right-hand cargo door if necessary. The left-hand door gunner would fire his twin M60s as soon as the patrol were all inboard, so as to suppress any likely danger by encouraging the enemy to keep their heads down.

The moments of confusion as the patrols piled onto the helicopters were amply covered by Bushranger Seven-Three's minigun run along most of the stretch of treeline to the west of the clearing. The door gunners commenced firing as the Hueys slowly began to gain height and forward momentum.

On Albatross Zero-One, Kevin Green and his co-pilot were ringside at a slow motion show. They saw Playboy and Crossbow break right as the slicks came to rest one behind the other a dozen metres from the treeline, adjacent to the dying smoke grenades. They watched the combined patrols dart from the edge of the clearing for the slicks, and saw Bushranger Seven-One break right at the bottom of his run as Bushranger Seven-Three hosed the area with 7.62 mm fire from its miniguns.

Then, to the astonishment of the pilots aboard Zero-One, a lone enemy came into view, looking little more than a toy figure at the south-west corner of the LZ. In a quick flurry of movement, he raised what appeared to be a stick to his shoulder. They realised the stick was an RPG when the propellant train from the rocket arced toward the slicks at the other end of the pad some four hundred metres away. The NVA soldier disappeared into the treeline as the hastily fired rocket impacted on the ground some distance to the rear of Albatross Zero-Three.

Bushranger Seven-Five, rolling in at the tail of the second pass, also witnessed the brave but foolhardy action of the NVA soldier. Flying Officer Mick Whatling at the controls fired a short burst from both miniguns into the area and decided that a hit was not a probability. He fired another long burst along the remaining length of the treeline and then broke right to fall in behind the two slicks that had lifted out of the pad midway through his final pass.

Kevin Green breathed a huge sigh of relief as he watched the slicks head east before turning hard right to follow Bushranger Seven-Three toward the south. He looked at his fuel gauge. He only had about four minutes of loiter time left and he gave a silent prayer of thanks that the gunships had left Nui Dat some time after he had. Otherwise they would have been lost to the extraction before they had a chance to participate in the final attack.

'Crossbow One-One,' Green said to the senior call sign of the Blackhorse gunships, 'thank you for hanging round and helping to get our blokes out. Much appreciated.'

'Hell, man, that's no problem. You guys have got good tactics and it's a pleasure to be in a shootout with ya. Remember to give us a call any time you got a good firefight going.'

'Roger that,' Green replied. 'If you're ever in Vung Tau with nothing to do, you know where to find us.'

'That's affirmative, man. See you all sometime! Crossbow . . . Out.' The channel closed and Green and his crew were left with their thoughts.

'Handing over,' Green said to his offsider, Pilot Officer Gavin Leaver.

'Taking over,' the young man responded quickly, grasping the controls gently. Green released control of the Huey and Leaver turned Zero-One steadily toward the south-west and set off to join formation with the remainder of the extraction agency. The helicopters had climbed to 1500 feet and were heading for Nui Dat with as much speed as possible.

'Better call Bravo Nine Sierra operations room,' Kevin Green advised the younger pilot, 'and let them know we've got their blokes.'

Epilogue

Documents in the satchel captured by Rowan Ashton's Bravo Nine Sierra patrol detailed the extent of Viet Cong infrastructure in the communists' Military Region Seven. The information enabled the Task Force Commander to mount a series of successful operations against the VC in Phuoc Tuy province. Operations conducted by the Australian and New Zealand forces based at Nui Dat led to the destruction of a number of VC staging camps and the location of four major arms and ammunition sites, creating a severe setback to the communist thrust for domination of the region.

Glossary

AK47	Assault rifle used by North Vietnamese forces
Albatross	Designator given to RAAF troop-carrying helicopters
AO	Area of operations
bait layer	Army cook
Blackhorse	American base in southern Long Khanh Province, 30 kilometres north of Nui Dat
boozer	Soldier's Club and canteen
Bushranger	Designator given to RAAF gunships
call sign	Combination of words, letters and/or numbers that identify a unit
Charlie	Abbreviated slang for Viet Cong (from 'Victor Charlie')
clicks	Slang for kilometres
CO	Commanding Officer
2IC	Second in Command
Comcen	Communications Centre
CP	Command Post
crawl trench	A narrow, shallow trench dug between bunkers for safe passage during an attack
CS gas	A noisome gas that causes tears, excessive salivation and breathing difficulties
Diggers	Colloquial term for Australian soldiers
dong	Monetary unit of Vietnam
Durrie	Slang term for cigarette

Dustoff	Term formed from the initial letters of 'Devoted and Untiring Service To Our Fighting Forces'. Adopted American term for the aero-medical evacuation system
Envoy	Codename for the SAS telephone switch at Nui Dat
FAC	Forward Air Controller. An airborne spotter for air and artillery strikes
FGA	Fighter ground attack
fire lane	A cleared area or strip (normally manmade) in front of a machine gun position
Firestone Trail	A 200 metre wide, 10 kilometre long strip hacked out of the jungle by US Army Engineers to facilitate the movement of armoured vehicles and enable reconnaissance flights to detect recent Viet Cong activity
Free-fire zone	An area inside which anyone is considered to be enemy
goffa	Soft drink
gooks	A collective slang reference to Asians used since the Korean War
gunship	A helicopter (armed with 2.75 inch rockets, miniguns, M60 door guns and sometimes an automatic 40mm grenade launcher) used for close air support
gunnie	Slang for gunship
HE	High explosive
HFT	Heavy fire team (a team of three helicopter gunships)
HMG	Heavy machine gun (50 calibre or 12.7mm)
horse collar	Canvas sling usually employed with a helicopter winch
Huey	Nickname for the 205 Iroquois HU-1 helicopter; in 1962 the designation changed to UH-1, but the name 'Huey' stuck
Jade	Designator given to forward air controllers working out of Vung Tau
Kabar	Term formed from the initial letters of 'Knife Assessory Browning Automatic Rifle'. Fighting knife issued to the BAR man in a US Marines

	section. The Baby Kabar is a smaller knife issued to US Navy Sea Air Land Forces
KIA	Killed in action
LFT	Light fire team (a team of two helicopter gunships)
LMG	Light machine gun
Local Force	Irregular soldiers recruited locally
long green	An area of high VC activity in the SE of Phuoc Tuy province. Also the nickname given to Victoria Bitter beer because of its green can
LRRP	Long Range Reconnaisance Patrol
LUP	Lying-up place
LZ	Helicopter landing zone
Main Force	Regular soldiers recruited regionally. Also called Regional Force
May Tao	A group of hills in the north-east of Phuoc Tuy Province and for many years a haven for the Viet Cong
mess	Bar and meeting place exclusive to the ranks denoted in its title; e.g. officer's mess: a club for officers
mess hall	Dining room
mm	Millimetre
mike mike	Slang for millimetres
M16	The M16A1 rifle. Standard infantry weapon of the US Army, adopted by Australians in Vietnam as a command and scouting weapon
MPC	Military Payment Certificate. A substitute for US currency with equivalent value
No-fire zone	A one kilometre wide strip around an SAS patrol AO
Nogs	Slang term for Vietnamese
NVA	North Vietnamese Army
OC	Officer Commanding
OP	Observation post
Ops	Operations
OPSO	Operations officer
Operations room	Place where operations are planned by operations staff
PRC	Designator for type of radio

PTT	Press to talk
PPSH	Russian sub-machine gun commonly known as a 'burp' gun
prop or propped	The act of stopping
QRU	Morse code abbreviation for 'no messages for you' or 'clear of traffic'
QSL	Morse code abbreviation for 'message received and understood'
RAAF	Royal Australian Air Force
recce	Reconnaissance
R&R	Rest and Recreation leave
R 'n C	Rest in Country leave
RPD	Russian-designed light machine gun used by communist forces
RPG	Rocket-propelled grenade launcher (RPG2 or RPG7)
RV	Rendezvous point or place
reggie	Abbreviated form of 'regimental'
SAS	Special Air Service
Seagull	Term denoting operations staff
shell dressing	Large, open-wound dressing issued to Australian forces
SKS	Russian-designed semi-automatic rifle used by communist forces
slick	Troop-carrying helicopter
SLR (pron. 'slur')	Self-loading rifle. The standard infantry weapon of the Australian Army at that time
SSM	Squadron Sergeant Major. A warrant officer responsible, among other things, for good order and military discipline
SO2	Staff Officer Grade 2 (normally a major)
stand to	Period of full alert
Sunray	Person in charge
tailend Charlie	Last man in a line of march
Task Force	Group approximately the size of a military brigade
TAOR	Tactical area of responsibility
Troop	Group approximately the size of a platoon
VC	Viet Cong; also 'Victor Charlie'

VR   Visual Reconnaissance, conducted by aircraft to reconnoitre a specific area

XM148   Prototype of the M203 grenade launcher (XM = Experimental Model)

yarpers   People who talk a lot. Local Force VC and village guerrillas were christened 'yarpers' because they were not well trained or disciplined and gave away their location to SAS patrols by talking loudly in the jungle (this did not affect the resolve they had in pursuing their cause)